D1564509

AGING, BUT NEVER OLD

Recent Titles in
The Praeger Series on Contemporary Health and Living

AGING, BUT NEVER OLD

*The Realities, Myths, and
Misrepresentations of the
Anti-Aging Movement*

JUERGEN BLUDAU, MD

The Praeger Series on Contemporary Health and Living
Julie Silver, Series Editor

 PRAEGER

AN IMPRINT OF ABC-CLIO, LLC
Santa Barbara, California • Denver, Colorado • Oxford, England

Library of Congress Cataloging-in-Publication Data

Bludau, Juergen.
 Aging, but never old : the realities, myths, and misrepresentations of the anti-aging movement / Juergen Bludau.
  p. cm. — (The Praeger series on contemporary health and living)
  Includes bibliographical references and index.
  ISBN 978-0-313-38018-1 (hard copy : alk. paper) — ISBN 978-0-313-38019-8 (ebook) 1. Aging. 2. Aging—Physiological aspects. 3. Older people—Health and hygiene. I. Title.
  QP86.B57   2010
  612.6'7—dc22   2010011188

ISBN: 978-0-313-38018-1
EISBN: 978-0-313-38019-8

14 13 12 11 10   1 2 3 4 5

This book is also available on the World Wide Web as an eBook.
Visit www.abc-clio.com for details.

Praeger
An Imprint of ABC-CLIO, LLC

ABC-CLIO, LLC
130 Cremona Drive, P.O. Box 1911
Santa Barbara, California 93116-1911

This book is printed on acid-free paper ∞

Manufactured in the United States of America

CONTENTS

SERIES FOREWORD

CONTEMPORARY HEALTH AND LIVING

Over the past 100 years, there have been incredible medical breakthroughs that have prevented or cured illness in billions of people and helped many more improve their health while living with chronic conditions. A few of the most important 20th century discoveries include antibiotics, organ transplants and vaccines. The 21st century has already heralded important new treatments including such things as a vaccine to prevent human papillomavirus from infecting and potentially leading to cervical cancer in women. Polio is on the verge of being eradicated worldwide, making it only the second infectious disease behind smallpox to ever be erased as a human health threat.

In this series, experts from many disciplines share with readers important and updated medical knowledge. All aspects of health are considered including subjects that are disease specific and preventive medical care. Disseminating this information will help individuals to improve their health as well as researchers to determine where there are gaps in our current knowledge and policy makers to assess the most pressing needs in healthcare.

Series Editor Julie K. Silver, MD
Assistant Professor
Harvard Medical School
Department of Physical Medicine and Rehabilitation

Foreword

As a 71-year-old woman, this I know for sure. What a wonderful moment to be alive. Modern medicine has reinvented the world of aging, making available new knees, hips, and shoulders, repairing hearts, and creating miracle drugs. However, physical rehabilitation is just one component of this aging journey. We must prepare mentally as well, and this can be a significant factor. The medical world can do just so much; the rest is up to us.

Whether we are the ones being cared for or the caregivers, this book encourages us to look forward, urging us to prepare ourselves for the unique challenges we will face as older citizens and, at the same time, assuring us that there are still opportunities for great joy and satisfaction. Yes, we will be facing a new reality, but dedicated physicians are working tirelessly to enrich and extend our lives.

This is not a one-size-fits-all book. It emphasizes the many variables among those in our age group. Some of us will age with minimal health issues, while others will struggle with chronic ailments. Yet, this is not the time to look back with regret. It is more a time to celebrate what still can be. Rejoice in what you have done in your life. Surround yourself with positive, active, fun, and grateful people. Our mission now is to keep relevant and useful, setting goals and doing good deeds.

Reading books like *Aging, But Never Old* arms us with the wisdom to understand and embrace this moment. Who better to entrust our health management to than specialists dedicated to the study of the unique issues of aging? Who better than geriatricians to look to for advice and counseling?

The new reality of our lives may not be a walk in the park; it may just be a walk on a walker. Just do what you can do; accept what is and move on. It is not too late to dream, to plan, or to do something remarkable. This is the key to never getting old.

Jo Ann K. Medalie
Chair, Broward County Library Advisory Board
Producer, Broward Meet the Press
Assistant to City Manager, Fort Lauderdale

Acknowledgments

My sincere thanks go first and foremost to all my elderly patients who have helped in teaching me the art of geriatric medicine and inspired me to write this book. In particular, I would like to thank my dear patient Eleanor Spingarn for her support and encouragement.

Another sincere thank you goes to a good family friend, Jo Ann Medalie, who was instrumental early on when the book was just an idea, who helped me to come up with the title, and who also so graciously wrote the foreword.

I would also like to thank my colleagues without whom I would not have succeeded in my efforts to write this book: Dr. Dae Kim and Dr. Jatin Dave for their careful review; and Dr. Alan Antman, Dr. Jerry Avorn, Dr. Margie Lachman, Dr. Jean Matheson, Dr. David Sinclair, and Dr. Robert Waldinger for allowing me to interview them. In addition, my thanks to Hank Santini for his perspective on life and on facing its challenges.

A special thank you goes to Dr. Julie Silver who inspired me to write a book and supported me in this endeavor.

And I would have never been able to write this book if it wasn't for the tremendous work and guidance of Dr. Susan Aiello, to whom I owe many thanks for keeping me organized, focused, and on top of my assignments.

Last but not least, I thank my family: my wife, Paola, and my children, Sebastian, Hannah, and Oliver, for their understanding on the many occasions when my thoughts were on this book instead of with them.

INTRODUCTION

I shall not mind
the whiteness of my hair,
or that slow steps
falter on the stair,
or what strange image
greets me in the glass . . .
if I can feel,
as roots feel in the sod,
that I am growing old to bloom
before the face of God.
Author unknown

Getting old is often considered an unavoidable dread. Old age in itself is not a disease, but rather a *wonder of the beauty of life.* Aging is a gift. Aging is unique to each person. Aging is a collection of life experiences that may bring wisdom and happiness to a person. Aging changes a person's perspective of life. What seemed important in younger years may no longer carry the same significance in old age. Older adults do not need to prove themselves anymore. They can enjoy life's moments more richly. And good health becomes the most important part of aging. However, being an older adult can mean being more vulnerable to certain states of ill health. Believe it or not, this is something that older adults and babies have in common. In infancy and childhood, most of the organ systems are in the process of reaching maturity and, therefore, are at times more susceptible to diseases. In old age, these same organ systems are trying to maintain their functional capacity through the wear and tear of decades of use.

Although bookstores are literally bulging with books on aging written for the general public, there is a surprising paucity of books that shed any light on the evidence-based scientific information about the process of aging and what it means for your health. Although grandma's advice might have had some merit in its day, current health recommendations and treatment options are based on the best available scientific data. Without such evidence, it is difficult to judge the risks and benefits of most therapies.

So, this book fills that gap. It will give you the real data—what we really know, and sometimes what we don't—in an understandable and practical way. It is based on my experience as a geriatrician, a physician who specializes in clinical care of older adults. It is not intended to be an exhaustive or comprehensive account of every disease related to old age, but rather an attempt to raise awareness about the major issues that affect us as we age, as well as how to manage these ongoing changes in our lives. For example, in the following pages, you'll find insight and guidance for having productive visits with your doctor and other members of the healthcare team, up-to-date information on medications and how to take them, the current recommendations for nutrition and exercise for older adults, and much more. Throughout, I offer practical tips on improving quality of life in old age.

If I can achieve even some of these goals, I will consider myself fortunate to have served one of the fastest-growing segments of our society—older adults and those who love and care for them.

1

THE SECRETS OF AGING

What is aging really? We hear about it and read about it almost every day. We see it in ourselves, and we recognize it with mixed feelings in our children and with trepidation in our parents. But when asked to explain aging, we fumble for the right words and are surprised how difficult it is to actually define. Does it refer to a time period? Is it the process of maturing? Or, more bluntly, is it just growing old? Whatever it is, today's Western society does not embrace aging as a value; in fact, it often tends to stigmatize it. Some of us cope by using adjectives like *successful* or *healthy* to try to feel better about it. Others hold tight to the messages of those in the anti-aging movement like the American Academy of Anti-Aging Medicine, proclaiming "anti-aging medicine is ushering in the Ageless Society."[1]

In this book, I'll try to shed some light on and insight onto aging. The more we understand aging, the better we will be at coping and adjusting to it instead of fighting it or looking for our lost youth. Hippocrates (430 BCE to ca. 370 BCE) suggested "that old age was cold and wet," referring to a failure of the heart with age, while the prominent Roman physician Galen (129–200 CE) felt "that old age was cold and dry."[2] Although we have a better understanding of aging today than our predecessors did thousands of years ago, there are still diametrically opposed views on aging. And despite incredible advances in science, medicine, and technology, we have been unable to stop the aging process. The quest for a cure for aging has been popular throughout the ages and still is. How ironic is it that in searching for the fountain of youth, Ponce de León discovered Florida, which is often referred to as the nation's nursing home? And how is it that despite the promises of myriad anti-aging businesses and the millions of dollars spent by consumers, we are still growing older?

If you are interested in really knowing what aging is about and what we can do about it and what is not yet possible, then this is the book you want to read. While I cannot guarantee you will always find upbeat information, and you definitely won't find incredible cures, I will give you honest, up-to-date, scientifically proven information.

Let's start then with some thought-provoking statements about aging. Unfortunately, I do not know the authors.

"Aging is relative. A mosquito is old in a day, a dog is old at 15 years, a human is old at 90. A tortoise can outlive humans by more than 200 years. A redwood tree can live more than 2000 years."

"Aging is activity-specific: 40 is old for baseball and young for politics; 18 is old enough for the army but too young for life."

"Aging is cultural. When most of the population was younger than 30, anyone older than 30 was old. Now we talk of the "young-old" as 65-74, "middle-old" as 75-84, and "old-old" as 85+. When more of us live to be 100, we will change the categories again."

AN ATTEMPT AT A DEFINITION OF AGING

Aging might best be described as "an irreversible process characteristic of each species" that "occurs over time independent of any specific disease or trauma to the body."[3] Another way of saying this is that aging is a "gradual deterioration of physiological function [normal functions of the body]," resulting in a "loss of viability and increase in vulnerability."[4]

In summary:

- Aging is not a disease or a collection of diseases.
- The aging process varies considerably in individuals.
- Aging makes our bodies more susceptible to various diseases.

THEORIES OF AGING

The question remains: What is the fundamental cause of aging? In a search for a single all-encompassing process, biologists, researchers, geneticists, physicians, philosophers, religious leaders and, of course, enterprising scam artists have managed to put forward hundreds of theories. Let's look at a few to give you a taste of how broad views are about the aging process. A popular viewpoint is the "Wear-and-Tear Theory," which portrays aging as a slow but steady wearing out of different parts of the body. A good example is the development of osteoarthritis in the hips and knees and the stiffening of the arteries. Another idea is the "Autoimmune Theory," which suggests that with increasing age, the body's immune system tends to malfunction and then starts attacking itself. This reminds me of the famous saying, "the revolution eats its own children." The "Aging Clock Theory" thinks of a clock, ticking away slowly and steadily within our bodies until it stops ticking altogether. A good example of this is the menstrual cycle, which runs its inevitable course over a woman's lifetime, coming to a programmed end. This theory sparked interest in hormonal therapy because some hormones are at higher levels in younger people than in older people. One of these hormones in particular is the growth hormone dehydroepiandrosterone (DHEA), one of the all-time favorites of the anti-aging business. More recently, researchers have discovered that the end tips of chromosomes, called *telomeres,* tend to get shorter each time a cell divides. Could they be the small ticking clocks that count down the time of a cell? I am surprised we have not seen any ads for replacement clocks offered by the anti-aging business.

Another similar theory that considers aging as a preprogrammed process is the "Cellular Theory" of aging, which is based on the idea that cells can replicate only so many times until they run out of steam. This theory dates back to the 1960s; it started in the laboratory, where cells were found to have a fixed life span. An interesting, albeit morbid, piece of information is that it was discovered that this fixed life span was a characteristic of normal cells, while cancer cells can seem to go on replicating forever. So it seems that the answer to the ever-burning question, "Can human bodies become immortal?" would therefore be yes, but that humans will "have to get cancer in order to do it." And "therein lies the rub" (borrowed from William Shakespeare, *The Tragedy of Hamlet, Prince of Denmark*).

Yet another theory, known as the "Cross-Linkage Theory," refers to the accumulation of waste products. Collagen, a protein found in many parts of our body, contains cross-linking compounds. These compounds result in the loss of elasticity of body tissues, which shows up in different ways. For

---

Life span is referred to as the "genetically determined absolute life of a specific animal species under the best of environmental circumstances."[6]
Life expectancy " . . . is the average number of years that a human population of a given age and sex can expect to live under current conditions."[6] Life expectancy has dramatically increased over the last 100 years from an average of 47 years in 1900 to around 80 years at the beginning of this century. Good public health initiatives, reduced infant mortality, better sanitation, clean water, and medicines like antibiotics have made this possible. Although the increase in life expectancy will not continue at this dramatic rate, we should see further slow improvement with more emphasis on preventive strategies. For example, heart disease and stroke can be reduced through smoking cessation, exercise and weight control, and better control of cholesterol and blood sugar.

Compression of morbidity

One hundred years ago, people died at all ages primarily from accidents and infectious diseases. Nowadays, we are shocked when we hear about a young person dying, and the cause is usually a tragic accident. Infectious disease is largely prevented by vaccination, and most cases that do develop can be cured. The vast majority of people die in old age from chronic diseases like heart disease, lung disease, or cancer. The result is that we have managed to push death to the later years of a person's life, in other words, we have compressed the morbidity.

example, it helps explain the fact that most of us at about age 45 start needing reading glasses because the lenses of our eyes start to stiffen. It also
explains our skin becoming less elastic and forming those dreaded wrinkles.

Along the same line of thought is the "Free Radical Theory," which advocates the idea that free radicals are formed in cells as by-products of cell
metabolism. These free radicals are toxic and damage the cells from within.
The cells respond to this insult by using antioxidants, which act as a garbage
collection service and "mop up" the free radicals. This is what has prompted
the craze in antioxidant supplements, headed by the now disgraced vitamin E.
It seems you cannot watch television, read the newspaper, or go to a super-
market without being inundated with the latest, and, of course the best, antioxidant supplement.[5]

AGING IS LIKE A HOUSE

I like to compare the aging of the human body to the aging of a house.
When the house is newly built, everything is in pristine shape, working well
and without problems (at least we hope so considering the size of our
mortgage).

But over the years, parts of the house wear out and sometimes major
repairs become necessary. The weather and the elements do their destructive
job on the outside of the house in a similar way the environment does to our
bodies. The sun, rain, wind, and snow make the paint crack and the wood
rot, just like our skin suffers from spending hours in the sun, even if we're
covered in tanning oil. While we can easily get a daily weather prediction on
the local news or online, we can't change it or its effects on our house. So, we
make sure to maintain our house by painting it regularly, cleaning the gutters,
and repairing the roof and other damage as soon as possible. The same holds
true for our health. If we maintain our bodies by not smoking, drinking alcohol carefully, exercising, and watching our diet, we'll keep ourselves in the
best shape possible for the years to come.

Likewise, there is daily wear and tear inside the house. Walls and floors
can get scratched, tiles may crack, appliances break, fuses blow, and pipes
burst. Certainly, we can't move out of the house to avoid any wear and tear,
so instead we take care of it and protect it as much as possible by keeping
appliances in good working condition, following maintenance instructions,
and calling the plumber as soon as we find a leak. Compare the interior of
the house to genetically determined disease in people, which is part of our
DNA, or genetic code. While we cannot alter our genetic code, we can screen
for certain diseases so that we can catch them early enough to treat them
more successfully (see Chapter 8, "Health Maintenance").

While our houses and bodies cannot remain in their original pristine conditions,
maintaining them well and practicing prevention will allow them both to age grace-
fully. Our house may eventually become a charming historic building, in much the
same way that we become fit and healthy octogenarians.

SKIP THE THEORIES—WHAT ACTUALLY HAPPENS?

Are you ready for the truth and nothing but the truth? Because, beware, this is not for the feeble. In the words of Bette Davis, "Old age is no place for sissies." So, you may want to sit back, put on some calming background music like Mozart's *Requiem* or Beethoven's *Symphony No. 5*, and take a deep breath before you continue to read. You can also skip this section or plan to read it later after you've read a few other chapters.

Fortunately, aging is a painless and amazingly slow process that we don't recognize on a daily basis, unless of course you have spent some time at 1600 Pennsylvania Avenue in Washington, DC. Again, aging is *not* a disease; rather, it predisposes us to diseases. Another important concept about aging is that every person ages differently. Whatever happens is most likely a combination of internal (genetic) and external (environmental) factors.

With that in mind, let's look at our bodies as they age ever so slowly, starting on the outside first. As we get older, we tend to shrink a little, meaning that our height tends to decrease while, unfortunately, our weight tends to increase. As you will surely have noticed, men have a propensity to get round in the waist, and women in the hips. Our skin gets thinner and more wrinkled. Our hair thins and turns white or gray. Mucous membranes become drier, and we have fewer sweat glands. As a result, we're not able to regulate our body temperature as well, and we tend to "feel the cold more."

Typically, our hearing ability declines steadily, especially for high-frequency sounds. Wouldn't you know it that men are more affected than women? And to add insult to injury, wax buildup tends to increase with age, too. In our eyes, the lenses become less transparent, which can lead to cataracts. The term *cataract* is derived from the Greek word *cataractos*, which describes rapidly running water. When water is turbulent, it is transformed from a clear medium to white and cloudy.[7] The pressure within our eyes may increase and damage the visual nerve. This condition is called glaucoma, also referred to as the "silent thief of sight."[8] Macular degeneration is another common eye disease in which the macula, "the central area of the retina, a paper-thin tissue at the back of the eye where light sensitive cells send visual signals to the brain," deteriorates.[9] Add some changes in color vision, especially greens and blues, to all this, and you will surely agree that we need a good ophthalmologist in addition to those designer reading glasses.

Our senses of smell and taste are not spared either. The nerves in the nose involved in smell slowly deteriorate, which also results in subtle changes in our taste sensation. The number of taste buds on our tongue also diminishes, leaving us with less ability to taste sweet and salty foods so that more of the sour and bitter tastes come through. Now doesn't that make you feel better?

Our joints tend to start to creak, ache, and get stiff from the constant wear and tear, and we can predict the weather better than most meteorologists. Just wait until it's time for you to cut your toe nails. They often become so thick that you may seem to need rose clippers instead of normal trimmers.

This is one very good reason to become friendly with a nearby podiatrist. And these are just some of the things we can easily notice or see! Now let's look at what happens on the inside of our body.

Our lungs tend to get stiffer as we age, and lung function diminishes. Adding smoking to an already declining lung function makes the situation far worse. Similar to our skin, the heart tends to become less elastic, and the heart valves become hardened. The arteries also harden, while the veins tend to expand and become more prominent, resulting in painful and unsightly varicose veins.

Our digestive system seems to mostly avoid the ravages of age except that it may move a little slower (known as reduced motility). No wonder we start to appreciate the television ads for constipation.

Age is not so kind when it comes to our kidneys. Kidney function is generally reduced by half by the time we celebrate our ninetieth birthday. This is a very good reason to be especially careful with all medications the older we get (see Chapter 4, "Medications and Older Adults").

As we age, the levels of the sex hormones—testosterone in men and estrogen and progesterone in women—slowly diminish. The uterus (womb) shrinks and the pelvic floor muscles tend to weaken, especially in women who have had several pregnancies. These changes in women and in the prostate gland in men (the prostate tends to get larger and harder) can cause problems with urination and interrupt nighttime sleep. If that isn't disruptive enough, the sleep pattern itself changes with age, with less deep sleep periods during the night. No wonder jokes like these are common: "People call at 9 PM and ask, 'Did I wake you?'" or "You wake up with that morning-after feeling and you didn't do anything the night before."[10]

That is still not all. In the brain and in the rest of the body, nerve cells degenerate, which is one reason why older adults often have changes in their gait. Even the immune system, with an overall decline in function, is not immune to the effects of aging. This is one reason why older adults need an annual flu shot, in addition to having other existing conditions that put them at risk of a more serious illness/infection. So now you know the truth and why with increasing age most address books "contain names ending in MD."[10]

Given this truth, I can understand how people are attracted to the amazing promises and reports generated by the anti-aging movement. However, the fact of the matter is that there is no "cure" for aging, and there cannot be one because aging is not a disease. Now is a good time to introduce you to the field of medicine that specializes in aging and age-related diseases known as geriatrics. Geriatricians are physicians who are experts on aging matters and who focus on the health and well-being of older adults.

Geriatrics is the specialty of medicine that focuses on the medical care of older adults, that is, those 65 years and older. The focus is primarily on management of chronic disease and supportive care of the patients and their caregivers.
Gerontology is the study of various aspects of aging.

A Short History of Geriatrics

Ignatz Leo Nasher, who was born in Vienna in 1863 and received his medical degree from New York University in 1885, coined the word *geriatrics*. The word was "derived from geronte, a group of men over 60 years who ran the legislative council (gerousia) of Athens." Marjory Warren (1897–1960), who has been credited with the development of modern geriatrics in the United Kingdom, "took over the aged beds at the West Middlesex Hospital and introduced among other changes 'active rehabilitation programs,'" In 1946, "Lord Amulree and Dr. Sturdee addressed the Houses of Parliament on the care of the aged and chronic sick. This led to the inclusion of the care of the aged as part of the National Health System." And, in 1965, Dr. Ferguson Anderson was awarded the first chair for geriatrics at Glasgow University. While the specialty of geriatric medicine was born in the United Kingdom, it was the work of researchers in the United States that "provided the scientific validation of the British methods and provided the next steps forward in the development of the science of geriatrics." The Josiah Macy Jr. Foundation in the United States was instrumental in supporting this research. And wouldn't you know that it took another woman on this side of the Atlantic to promote geriatrics. Mrs. Kate Macy Ladd, who formed the foundation, "chose aging as one of the five areas to be focused on for future support." I dare say that geriatrics would not be here today if it weren't for the intuition of women. With a grant from the foundation supporting the research, Edward J. Stieglitz "was appointed the first head of the Unit on Aging with the Division of Chemotherapy at the National Institute of Health" in 1940. In 1950, President Truman called for the first National Conference of Aging, and in 1965, "Medicare and Medicaid were introduced, providing finances to drive high-quality medical care for older adults." It was Les Liebow from New York, at the Jewish Home and Hospital for the Aged, who has been credited with "creating the first fellowship in geriatric medicine at City Hospital Center (a Mount Sinai School of Medicine affiliate) in 1966." The Veterans Administration system, with its Geriatric Research, Education and Clinical Centers (GRECCs), has been described as being the "single most important institution in the development of geriatrics in the United States."[2] In these GRECCs, fellows in geriatric medicine and psychiatry are trained, and research has led to better assessment methods and the use of a team approach in geriatrics. Formal geriatric fellowship training started in the late 1970s, and the first certifying examination in geriatric medicine was offered in 1988.[2]

Geriatrics Today and Moving Forward

Now here at the beginning of the twenty-first century with almost 30 years of formal geriatric training in the United States, you would think that geriatric medicine is a well-established medical specialty. Unfortunately, that is not the case. Our health care system has a serious shortage of geriatricians; more physicians chose not to renew their boards in geriatric medicine; and hospital administrators, medical school deans, and politicians still ignore the growing need for geriatric programs. Shortly after publishing a study "demonstrating how much better people's lives were with specialized geriatric care, the university [University of Minnesota] closed the division of geriatrics," explaining financial losses as the reason.[11] And Harvard Medical School went as far as dissolving its Division on Aging a few years ago. This does not bode well for the future of geriatrics in our current health care system, which has sent vague and often inconsistent messages, and even worse, only haphazardly supports appropriate care for older patients.

Compare this system with the clear fight-against-aging message of the anti-aging movement. In Chapter 2, we start by examining the differences between the practices of geriatric medicine and the anti-aging movement, two competing forces not unlike the ones in Steven Spielberg's epic movie "Star Wars."

After that, we'll look at the most common issues and questions that almost all older adults have about their health. Chapter 3 will tell you how to work with your physician to make the best of your office visit. Chapter 4 discusses the hot topic of medications. Chapter 5 explains the significance of nutrition, while Chapter 6 introduces you to the need for regular exercise. Chapter 7 deals with the aging brain and the dreaded diagnosis of dementia. In Chapter 8, I will introduce you to the ever more important field of health maintenance, which is followed by five chapters on specific conditions common in older adults. Chapter 14 will demystify sexual activity in older adults. Chapter 15 describes the significance of the three S's—social connectedness, support through caregiving, and the power of spirituality—while Chapter 16 helps you be prepared for all events of life. Finally, Chapter 17 reminds all of us to appreciate and enjoy the passage of time in what can be a remarkably fulfilling time of life.

REFERENCES

1. Robert H. Binstock, "Anti-Aging Medicine and Research: A Realm of Conflict and Profound Societal Implications," *The Journals of Gerontology Series A: Biological Sciences and Medical Sciences* 59 (2004): B523.
2. John E. Morley, "A Brief History of Geriatrics," *Journal of Gerontology: Medical Sciences* 59A (2004): 1132.
3. Harry Moody, *Aging, Concepts and Controversies* (Thousand Oaks, CA: Pine Forge Press, 2009), 130.
4. Joao Pedro de Magalhaes, Integrative Genomics of Ageing Group 2008, "What Is Aging?" http://www.senescence.info/definitions.html.
5. Harry Moody, *Aging, Concepts and Controversies* (Thousand Oaks, CA: Pine Forge Press, 2009), 57.
6. Judith Estrine, *Is There an "Anti-Aging" Medicine?* (AARP Andrus Foundation and the International Longevity Center-USA, 2001), http://www.ilcusa.org/pages/publications/healthy-aging/is-there-an-anti-aging-medicine.php.

7. David Paine, "Practical Guide to Health, Cataracts," eMedicine Health, http://www.emedicinehealth.com/cataracts/article_em.html.
8. National Eye Institute, "Watch Out for Glaucoma, the Thief of Sight, Early Detection Is Key to Saving Vision," National Eye Institute, http://wwwpioneerthinking.com/ara-glaucoma.html.
9. American Health Assistance Foundation, "About Macular Degeneration," American Health Assistance Foundation, http://www.ahaf.org/macular/about.
10. C-boom, "Where the Coolboomers Surf, You're Know You're Getting Old When . . . , Trivia, Nostalgia, Memory Lane, and Aging Humor Jokes," C-boom, http://www.c-boom.com/humor2.htm.
11. Atul Gawande, "The Way We Age Now, Can Medicine Serve an Aging Population?" *New Yorker*, April 30, 2007, 50.

2

GERIATRIC MEDICINE VERSUS THE ANTI-AGING MOVEMENT

In the first chapter, you heard about the secrets of aging and a short history of geriatric medicine. I also hinted at the raging battle between the established field of geriatric medicine and the rebel anti-aging movement. This chapter will shed some light on the workings of both, so that you will be able to distinguish between what is sound and based on good science and what is nothing but smoke and mirrors.

Let's start by looking more closely at the field of geriatric medicine. Why is there a need for this specialty? How does it differ from general internal medicine? What do geriatricians do differently when they evaluate and treat an older adult? These are common questions among patients and physicians alike. Many internists and family practitioners argue, not unjustifiably, that they have experience in treating and caring for older patients, especially since older adults make up almost half of all doctors visits. So do we really need another type of physician to care for older adults? It is true that geriatricians may not necessarily treat older patients differently per se. But there is a very large and important difference in that the focus of the treatment is different. In order to appreciate how significant this is, we need to look at what makes an older adult different from a younger patient.

WHAT MAKES OLDER PATIENTS DIFFERENT?

Older patients differ from younger ones in five major ways: heterogeneity, homeostenosis, comorbidities, different disease presentations, and the difference between acute and chronic diseases. As a result of these five major differences, older patients cannot simply be treated like their younger counterparts. Unfortunately, this is exactly what happens all too often, and it should therefore be no surprise that the care of older patients is often suboptimal. This is where geriatricians can help. Let's explain each of the five differences in more detail.

Heterogeneity

As people age, they become more *heterogeneous*, meaning that they become more and more different, sometimes strikingly so, with respect to their health and medical needs. Imagine for a moment a group of 10 men and women, all 40 years old. It is probably safe to say that most, if not all, have no chronic diseases, do not see their physicians on a regular basis, and take no long-term prescription medications. From a medical point of view, this means that they are all very similar. Compare this to a group of 10 patients who are 80 years old. Most likely, you will find an amazingly fit and active jet-setting gentleman who may not be taking any prescription medications. On the other end of the spectrum, you may find a frail, memory-impaired, and wheelchair-bound woman who lives in a nursing home. In between these two extremes, there will be those with gait problems as a result of a stroke or crippling arthritis to those suffering from advanced heart and chronic lung diseases. Some will take five prescription medications, others up to 15 or even more. Some need daily help, while others can manage with only occasional support from family members.

Homeostenosis

This tongue twister refers to a narrowing or *stenosis* of our internal body reserves to withstand stress.[1] This means that as we grow older, our bodies are increasingly more susceptible to any stressor, such as an infection, trauma, and the effects of medications. For example, let's consider the effects of an annoying case of the common cold. A younger person may feel run down and achy, have little appetite, and sleep poorly. Most over-the-counter cold remedies can help a younger person get through the day, although they can also induce sleepiness, dry up secretions, and lead to constipation. The same viral illness and these same effects can cause far more havoc in an older person. A poor appetite can result in significant dehydration and cause dizziness or even a fall, especially if the person is taking medications for high blood pressure. Just a day or two lying in bed and not walking much will make an older person noticeably weaker, again increasing the risk of falls. Many over-the-counter cold medications can cause confusion in addition to constipation. They may also interact with other medications that many older adults are taking (read more on this important concept in Chapter 3, "Doctor Talk").

Comorbidities

The third important difference in older people is the number of *comorbidities*, or other medical conditions that are present at the same time. Older patients typically don't arrive at the doctor's office with one medical problem. Instead, they usually have a variety of concerns and illnesses, many (if not all) of which need some type of treatment. The importance of this is that sometimes treatments interfere with one another, or the treatment for one problem might even make another condition worse. This is an excellent

A lovely 86-year-old female patient of mine had heart failure, which causes fluid to build up in the lungs and legs. She was being treated with a diuretic medication (or "water pill") to remove the excess fluid from her body. She also had a poor gait and some problems with balance because of bad arthritis in her left knee and a weak right leg from a previous stroke. So, walking was a challenge for her. Because of the diuretic pill, she needed to visit the bathroom quite often. On one of those urgent calls, she fell and fractured her hip. I will spare you the unhappy ending. The point is that many conditions in older patients cannot simply be treated according to the standard recommendations made for and used in younger patients.

example of how the expertise of a geriatrician can help prevent the far too common and at times tragic example of bad interactions among multiple medical conditions.

Different Disease Presentation

The fourth difference is that diseases may show up in older adults in very unusual ways. The crushing chest pain and feeling of impending doom so commonly thought of as the symptoms of a heart attack are rarely present in an older patient. Instead, an older person may have a stomach ache and feel nauseous or simply feel extremely tired. The cough, breathlessness, and fever that are hallmarks of pneumonia in younger people may instead be replaced by confusion, poor appetite, and even a propensity to fall in older adults. Therefore, the medical history of older patients often needs to be much more thorough than that of younger patients. Sir William Osler's (1849–1919) wise remark, "Listen to the patient, he'll give you the diagnosis" holds even more true in older patients.[2]

Chronic versus Acute Diseases

Finally, the types of diseases of older patients are often very different from those of younger patients. Older patients often visit their physician for a worsening of a chronic condition. This can pose challenges in diagnosis and require careful consideration of treatment options because usually these patients are already on some kind of treatment regimen for their chronic condition.

Memory impairment, another common condition among older patients, also makes assessment more complicated. For example, the history may be incomplete and/or need to be corroborated by a caregiver.

GERIATRICS AS THE MIRROR IMAGE OF PEDIATRICS

As mentioned previously, geriatricians use the same medications and treatment options as other physicians, but our approach and focus is very different.

One could say that geriatricians have a more holistic approach to patient care that is very similar to the approach in another specialty of medicine.

Think of geriatric medicine as being the "mirror image" of pediatric medicine. Listlessness and poor appetite would be considered general or vague symptoms in young adults, but these symptoms in babies would be recognized by pediatricians as signs of a possible urinary tract infection. Likewise, geriatricians recognize different disease presentations in older adults as described before.

Another similarity to pediatrics is the involvement of the primary caregiver of the patients. The golden rule in pediatric medicine—the mother is always right until proven otherwise—also applies to the caregivers of older patients. Geriatricians work closely with our patients' caregivers, recognizing that their involvement is critical to providing good care. No one knows the very young or the older patient better than the immediate caregiver, whether a parent, spouse, adult child, and so forth.

Another central principle of geriatric medicine is the focus on function. Instead of treating each of the many medical conditions separately in older patients, geriatricians focus specifically on those conditions that affect a patient's functional abilities. In the tragic case report in the sidebar of the older lady with the water pills, a better option would have been less aggressive treatment of her heart failure, considering how her difficulty in walking made the frequent bathroom trips burdensome. Even though she might have continued to have some symptoms of heart failure, adjusting the dosage of medication could still have kept her as comfortable as possible, able to walk around her apartment without becoming short of breath, but with fewer bathroom trips. Put another way, geriatricians monitor patients' chronic conditions by watching for any changes in function and treating these conditions keeping in mind the goal of improving function. This is not unlike pediatricians, who carefully monitor the developmental stages of their pediatric patients to quickly address any problems when certain developmental milestones are not attained. The similarities go even further in that the treatment of older patients follows some of the same principles as those in pediatric medicine. In older patients, just like in very young patients, certain medications should be avoided, and reduced dosages and/or different routes of administration may be needed.

By following these principles, geriatricians are able to improve the quality of life of older patients even though we cannot cure many chronic diseases. And neither can those apparent anti-aging medicine specialists. Let's then take a closer look at what the anti-aging movement really has to offer.

THE ANTI-AGING MOVEMENT: MEDICINE OR BUSINESS?

The answer is both. With the establishment of the National Institute of Aging in 1974, long overdue serious research on aging began. Just as aging research finally "achieved scientific and political legitimacy in the late 20th century, the 'anti-aging medicine' movement literally took off in the 1990s and started to challenge conventional aging research."[3] It has been speculated that the aging baby boomers in our youth-oriented culture may have sparked the fuse. An explosion in the use of anti-aging products came with the 1994 Dietary Supplement Health and Education Act, which "relaxed the regulation of such products." This was quickly followed by many books on anti-aging topics, journals, various Web sites, and businesses, which have resulted in a booming anti-aging market of over $60 billion dollars in 2007. The most influential organization in the anti-aging movement is the American Academy of Anti-Aging Medicine, or A4M for short, which was founded in the early 1990s by two Chicago-based osteopaths, Ronald Klatz and Robert Goldman. But there are many more businesses offering a dazzling array of unconventional and unproven treatments and promises that sound too good to be true for anyone who has a healthy sense of skepticism. The only way to understand what this anti-aging medicine is, what Dr. Tom Perls (Director of the New England Centenarian study, funded by the National Institute of Health) calls "anti-aging quackery," is to look at what it actually has to offer.[4]

Broadly speaking, the anti-aging market comprises five categories: cosmetic treatments and surgery; exercise and therapy; food and beverages; vitamins, minerals, and supplements; and cosmetics and cosmeceuticals. Could it really be true that all these claims of guaranteed youth are nothing more than getting at our money? Of course it is—an age-old trick of promising everything we want to hear and believe in so badly. And it is working like a charm. My suggestion is to be very careful about Web sites that offer any anti-aging remedies.

But there are other reasons why the anti-aging business is thriving these days. Without doubt, its advertising skills are remarkable. If only health care providers and insurance companies could learn to advertise the benefits of health maintenance as well (see Chapter 8). The use of the word *medicine* and the establishment of a subspecialty board by the A4M also help to elevate its profile considerably. Furthermore, anti-aging is now an accepted term in the Merriam-Webster Dictionary, and it has been used in a number of recognized professional journals. All of this has also lent the anti-aging business some serious credibility, which it is quick to use in its marketing strategies.[4]

SNAKE OIL AND BEYOND

The story behind the birth of snake oil reads like a historic novel. Many ready-made concoctions were later interestingly referred to as patent medicines, a term used to describe all "self-prescribed nostrums and cure-alls." Originating in England, these patent medicines became a true American icon. American entrepreneurs, not unlike their modern-day colleagues seeing a great business opportunity, took over the booming business when the Revolutionary War stopped all shipments of these patent medicines to the colonies. There are fascinating tales of medicine peddlers who organized elaborate traveling shows to trick and swindle people into buying their bogus tonics. Over time, these "worthless cure-alls came to be known as snake-oil."[5] But back to our own day and time. Although we do not usually attend traveling shows and we think of the twenty-first century as being more sophisticated, not much has really changed. Instead of watching shows in town squares, we are fascinated by Web sites and elaborate health food stores where we continue to buy "snake oil."

Cosmetics

Let's start with the dazzling array of anti-aging creams, lotions, and potions. The FDA classifies these products as cosmetics, which means that they have no medical value and no rigorous testing is required for these products. One of the most common ingredients in these anti-wrinkle products is retinol, which is a vitamin A compound that is less potent than its prescription cousin tretinoin. Hydroxy acids are another common ingredient in these products. They work by removing old and dead skin, but can also worsen sun damage. For this reason, they should always be used together with sunscreen. Coenzyme Q_{10} is an antioxidant, used as a dietary supplement that has shown some benefit in protecting against sun damage; it is also available in pill form. Copper peptides, which are a combination of the trace element copper and small protein fragments called peptides, enhance wound healing. Kinetin is a plant growth factor, the exact mechanism of action of which is unclear. Tea extracts, especially from green tea, are also commonly included.

There is no guarantee that these over-the-counter creams actually work. Many are quite costly and may cause rashes and serious skin irritations. However, some prescription anti-wrinkle products have shown some beneficial effect. If you are interested in using them, I would recommend that you speak to a dermatologist who is knowledgeable about these products and can select the appropriate therapy for you.[6] Keep in mind that these creams do not really treat aging but just cover up a normally occurring phenomenon of aging. Sorry, but this is no real anti-aging therapy.

Antioxidants and Vitamin Supplements

Antioxidant and vitamin preparations are another favorite in the treatment repertoire of the anti-aging business. Please see Chapter 5, "Nutrition," for more discussion and recommendations on the use of these supplements. Again, these products are not regulated by the FDA, and so you cannot be sure what each of the vast array of available products contains or how effective they are. There is no way for you to know what you are really swallowing, how it might interact with other medications you are taking, or what effect it could have on your medical conditions.

Megavitamin products are also bogus. Each vitamin has a specific recommended daily allowance, or the amount needed for good health and body function. Mega dosages will not enhance the beneficial effects and, in fact, can be harmful. Is there an "anti-aging" medicine?[7] None of the antioxidant or megavitamin products have been shown to have any real anti-aging properties.

Hormone Replacement Therapy

We know that certain hormones like testosterone, estrogen, growth hormone, and dehydroepiandrosterone (DHEA) decline with advancing age and that certain hormones have been used to treat medical conditions. However, no hormone has as of yet been shown to stop, slow, or reverse aging. In fact, quite the opposite is the case when you look at estrogen replacement therapy. Consider the Women's Health Initiative study, a very large, well-known, multicenter study of 16,000 healthy postmenopausal American women between the ages of 50 and 79 that was designed to look at the benefits of hormone replacement therapy. Participants were given either a combination of estrogen and progesterone, or a placebo. Researchers had to stop the study prematurely in 2002 because of the large number of side effects women started to suffer. The risk of heart attack, stroke, breast cancer, and blood clots all increased. This was unfortunate news for women suffering from menopausal symptoms, but welcome news and business for lawyers specializing in hormone replacement side effects. In summary, not only is it fair to say that hormone replacement therapy does not qualify as an anti-aging therapy, but it can have serious life-threatening complications.[8,9,10]

Human Growth Hormone

Despite the known risks of hormone replacement therapy, a top seller for the anti-aging business is still the famous human growth hormone (HGH). If you enter "growth hormone" into any search engine on the Internet, you will be overwhelmed by the sheer number of Web sites offering various versions, from injections to sprays and pills, and of course so-called naturally occurring herbs. HGH is produced by a small gland in the brain, and it is important for normal organ function. HGH is used successfully in patients who have a known growth hormone deficiency when administered by injection. As an aside, there are no studies to show that HGH can actually be given in pill or spray form. There are also no studies to show that giving HGH in any form to older adults who have no hormone deficiency is of any benefit at all. Instead of making you look and feel younger, you could end up with joint and muscle pain, diabetes, or even heart disease, none of which qualify as successful anti-aging effects. My advice is to stay away from any products claiming to include HGH and from physicians charging outrageous prices for injections of HGH.[11]

Caloric Restriction

Among all the strategies of the anti-aging movement, caloric restriction may be the best bet. In animal studies, limiting daily calorie intake resulted in longer life in some animals. Whether this really resulted in maintaining the youthful appearance of some mice is questionable, but age-related diseases did seem to be postponed. There are no large scientific studies in people that have shown similar effects, but we already know that a proper diet can lower blood pressure and cholesterol and help in managing diabetes (see Chapter 4, "Medications and Older Adults"). Losing weight is also beneficial in the treatment of heart disease and arthritis. It also will reduce the risk of complications of all these diseases, and chances are, will reduce the risk of death and debility. Unfortunately, it will not automatically guarantee you a long life.[9]

Resveratrol—the New Wonder Supplement

The new wunderkind of the anti-aging business is the one and only resveratrol. "Resveratrol is a molecule which is produced by several plants and found in the skin of red grapes in minute amounts and thus is present in red wine."[12] "When the resveratrol molecule enters the cell, it activates an enzyme called SIRT1. As a consequence, SIRT1 engenders new mitochondria [power source of cells] in the muscle and other tissue. As a result, the new mitochondria boost the metabolic rate of the body." The resveratrol.org Web site states that this could result in "less weight gain, prevention of diabetes, prevention of cancer, increase exercise endurance, prevent strokes and heart disease, [and] prevents Alzheimer's and Parkinson's diseases."[12]

What is different about resveratrol versus many other anti-aging products is that it was discovered in 2003 by David Sinclair, a professor of pathology at Harvard Medical School and cofounder of Sirtis Pharmaceuticals. As of the spring of 2009, results from the first human trials have shown that resveratrol reduced blood glucose. Data from further human trials is not yet available.

While Sirtis Pharmaceuticals is carefully testing the molecule according to industry standards, the greater anti-aging business world is already promoting and selling resveratrol capsules as if their beneficial effects have already been well established. Not only is this unethical and downright deceiving, but some Web sites are even using the Harvard connection to boost the significance of this wonder drug that apparently "Unlock(s) Your ANTI-AGING Potential."[13]

From Genes to Stem Cells

Other proclaimed anti-aging therapies include gene manipulation and stem cell therapy. Tinkering with genes has indeed resulted in life extension in organisms such as yeast, fruit flies, nematodes, and mice. How exciting is it when these organisms are in your kitchen? Stem cell therapy is at its dawn, and while we as a country are still struggling with the ethics of harvesting and using human stem cells, I think it is fair to say that we are far from commercially using stem cells to treat aging or aging-related diseases.

THE FINAL ANALYSIS

In summary, none of the anti-aging products can truly treat aging or reverse it. Although it is important to keep an open mind, it is equally important to be critical and prudent. I hope that with this book and careful evaluation of other reputable sources, including your personal physician, you will agree that geriatric medicine has much more to offer older adults than the dubious anti-aging business and its collection of bogus products. Anti-wrinkle creams can cover some of the blemishes of aging, but they cannot make you younger inside.

With this in mind, I invite you to continue with me on a journey through the field of geriatric medicine in the chapters to follow.

REFERENCES

1. The University of Oklahoma Health Sciences Center, "Homeostenosis," University of Oklahoma, http://www.ouhsc.edu/geriatricmedicine/Education/Homeostenosis/HomeostenosisIndex.htm.
2. Robert Kane, Joseph Ouslander, and Itamar Abrass, *Essentials of Clinical Geriatrics*, 5th ed. (New York: McGraw-Hill, 2004), 3–70.
3. Robert H. Binstock, "Anti-Aging Medicine and Research: A Realm of Conflict and Profound Societal Implications," *The Journal of Gerontology Series A: Biological Sciences and Medical Sciences* 59 (2004): B523.
4. Robert Arking, et al., "Roundtable Anti-Aging Teleconference: What Is Anti-Aging Medicine?" *Journal of Anti-Aging Medicine* 6 (2003): 91.
5. Joe Nickell, "Peddling Snake Oil," http://www.csicop.org/sb/9812/snakeoil.html.
6. Mayo Clinic Staff, "Wrinkle Creams: Your Guide to Younger Looking Skin," http://www.mayoclinic.com/health/wrinkle-creams/SN00010.
7. Judith Estrine, *Is There an "Anti-Aging" Medicine?* (AARP Andrus Foundation and the International Longevity Center-USA, 2002), http://www.ilcusa.org/pages/publications/healthy-aging/is-there-an-anti-aging-medicine.php.
8. Robert Butler, "Is There an Anti-Aging Medicine?" *Journal of Gerontology Series A: Biological Sciences and Medical Sciences* 57 (2002): B333.
9. Position Statement of 51 Top Scientists on Fad Anti-Aging Products, "Fad Aging Cures Exposed, by Leading Scientists," http://www.healthfully.org/lgev/id7.html.
10. Project Aware, "Benefits, Risks, and Side Effects of ERT, HRT, and NHRT," http://www.project-aware.org/Managing/Hrt/benefits-risks.shtml.
11. Mayo Clinic Staff, "Human Growth Hormone (HGH): Does It Slow Aging?" Mayo Foundation for Medical Education and Research, http://www.mayoclinic.com/print/growth-hormone/HA00030.
12. "Is Resveratrol the New Wonder Supplement?" http://resveratrol.org.
13. "Turn on Your Anti-Aging Gene," http://www.resveratrolmiracle.com.

3

DOCTOR TALK

YOUR ROLE AS A PATIENT

Some changes in our aging body cannot be reversed no matter how much we would like to believe the promises we hear on television or read in magazines and newspapers. The best way to accept this fact of life is to become an informed partner in your health care.

First, learn as much as you can about your medical condition. However, be sure to choose your sources carefully. The amount of information on the Internet is overwhelming, and some of it is not based on facts but rather on someone's attempt to make a quick buck. (See the Appendix for some reputable and useful sites.)

Quality of Health Care Delivered to Adults: A 2003 national study, published in the *New England Journal of Medicine*, showed that less than 55 percent of patients interviewed received the recommended care for their medical conditions.[1]

Second, ask questions. Do not be afraid to ask your physician if you do not understand something. Medicine is often very complex and difficult to understand.

Third, if you are concerned about the plan of care, go for a second opinion. Sometimes, speaking to another physician can help you better understand your options and alleviate your concerns. However, do not fall into the trap of going from one physician to another looking for answers that do not exist.

COMMUNICATION AND TRUST

In real estate, the motto is "location, location, location." When it comes to working with your doctor, the motto is "communication, communication,

communication." In addition to being well informed, you must be able to speak openly with your physician for a successful partnership. Open communication requires both trust and honesty from both you and your doctor. Tell your doctor what you can and are willing to do, and what you can accept and live with. Ask for straight answers to your questions: "Is my condition treatable? Is there anything I should be doing differently? Why do I need this medication? Are my concerns justified and my expectations reasonable?"

Three tips to form a better partnership with your doctor:

1. Learn what you can about your medical condition(s).
2. If you do not understand something, ask about it—and keep asking until you do!
3. Speak openly and honestly with your doctor.

THE BEST 15 MINUTES

Typically, the time you have with your physician during an office visit is very limited. According to the U.S. Department of Health and Human Services, 90 percent of office visits in 2004 lasted between 6 and 30 minutes, with an average of about 18.7 minutes.[2] This is not a long time to discuss several medical problems. Therefore, being prepared can help you "stretch" the time. Plus, you should remember that during this time, your doctor needs to ask certain questions, as well as examine certain parts of your body or do a more thorough physical exam.

Paying attention during office visits to falls, functional abilities, memory problems, medications, nutritional concerns, and personal support systems (friends, family) improves the health of both patients and caregivers, improves patient function, and may lead to fewer hospital stays and delayed nursing home placement.

Being organized and writing down your questions before your visit can help you and your doctor make the most of the time. Prioritize by listing your most pressing questions and concerns first. You may even want to give your doctor a copy of your questions for his or her notes. During every office visit, make sure to mention if you have seen any specialists, if you have had any changes in your medications, and if you have noticed any functional changes. Ask your doctor if you need any health screening exams or tests. If you are accompanied by a caregiver, ask him or her to voice any concerns or changes about your caregiving needs. Encourage your caregiver to be honest about his or her own needs and limitations in providing care and support. Also make sure your doctor knows your wishes regarding life-prolonging measures (i.e., resuscitation or intubation).

Make sure to bring copies of any laboratory results or reports from specialists you have seen since your last visit. It is much better for you to personally bring a copy than to rely on reports being faxed or mailed to your primary care doctor. Often, this will mean your doctor will not have to repeat a test that you may have taken recently elsewhere. Plus, having the results available may mean you can get started on a treatment program right away.

Most importantly, listen carefully to any explanations and recommendations. Studies have shown that patients with chronic medical conditions have a poor recall of their physician's recommendations. Taking notes during your visit can help you remember your doctor's advice so you can follow the instructions. If taking notes seems to intimidate your physician, explain that your intent is to keep your visit organized and to make the most of it, not to plan a lawsuit. You can also ask for written instructions for later reference. Bringing along a relative or friend is helpful because "four ears hear better than two." And again, do not be afraid to ask if you do not understand something.

Three tips to help you prepare for your office visit:

1. Have a goal for your visit, even if it is only to report that you are feeling well.
2. Write down your questions, listing the most important ones first.
3. Keep a set of all your medical records, including copies of test results and visits to specialists.

GERIATRICIANS ARE NOT MAGICIANS

Often, patients come to a geriatrician for help with a particular problem. Even more often, the problem has been there for a long time and the patient has already seen several physicians, including other specialists for the same problem. Despite amazing advances in medicine and technology, there is no magic. If promises of a cure sound too good to be true, it's because they usually are. False hopes and unrealistic expectations are sure to lead to disappointment and frustration. If there really was a cure-all treatment or pill, everyone would be using it!

According to the Centers for Disease Control and Prevention, more than two-thirds of all deaths in the United States are caused by five chronic diseases: heart disease, cancer, stroke, chronic obstructive pulmonary (lung) disease, and diabetes.[3]

Geriatric medicine emphasizes care and careful management of chronic conditions when a cure is not possible. Geriatricians often do this not by prescribing yet another medication, but by individualizing medical care to the needs and wishes of the patient. As specialists in the care of older patients, our goal is to treat with a focus on the patient's daily functional abilities, such as taking a shower, getting dressed, or preparing a meal. We tend to look for the one medical condition that causes the greatest problem for a patient in his or her daily life.

A colleague asked me to see an older man who rather suddenly was having a much harder time walking. Although this man had had a major stroke several years earlier, he had been managing quite well living on his own with some support from his children. He recently had seen his primary care physician because he felt weak, was losing weight, and became short of breath when walking. His primary care physician had sent him to a cardiologist because he was concerned about heart disease, and to a psychiatrist because his weight loss may have been a sign of depression.

It was clear that this patient had great difficulties looking after himself, and he was afraid he might have to move out of his house. He did not have either severe heart disease or depression. His real problem was that he had been falling a lot recently, and he had become very fearful. He realized that a hip fracture would more than likely put him in a nursing home for good. So, he curtailed his walking, rested on the sofa or bed most of the day, and became what is called "deconditioned." This made him even more susceptible to falling.

He didn't need new medications or further tests—he needed a well-designed outpatient rehabilitation program to improve his balance and gait. Over time, his shortness of breath improved because he exercised more, and he became more confident in his balance and ability to walk.

Three tips to help you better manage your medical conditions:

1. Do not be afraid to tell your doctor about problems that seem minor (like a recent slip in the shower or an occasional memory lapse).
2. Be realistic, but do not give up hope.
3. Have a family member or friend accompany you to the visit. They may be able to remember things that you do not—"four ears hear more than two."

Pill Salad or a "Pill for Every Ill"

Be careful what you swallow! This advice holds true for both prescription and over-the-counter medications. We do not have a pill for every problem, and, in general, pills do not heal a disease. Medications are important to help you manage your conditions, but they are only one part of your medical care, and often not the most important part. Many patients take so many pills they could put them in a bowl, add milk, and call it their breakfast cereal! Others are so concerned about taking pills that they resist every attempt to take medications, even when they could greatly benefit from the drug. Yet others will not take any prescription medications for fear of side effects but readily buy every available herbal supplement in health food stores.

Studies have reported that older adults living in the community take, on average, four or five medications on a regular basis. It is estimated that as many as 18 percent of patients take medications that are not appropriate.[4]

According to an article published in the *Journal of the American Medical Association*, patients frequently do not take into account the fact that many "natural" supplements are not regulated for safety or effectiveness, especially in patients undergoing surgery. Often, there is little or no basis for the claims made. In addition, these supplements can interact with many other medications. For example, warfarin (Coumadin), *Ginkgo biloba*, and vitamin E can all thin the blood; if taken together, they can lead to internal bleeding. Some supplements, such as sleep aids that contain valerian, need to be stopped before a scheduled surgery because they may interact with anesthetic agents. Both *Ginkgo biloba* and ginseng can result in postoperative bleeding complications.[5]

A study at the Mayo Clinic suggests that as many as 61 percent of people take dietary supplements, most commonly multivitamins (41.5 percent), vitamin E (24 percent), and vitamin A (23 percent).[6]

Side Effects versus Benefits

All pills have side effects, but, fortunately, this doesn't mean that every patient will experience every possible side effect. In fact, quite the contrary. The vast majority of patients never complain of any side effects. Medications also interact with one another, and we do not always have a clear understanding of all the potential side effects and interactions of the endless combinations of drugs. This is especially true in older patients because they often have to take multiple medications. Medications can also interact with certain types of foods, as well as herbal supplements.

So, why take medications at all if their side effects and interactions are numerous and, in many cases, unknown? Because their benefits usually outweigh their risks, and they help people live with and manage their medical conditions. This *risk-benefit relationship* is important to understand. If the benefit of treating an infection with an antibiotic outweighs the risk of affecting kidney function, then clearly the infection should be treated. However, at the same time, careful monitoring is important, and dosages of medications may need to be adjusted in older patients. Sometimes, this may make the treatment inconvenient, but there is good reason for being especially careful with some medications in older patients.

Minimizing the Number of Medications

In many cases, there are ways other than pills to take care of a particular problem, such as constipation. Older people often suffer from constipation

An angry patient phoned me, complaining about how difficult it was for him to cut his pills in half. Initially, I was irritated because I had spent a lot of time with this patient, as I was particularly concerned about his condition. However, later, I realized that maybe I hadn't properly explained the need to adjust his medications. This highlights again the need for good communication between the physician and the patient. With few exceptions, good communication on the need for and possible side effects of a medication is probably the most important aspect of any patient-doctor relationship.

because of another medical condition, such as Parkinson's disease, or because it is a side effect of certain medications (e.g., medications to lower blood pressure). Instead of adding another medication, it is often easiest and best to try a remedy such as prune juice or warm water.

Do not immediately reach for the bottle of ibuprofen in the medicine cabinet when you have a headache. Instead, try resting for a moment or going for a walk. And when your back acts up after a day in the garden, try soaking in a warm bath rather than taking another painkiller. Painkillers like ibuprofen can raise your blood pressure, worsen your reflux disease, and cause havoc in your kidneys.

Some people may need to take multiple medications, while others take none or very few. In certain diseases, such as heart disease, more than one medication is needed for effective treatment. Regardless, the number of medications should be limited to those that are actually needed, especially if a patient has underlying liver or kidney disease. This is because most drugs are processed in the body and then eliminated by the liver and kidneys.

Three tips to make sure you are taking the right medications:

1. Tell your doctor *everything* you are taking, including herbal supplements, and discuss the need for all your medications.
2. Do not believe everything you hear or read.
3. Think twice before using over-the-counter medications.

SENIORS AND HOSPITALS—LIKE OIL AND WATER

Most older people should go to the hospital only when they have to. While many lives are saved daily in hospitals, older patients in particular regularly experience severe and even life-threatening complications. A Harvard Medical Practice Study showed that patients older than 65 had a higher risk of infections, falls, pressure ulcers, delirium, side effects from medication, and complications both during and after surgery.[7] This is not because doctors and nurses do a poor job of taking care of older patients in the hospital. On the contrary, every year, more and more older patients are treated in hospitals, and those treatments become more and more sophisticated. So, why this contradiction? The fact is that older patients are at higher risk of developing major complications because of other medical conditions and diminished reserves to withstand the stress of an illness.[7]

A healthy 95-year-old woman fell and underwent surgery to repair a hip fracture. Initially, she did well after the operation, but then heart failure developed because of the intravenous fluids she had received. Because she became a little confused on the pain medications, these medications were held back. As a result, her pain was not well controlled, walking was difficult and painful, and her progress was slow. When she had to stay at the rehabilitation facility longer than expected, she became very depressed.

To understand what went wrong in this case example, you need to be aware of and understand the concept of *iatrogenesis*. This refers to the unintentional harm to patients that is caused by doctors and nurses during treatment.[8] An example of this is the problem that developed after the older woman in the case illustrated above was given intravenous fluids. It is standard procedure and good medicine to administer fluids to patients undergoing and recovering from surgery, but this patient had had heart disease for years. Her weak heart could not handle that much fluid, and it started to fail. Another example is the confusion that can result in a patient taking pain medications. Certainly, pain management is an important part of care, but pain medications need to be given very carefully, anticipating the possibility that an older patient may become confused. Withholding pain medications for fear of confusion can equally cause problems, and as this case shows, can be responsible for an overall poor recovery.

Three tips to help when a loved one is in the hospital:

1. Visit as often as possible and stay as long as possible.
2. Talk regularly to the nurses and doctors who are looking after your loved one.
3. Be patient and supportive while your loved one is recovering.

Not Enough Geriatric Training

Unfortunately, the lack of understanding the specific needs of older patients is widespread. Older patients need to be cared for differently than younger ones, but few hospitalists, residents, and specialists have any geriatric training.[9] Equally serious in the care of older hospital patients is the lack of specialized nursing care. Younger patients can make their needs known, but a confused or weak older patient often cannot.

The two important factors that determine how well an older patient does after being discharged from the hospital are good nutrition and the ability to move around.[10,11] Older patients often have difficulty eating and don't eat well simply because some nurses do not recognize the need to monitor or help these patients with their meals. Some patients simply lose their appetite because they haven't had a bowel movement for days and become bloated lying in bed. The unfortunate result is that most of the time, older patients do not eat properly and lie in bed for many days.

Delirium—A Common Complication

Another common and often devastating consequence of hospitalization in older patients is the development of delirium. This medical condition is very serious and can occur after operations and in the case of serious infections. Delirium is a sudden and dramatic state of confusion in previously alert patients. Patients are often unable to recognize their families, and they become either very agitated or sedated and listless. Some do not want to take their medications, do not eat well, and will not participate in their care. Often, a delirious patient will sleep during the day and stay up all night.

Any older patient can develop delirium, but patients who already have a dementia or even a mild memory problem have an especially increased risk of delirium. If your loved one has a memory problem, even if it is mild, it is important to let doctors and nurses know. Families should alert the hospital staff if problems like this have developed during previous hospitalizations or when certain medications (such as pain medications) have been used.

The treatment for delirium is limited. Although several medications are available, they all have significant side effects, including more confusion. More commonly, the medical condition that is most likely causing the confusion is treated; this might be an infection or a side effect of another medication. Often, neurologists or psychiatrists are called in to help care for these patients.

Most important in the treatment of delirium is good and attentive nursing care, including ensuring that the patient drinks enough fluid and has a good nutritional intake. Attention to bowel and bladder care is needed to avoid constipation and urinary tract infections. Families play a very important role in the care of a patient with delirium. Patients do better when a familiar person is around as much as possible during the day and sometimes at night. Having a family member available at mealtime is especially helpful.

Only time can tell how much memory and function a patient will regain. Recovery from delirium can take days to weeks and even months. Patients often need to be transferred to rehabilitation units, but this poses another problem in that they are often not able to participate fully in their therapy. Sadly, as a result, many patients are not able to return home. Because delirium is not always preventable, it is important to anticipate and minimize its severity with early medical treatment and excellent nursing care.[12]

REFERENCES

1. Elisabeth A. McGlynn, "The Quality of Health Care Delivered to Adults in the United States," *New England Journal of Medicine* 348 (2003): 2635.
2. Esther Hing, "National Ambulatory Medical Care Survey: 2004 Summary—Providers Seen and Outcomes," *Advance Data: From Vital and Health Statistics* 374 (2006): 6.
3. National Center for Chronic Disease Prevention and Health Promotion, "The Burden of Chronic Diseases as Causes of Death, United States," http://www.cdc.gov/nccdphp/burdenbook2004/Section01/tables.htm.
4. Joseph H. Flaherty et al., "Polypharmacy and Hospitalization among Older Home Care Patients," *The Journals of Gerontology Series A: Biological Sciences and Medical Sciences* 55 (2000): M554.
5. Michael K. Ang-Lee, Jonathan Moss, and Chun-Su Yuan, "Herbal Medicines and Perioperative Care," *Journal of the American Medical Association* 286 (2001): 208.
6. Donald D. Hensrud et al., "Underreporting the Use of Dietary Supplements and Non-Prescription Medications among Patients Undergoing a Periodic Health Examination," *Mayo Clinic Proceedings* 74 (1999): 443.
7. Jeffrey M. Rothshild, David W. Bates, and Lucian L. Leape, "Preventable Medical Injuries in Older People," *Archives of Internal Medicine* 160 (2000): 2717.
8. Lisa S. Lehmann et al., "Iatrogenic Events in Intensive Care Admissions: Frequency, Cause, and Disclosure to Patients and Institutions," *American Journal of Medicine* 118 (2005): 409.
9. Margaret A. Drickamer et al., "Perceived Needs for Geriatric Education by Medical Students, Internal Medicine Residents, and Faculty," *Journal of General Internal Medicine* 21 (2006): 1230.
10. Rebecca Gary and Julie Fleury, "Nutritional Status: Key to Preventing Functional Decline in Hospitalized Older Adults—Promoting Functional Status through Interdisciplinary Collaboration," *Topics in Rehabilitation* 17 (2002): 40.
11. Jane E. Mahoney, Mark A. Sager, and Muhammad Jalaluddin, "New Walking Dependence Associated with Hospitalization for Acute Medical Illness: Incidence and Significance," *The Journals of Gerontology Series A: Biological Sciences and Medical Sciences* 53A (1998): M307.
12. Beatriz Korc, "Delirium in Hospitalized Patients May Be Preventable," *American Medical News* (2009), http://www.ama-assn.org/amednews/2009/09/21/prca0921.htm.

4

MEDICATIONS AND OLDER ADULTS

Much of the time, doctors have little to offer our patients other than medications. Certainly, some conditions can be cured with surgery or managed with nursing care or physical therapy, but older adults often have chronic medical conditions that cannot be treated effectively without the use of medications. So, in addition to your doctor's good advice, most of your visits probably end with one or more prescriptions. Patients play a part, too, often wanting some "magic pill" that will be a cure. The fact is, though, that all medications can interact with one another and can cause side effects that may need to be treated with yet another medication. The result is that older adults are the largest per capita users of prescription medications and consequently are most at risk of medication-related adverse events.[1,2]

A study published in December 2008 in the *Journal of the American Medical Association* showed that among a sample of "community-dwelling older adults, prescription and nonprescription medications were commonly used together, with nearly 1 in 25 individuals potentially at risk for a major drug-drug interaction."[3] The use of multiple—usually five or more—medications is referred to as *polypharmacy*. To complicate matters even more, some medical conditions like heart disease are at times treated best only by using multiple medications. This situation is called rational polypharmacy.

A **medication** is a substance used to treat or control a disease or to help prevent or even diagnose a disease. Medications come in many shapes and forms, from pills or liquids that are taken by mouth or injected into a vein, to ointments, creams, or even patches that are applied to the skin.

Polypharmacy is derived from the words *poly*, which means many, and *pharmacy*, which means medications, and it literally means the use of more medications than are necessary.

Rational polypharmacy refers to the use of many medications that act together to better treat a medical condition.

THE NAME GAME

Many medications have two names: a generic name and a brand name. This confuses not only patients but also sometimes doctors and even insurance companies. The generic name usually refers to the chemical name of the medication, whereas the brand name refers to the name registered by the company that makes it and under which it is sold. A common example is furosemide, which is a "water pill" (or a diuretic), that is sold under the brand name Lasix. Even more confusing is that in some cases, many companies make the same drug, and so there can be many brand names for the same medication. A common example of this is aspirin, which is sold both simply by its generic name as well as under many different brand names, including Bufferin, Anacin, and Excedrin. If this wasn't bad enough, some names sound and look very similar. This was the case for an antidiabetic agent called Amaryl and a medication for Alzheimer's disease called Reminyl. This potentially deadly confusion prompted a name change of the medication for Alzheimer's disease to Razadyne in 2004.[4] The generic names of medications will mostly be used in this chapter. For your convenience, at the end of this chapter there is a list of some common and important drugs with their brand names.

A few days after a patient of mine was discharged from the hospital after a short stay for control of his high blood pressure, his wife phoned me to report that he was very weak, his blood pressure was barely measurable, and his pulse rate was low. I advised her to take him to the emergency room immediately. What had happened was simple but scary. He had been discharged on a medication to lower his blood pressure called metoprolol (Lopressor, Toprol). What the physician in the hospital did not know was that the patient had already been taking a similar medication called atenolol (Tenormin). When the patient was discharged, he had been given instructions to continue his new medication and to restart all his regular medications. Taking these two medications that had the same effects landed the patient back in the hospital with a very slow heart rate and dangerously low blood pressure.

MORE MEDICATION COMPLICATIONS

In addition to possibly having similar names, many pills also look alike—small, round, and often white. Make sure you know what you are taking!

An excellent book by Jerry Avorn, MD, professor of medicine at Harvard Medical School and the chief of the division of pharmacoepidemiology and pharmacoeconomics at the Brigham and Women's Hospital in Boston, entitled *Powerful Medicines: The Benefits, Risks, and Costs of Prescription Drugs,*[5] describes how a lack of medication oversight often leads to more complications. In an interview with Dr. Avorn, he also states that pharmacy shopping and doctor shopping by patients adds to the confusion and lack of oversight in that "nobody is minding the store." How does this happen? The side effects of a medication prescribed by one doctor become a "newly diagnosed disease" by another doctor that the patient sees at a later time. The second doctor prescribes another medication for this "new disease."

An unfortunately common example of this is caused by the use of haloperidol (Haldol), a medication for elderly patients with dementia and agitation. Unfortunately, many elderly people are treated with dosages that are too high, and they end up being sedated and appearing like patients suffering from Parkinson's disease. These patients do not need more medication, but rather a lower dosage of haloperidol, or maybe none at all. Another example is the use of a drug called amitriptyline (Elavil), which has such a severe "drying effect" that it leads to a dreadfully dry mouth, severe constipation, or even worse, difficulty urinating. It's much better to reevaluate the need for this medication before a trip to the neighborhood drugstore to buy an over-the-counter medication for constipation or to the emergency room because of difficulty with urinating.

Or what about the poor patient who became incontinent of urine when treated with furosemide (Lasix) for a mild increase in her blood pressure? She started becoming overwhelmed by the sudden urge to urinate, and because of her difficulties walking, she couldn't quite make it to the bathroom. Several blood and urine samples were taken to look for a urinary tract infection, and a new medication was prescribed to calm the bladder. What made things even worse was that she became so depressed and homebound that her physician wanted to start yet another medication, an antidepressant. Fortunately, a smart medical student figured it all out, realizing that her increased urination was being caused by the strong "water pill" all along.

A word about drug allergies. An allergy to a particular medication is not the same thing as an adverse event or side effect of that medication. Allergic reactions occur when the body has made antibodies to a medication on a previous encounter. In people who are allergic, if the same medication is taken again, the immune system is activated, which can result in reactions ranging from a simple rash to life-threatening anaphylactic shock. In contrast, feeling dizzy or nauseated after taking a pain medication or having some diarrhea after taking an antibiotic is *not* an allergic reaction. These reactions are side effects that are common but not invariable.

THE WONDERS OF MODERN MEDICINE

After hearing all this, you may feel ready to flush all those expensive pills right down the toilet. But that would not be the best course of action. Medications are among the wonders of modern medicine, and they have saved and improved millions of lives.

What would medicine be like without the accidental discovery of the antibiotic penicillin? In 1928, Alexander Fleming, a doctor and researcher at St. Mary's Hospital in London, accidentally contaminated a culture of a bacteria called *Staphylococcus aureus* with a mold named *Penicillium notatum.* Dr. Fleming noticed that the mold inhibited the growth of the bacteria, and efforts to produce the new antibiotic began. By 1941, penicillin was commercially available.[6,7] Its ability to fight against the bacteria that are commonly involved in pneumonia and wound infections, which often cause septicemia (also known as blood poisoning) that leads to death, saved the lives of thousands of soldiers toward the end of World War II. Since then, this "miracle drug" has been used to successfully treat serious strep throat infections, the horrible childhood disease of diphtheria, life-threatening meningitis, and sexually transmitted diseases like gonorrhea and syphilis. Napoleon Bonaparte, Al Capone, Leo Tolstoy, Vincent Van Gogh, and Oscar Wilde are just a few notable patients with syphilis who would have appreciated a prescription for penicillin and a neighborhood drugstore in their time.[8] Other antibiotics would have been wonder drugs in Europe in the fourteenth century when the "Black Death," as the bubonic plague has been called, killed 20 to 30 million people.[9] As important as antibiotics have been historically, let's not forget vaccines, which have eradicated smallpox worldwide and polio from most countries.

Steroids, although often associated with undesirable side effects, have also saved and improved the lives of millions of patients. They are useful in treating diseases ranging from A for asthma and many autoimmune diseases, to X for xerostomia, or dry mouth, in its severest form.

A drug that is used nowadays frequently and successfully to prevent strokes in patients with abnormal heart rhythms or to prevent and treat blood clots that have formed in our body (e.g., blood clots in the legs are called deep venous thrombosis, or DVT) "was actually first marketed as a rat poison in the 1940s. In 1999, warfarin was the eleventh most prescribed drug in the USA, with annual sales of approximately $500 million dollars."[10] In 1785, the English physician William Withering used an extract of foxglove leaves to treat patients with heart failure. For more than 200 years now, digoxin (Lanoxin and Digitek), a medication made from the foxglove plant, has been used to help weak heart muscles pump blood more effectively.[11]

Medications to treat high blood pressure have improved countless lives in our day and age. The connection between high blood pressure and the risk of stroke and heart attack is well known. A recent article in the *New England Journal of Medicine* confirmed the importance of treating high blood pressure, even in patients who are 80 years and older.[12]

More recently, we have become aware of the importance of statins, the lipid-lowering medications that seem to be in the news so often. We know that the risk of developing coronary artery disease, in which the arteries that supply blood to the heart itself become stiff and harden, increases with higher levels of cholesterol in the blood. The evidence showing benefits of statins in younger adults is excellent. In a 2007 article in the *Journal of Gerontology* in which the literature was carefully reviewed, statins to lower cholesterol levels were shown to benefit older adults as well.[13] "Happy Hour" might just be renamed "Statin Hour," with those little pills served with crackers and cheese. Cheers!

THE CONCEPT OF RISK–BENEFIT

As we've already seen, the picture is not that simple. All these wondrous medications also have some possible side effects. Antibiotics can cause life-threatening allergic reactions; steroids can cause muscle weakness, brittle and easily fractured bones, thinning of the skin, and even some psychiatric problems. Warfarin and other anticoagulants, or drugs to thin the blood, can cause bleeding from the bowels and life-threatening bleeds in and around the brain. A little too much digoxin can make you feel like James Bond—nauseated, having vision problems, and feeling strange heart rhythms—in the 2006 movie *Casino Royal* when he was intentionally poisoned with the drug during a high-stakes poker game. Medications that lower blood pressure can also do a job on your kidneys and make you feel dizzy, while those wonderful statins can make your muscles weak and ache.

So how do we decide whether or not to take a medicine that is potentially so dangerous? The answer lies in the concept of risk-benefit. In other words, the benefit of these medications, far more often than not, greatly outweighs the risk of possible side effects. Please note that the word here is *possible.* Side effects are not automatic. In fact, many people taking various medications experience no side effects at all.

One way of thinking about this is to think about something that most of us do every day: driving. We all know that driving can be very hazardous—there is always the possibility of being involved in a car accident. But we accept that because we know the benefits of driving far outweigh the risks. Now let's take this analogy a little bit further. The driver of a car may feel more secure because of safety features like side-impact airbags, antilock brakes, and rollover protection, but he or she still needs to take responsibility for driving carefully. The same holds true for the patient taking any medications. Using the medications as they were prescribed (e.g., taking the correct amount at the correct times) can help reduce the possibility of side effects.

Why then in today's age of amazing technological advances and with millions of dollars spent by the pharmaceutical industry and supposedly careful FDA oversight do we still have to worry about medication side effects? And why are older adults (besides the very young) the "most vulnerable population" as Dr. Avorn points out?[5] To answer all these questions, we need to

---

Three things to remember:

1. Become familiar with both the generic and trade names of all the medications you take.
2. Always keep an accurate list of all your medications with you or have it readily available.
3. Many possible side effects are listed on the medication label and other information you receive from your pharmacy when you fill your prescription. **This does not mean you will experience them.**

look carefully at what actually happens to the pills we swallow obediently every morning at the breakfast table.

A PILL'S BRAVE AND HAZARDOUS JOURNEY

Knowing what happens to a pill once you swallow it can help you better understand why medications need to be taken carefully. There are many ways of taking medications, but to keep it simple, let's consider a pill taken by mouth. Once we swallow that little pill, it starts on its arduous journey through our gastrointestinal tract. The pill is propelled by muscle contractions down the esophagus, which connects the mouth and the stomach. It's important to drink enough water while taking a pill, especially if you're literally trying to swallow your entire medication list, because pills can "stick" to the sides of the esophagus. This can feel very uncomfortable and possibly even cause ulcers in the esophagus, because its lining is not made to protect against dissolving pills. Some medications such as aspirin are absorbed into the bloodstream in the stomach. Most medications continue their journey a little further into the small bowel, where they are finally absorbed. This explains why some medications need to be taken on an empty stomach; otherwise, they simply do not get absorbed properly.

Some medications can be affected by other medications if taken at the same time. For example, the absorption of the antibiotic ciprofloxacin (Cipro) can be reduced when iron, calcium, or magnesium (found in vitamin supplements), antacids, or dairy products are taken at the same time. Popular antacids available over the counter, such as ranitidine (Zantac) or omeprazole (Prilosec), can change the acidity of the stomach and actually increase the absorption of other medications, such as amoxicillin (an antibiotic) or nifedipine (a medication to control high blood pressure; Adalat, Procardia). A most unfortunate interaction occurs with what would seem to be a healthy morning glass of grapefruit juice and several medications, including those used to treat high blood pressure, high cholesterol, and abnormal heart rhythms. A chemical in the grapefruit juice interferes with the absorption of these medications, which can result in higher concentrations of these medications and an increase in the possibility of side effects.[14]

Already you can see that many medications encounter many obstacles shortly after being swallowed, before they have a chance to do their work. But usually, the medication is absorbed into the bloodstream and taken to the liver. A good way to think of the liver is as the port of entrance to the body where every drug undergoes a rigorous immigration screen. The lucky ones immediately gain access to the main circulation to continue their journey. Others undergo the equivalent of being picked out at the customs counter where they undergo partial metabolism by the dreaded cytochrome P450 system, which acts as a custom officer. Anything that makes the cytochrome P450 more active (or more angry!) can result in less of the drug being available for the body. For example, when the popular herbal medication St. John's wort is taken with other medications, the P450 enzyme is activated, lowering the levels of warfarin, digoxin, and simvastatin (Zocor) in the body, and so making these common medications less effective. It can work the other way, too. Some medications like the over-the-counter acid reducers omeprazole (Prilosec) and cimetidine (Zantac), some antibiotics, and some antidepressants reduce the effectiveness of the P450 enzyme and, therefore, cause the levels of some medications to be higher than normal. This is one of the reasons why you should always tell your physician about any over-the-counter medications and supplements you are taking.

Once the drugs have been absorbed into the bloodstream, some go almost directly to their final destination, while others are transported by being bound to proteins in the blood. This means that only unbound drugs are active to work at their destination. So the more a drug is attached to a protein, or should we say "sitting in a taxi," the less it can do its work. Makes sense, doesn't it?

The liver is also where many drugs are ultimately metabolized, that is, broken down and prepared to be eliminated from the body. The form of some drugs needs to be changed so they can dissolve in water to be excreted either by the kidneys through the urine or by the gastrointestinal tract through the bile. Any problems with the kidneys can result in less of a drug being excreted in the urine, which means it may be left in the body at higher levels. Some medications, like certain antibiotics or blood pressure-lowering medications (like lisinopril [Prinivil or Zestril] or enalapril [Vasotec]) can reduce the effectiveness of the kidneys, which slows down the excretion of other drugs. This is why blood samples need to be taken so frequently in older adults; kidney function must be monitored closely to determine whether the dosages of many medications need to be reduced. This is also why it is critically important for you to drink enough fluid every day to keep your kidneys well flushed. Unless you need to restrict your fluid intake for a known medical reason, you should drink at least five eight-ounce glasses of any liquid other than alcohol every day.[15]

Not the Same Old Body

So now that you know what actually happens to all those pills once you swallow them, let's look at how the normal changes of aging within the body affect how the medications are handled.

As we get older, many normal age-related changes occur. Some changes, like wrinkled skin and thinning hair, are far too easy to see. But there are other changes—ones we cannot see—that have a significant effect on the way our bodies handle medications. The absorption of a drug in the bowels, as described previously, is not affected, but the transportation and distribution of medication is different in older adults than in younger people.

As we age, lean muscle mass and total body water decreases, while total body fat increases. This does not mean that with age we will all get fatter! Rather, it reflects a change in our overall body composition.[16] As a result, drugs that can be dissolved in fat are stored more easily in the body and so stay around longer. An excellent example of this type of drug is diazepam (Valium), which can take a week to be cleared from the body. On the other hand, drugs that can be dissolved in water, like digoxin and your scotch at happy hour, do not stick around as long, but can easily reach higher levels in the body and cause side effects very rapidly. You may have noticed that you cannot drink as much scotch or wine as the years go by—this is the reason. In addition, alcohol commonly interacts with other medications you may be taking. Does this mean you cannot enjoy a drink anymore? Absolutely not. But it does mean that you should talk honestly with your doctor about your alcohol intake.

As our bodies age, and especially if we have a serious illness, the proteins that bind drugs and shuttle them around the body in the bloodstream start to behave like taxis in New York City on a rainy day, disappearing right when you look for one. This means that more of drugs are unbound and so are more active in the body. As we've already discussed, one of the most significant changes with aging is that the kidneys get old and rusty and cannot excrete those drugs from the body as efficiently as before. And if that weren't enough, certain conditions that are common in older people, like hypertension and diabetes, along with some particular medications, decrease kidney function even more.

HOW TO TAKE YOUR MEDICATIONS RESPONSIBLY

Now that you appreciate a few of the reasons why older patients need to take their medications so carefully, what can you do to protect yourself from possible side effects and medication errors? First, being organized and knowing some important facts about common medications, especially about the ones you take, are very helpful in avoiding many common problems. Second, remember that taking daily medications is a serious business. It is up to you to make sure you're taking your medications correctly to get the most benefit from them. In addition to leading a healthy lifestyle, such as eating a good diet and getting the right amount of exercise, using medications properly is one of the most important things you can do for your health.

It's helpful to know a few important facts about some common over-the-counter and prescription medications. Table 4.1 includes some of the common medications taken by older adults. Of course, many more medications should be avoided by older adults, and the best sources of information are your physician and your pharmacist.[17]

Some Practical Tips

The following tips may come in handy and help you take your medications safely. With a little luck, you might save some money, too!

I remember a lovely Italian patient of mine who was an outstanding cook. One day, she proudly showed me her collection of recipes for various pasta dishes. She had carefully organized a notebook containing recipes on small pieces of paper with hand-written notes made by her mother and grandmother years ago. I was amazed at how meticulously she had put together her little cookbook. But when it came to her medications, she usually carried her daily pills in a zip lock bag and took one after the other during the course of the day. I explained to her that she really needed to be every bit as careful with her medications as she was with her recipes, and I was delighted to see on her next visit how she had organized and labeled her medications in a weekly pill minder. She lived to be almost 95 years old. Now, although I would like to think that her great longevity was related to the wonders of modern medicine, I am inclined to think her good health had something to do with the many delicious pasta meals she made over the years. I would still love to get my hands on that book.

At the Doctor's Office

- Ask your doctor to write down all your medications or ask for a printout.
- Ask your doctor to explain what each medication is for.
- Do not be afraid or ashamed to ask again if you do not understand something.
- Ask your doctor to make the drug regimen as simple as possible.
- At each visit, review your medications with your doctor and ask if all medications are still necessary.
- Tell your doctor about any new medications that you have received from a specialist.
- Tell your doctor if you are taking any over-the-counter medications or herbal supplements.
- Be honest and let your doctor know if you cannot afford the medications.

At the Pharmacy

- If at all possible, buy all your medications at one pharmacy.
- Ask the pharmacist to keep a medication profile on you.
- Ask for large print on labels if needed.
- Ask for easy-to-open containers if needed.
- Ask your pharmacist to check all your medications for any potential interactions.

At Home and on the Road

- If you miss a dose, call your doctor, and ask what you should do.
- Use a weekly medication dispenser.
- Ask for help filling the dispenser if you need it.
- Keep all your medications with a list from the doctor's office in *one* place.
- Make sure your spouse, children, caregiver, or a friend has a list of your medications and knows where to find them.
- Once a month (e.g., the first or fifteenth of each month), check if you need refills.
- When you travel, always keep your medications in your carry-on luggage and have an accurate list of all medications on you at all times. Make

sure to have the telephone numbers of both your doctor's office and your pharmacy with you.

Specific Tips about Pain Medication

- If you are on pain medication, take it on a regular basis. Do not wait until the pain gets worse. When taken regularly, the medications work better to keep your pain under control.
- If you take pain medication regularly, always take a laxative (e.g., Senokot) and a stool softener (e.g., Colace) to avoid severe constipation.
- If you suffer from severe pain and your doctor has prescribed morphine or morphine-like medications (also referred to as opioids), take them as directed. If you have fears or concerns about becoming addicted to these medications, please talk to your doctor—there is no need for anyone to suffer from severe pain.

Table 4.1
Medications and Their Side Effects

Medication	Potential Side Effects	Use Carefully in Case of
Nonsteroidal anti-inflammatory drugs (e.g., ibuprofen)	Fluid retention	Heart failure, hypertension
	Stomach irritation	Stomach ulcers, acid reflux
	Kidney function worsens	Decreased kidney function
Diphenhydramine or medications containing diphenhydramine	Sedation and confusion	Memory problems
	Low blood pressure	High blood pressure
	Difficult urination	Enlarged prostate
	Blurred vision	Glaucoma
Many cough and cold preparations containing antihistamines	Similar to those of diphenhydramine	
Benzodiazepines used as sleeping aids and for their antianxiety effects	Sedation and confusion	Memory problems
	Unsteady gait, falls	Gait and balance problems
Persantine	Hypotension	Should not be used in older adults unless specifically prescribed
Doxepin	Sedating and similar to diphenhydramine	
Oxybutynin	Sedating and similar to diphenhydramine	
Cyclobenzaprine	Sedating	Confusion and gait problems

Some Generic and Brand Names of Common Medications

Table 4.2 will give you some examples of brand names for each generic drug. The medications are divided into groups by their purpose or function. This list is far from exhaustive but includes some of the most commonly used medications in older adults.

Table 4.2
Some of the Most Commonly Used Medications in Older Adults

Generic Name	Brand Name
Pain medications, non-narcotic	
Ibuprofen	Motrin, Advil
Diphenhydramine	Benadryl, or as the "PM part" of Tylenol PM
Acetaminophen	Tylenol
Diclofenac	Voltaren
Indomethacin	Indocin
Naproxen	Aleve, Anaprox
Salsalate	Disalcid
Tramadol	Ultram
Pain medications, narcotic	
Fentanyl (patch)	Duragesic
Hydrocodone plus acetaminophen (combination)	Vicodin
Hydromorphone	Dilaudid
Oxycodone	OxyContin
Oxycodone plus acetaminophen (combination)	Percocet
Pentazocine	Talwin
Propoxyphene	Darvon
Antispasm medications for the gastrointestinal tract	
Dicyclomine	Bentyl
Hyoscyamine	Levsin, Cystospaz
Antispasm medication for the urinary tract	
Oxybutynin	Ditropan
Beta-blockers	
Atenolol	Tenormin
Metoprolol	Lopressor, Toprol XL

Generic Name	Brand Name
Bronchodilators	
Albuterol	Proventil, Ventolin
Salmeterol	Serevent
Osteoporosis medications	
Alendronate	Fosamax
Risedronate	Actonel
Blood pressure and heart medications	
Amlodipine	Norvasc
Diltiazem	Cardizem
Verapamil	Calan, Verelan, Isoptin
Nifedipine	Adalat, Procardia
Lisinopril	Prinivil, Zestril
Enalapril	Vasotec
Ramipril	Altace
Captopril	Capoten
Irbesartan	Avapro
Losartan	Cozaar
Valsartan	Diovan
Diuretics ("water pills")	
Furosemide	Lasix
Spironolactone	Aldactone
Triamterene plus hydrochlorothiazide (combination)	Dyazide, Maxzide
Ulcer and reflux medications	
Famotidine	Pepcid
Ranitidine	Zantac
Omeprazole	Prilosec
Cholesterol-lowering medications	
Lovastatin	Mevacor
Pravastatin	Pravachol
Simvastatin	Zocor
Sleeping and anti-anxiety medications	
Zolpidem	Ambien
Lorazepam	Ativan
Flurazepam	Dalmane

(*Continued*)

Generic Name	Brand Name
Temazepam	Restoril
Diazepam	Valium
Diabetic medications	
Glyburide	Micronase
Glipizide	Glucotrol
Metformin	Glucophage
Antipsychotic medications	
Haloperidol	Haldol
Olanzapine	Zyprexa, Zydis
Risperidone	Risperdal
Antidepressant medications	
Fluoxetine	Prozac
Sertraline	Zoloft
Paroxetine	Paxil

REFERENCES

1. Aaron Catlin et al., "National Spending in 2006: A Year of Change for Prescription Drugs," *Health Affairs. The Policy Journal of the Health Sphere* 27 (2008): 14.
2. Jerry H. Gurwitz et al., "Incidence and Preventability of Adverse Drug Events among Older Persons in the Ambulatory Setting," *Journal of the American Medical Association* 289 (2003): 1107.
3. Dima M. Qato et al., "Use of Prescription and Over-the-Counter Medications and Dietary Supplements among Older Adults in the United States," *Journal of the American Medical Association* 300 (2008): 2867.
4. Institute for Safe Medication Practices, "Medication Safety Alert! Potential Confusion with Amaryl (Glimepiride) and Reminyl (Galantamine)," 2004 issue, http://www.ismp.org/newsletters/acutecare/articles/20040909.asp.
5. Jerry Avorn, *Powerful Medicines: The Benefits, Risks, and Costs of Prescription Drugs* (New York: Alfred A. Knopf, 2005), 172.
6. Fun Facts about Fungi, "Penicillin: The First Miracle Drug," Utah State University, http://www.herbarium.usu.edu.
7. The University of Hawaii System, "Penicillin: The Wonder Drug," http://www.botany.hawaii.edu/faculty/wong/BOT135/Lect21b.htm.
8. Patrick French, "Clinical Review: Syphilis," *British Medical Journal* 334 (2007): 143.
9. The Middle Ages Web site, "Black Death," http://www.middle-ages.org.uk/black-death.htm.
10. Mike Scully, "Warfarin Therapy: Rat Poison and the Prevention of Thrombosis," *The Biochemist* February 24 (2002): 15.

11. Work by Withering, "An Account of the Foxglove, and Some of Its Medical Uses," *Encyclopedia Britannica*, http://www.britannica.com/EBchecked/topic/3023/An-Account-of-the-Foxglove-and-Some-of-Its-MedicalUses.
12. Nigel S. Beckett et al., "Treatment of Hypertension in Patients 80 Years of Age or Older," *New England Journal of Medicine* 358 (2008): 1887.
13. Caroline G. Roberts, Eliseo Guallar, and Annabelle Rodriguez, "Efficacy and Safety of Statin Monotherapy in Older Adults: A Meta-Analysis," *Journal of Gerontology: Medical Sciences* 62A (2007): 879.
14. Katherine Zeratsky, "Grapefruit Juice: Can It Cause Drug Interactions?" Mayo Clinic.com, http://www.mayoclinic.com/health/food-and-nutrition/AN00413.
15. Todd P. Semla and Paula A. Rochon, "Pharmacotherapy," in *Geriatric Review Syllabus*, ed. Peter Pompei and John B. Murphy (New York: American Geriatrics Society, 2006), CD-ROM version.
16. Richard N. Baumgartner, "Body Composition in Healthy Aging," *Annals of the New York Academy of Sciences* 904 (2000): 437.
17. Todd P. Semla, Judith L. Beizer, and Martin D. Higbee, *Geriatric Dosage Handbook*, 9th ed. (Hudson, OH: Lexi-Comp Inc., 2003), 1322–1324.

5

NUTRITION

NUTRITION IS LIKE FASHION

It changes constantly. There is always something new, while something highly praised a year ago is suddenly no longer in vogue, and other long-outdated ideas are back with a fanfare. It often leaves us confused and possibly with a case of heartburn.

Part of the confusion about "right" and "wrong" nutrition was caused in the early 1980s when the National Academy of Science issued its "landmark report on diet and cancer." According to Michael Pollan in his witty January 28, 2007, *New York Times* article "Eat food. Not too much. Mostly plants." the "industry and media followed suit, and terms like polyunsaturated, cholesterol, monounsaturated, carbohydrates, fiber, polyphenols, amino acids and carotenes soon colonized much of the cultural space previously occupied by the tangible substance formerly known as food. The Age of Nutritionism had arrived."[1]

Nutrients and More

Simply stated, "nutrients are chemical elements and compounds found in the environment that plants and animals need to grow and survive."[2] Nutrients that are required in large amounts are called macronutrients. Examples are carbohydrates, fats, and proteins. Vitamins and minerals, which are needed in much smaller quantities, are considered micronutrients.

Supplements

A dietary supplement was legally defined by Congress in 1994 as "a product that contains vitamins, minerals, herbs . . . and other ingredients intended to supplement the diet." The Food and Drug Administration has general labeling requirements for dietary supplements.[3]

Herbal supplements are a type of dietary supplement that contains herbs. Herbs are derived from a plant or part of a plant and have potential healing properties.[3]

Since then, our relationship to food has changed forever. It seems we no longer eat food, but nutrients instead. We now talk about low-fat, low-carbohydrate, nutrient-enriched foods.

WHAT IS ALL THE FUSS ABOUT NUTRIENTS?

The answer, as it so often is, can be found in history. Scurvy is most likely the first disease to be definitely associated with a dietary vitamin deficiency. Scurvy, caused specifically by vitamin C deficiency, results in weakening of the capillaries, resulting in bleeding of the gums and anemia. In its severe form, it can lead to death. Centuries ago, it was dreaded by all sailors. More than half of Vasco da Gama's crew died of scurvy while they were on his first journey around the Cape of Good Hope in 1497–1499. When James Lind, a Scottish naval officer, treated afflicted sailors with rations of lemons and oranges, he literally worked miracles.[4]

Some 500 years later in 1992, an article in the *New England Journal of Medicine* titled "Prevention of the first occurrence of neural-tube defects by periconceptional vitamin supplementation" radically changed the treatment of pregnant women. This confirmed the need for vitamin supplements, especially folic acid, during pregnancy.[5]

Besides vitamins, other nutrients have been shown to be directly linked to common medical conditions. Studies in the late 1970s and 1980s noted a relationship between calcium and osteoporosis, a common condition found in postmenopausal women and in some older men, too. The bone essentially becomes very brittle and, as a result, fractures easily, especially in the lower back and hip areas. We now know that vitamin D is also crucial in the treatment and prevention of osteoporosis.[6] Disease can be caused not only by the lack of a nutrient but also in some cases by too much. An excellent example of this is cholesterol. In July 1961, Dr. William Kannel and his colleagues published a landmark article describing high cholesterol, among other risk factors, as being associated with coronary heart disease.[7]

The same holds true for vitamins. In fact, the current recommendations are not to take high-potency vitamins, which are commonly sold in health food stores and on the Internet. The recently very popular vitamin E has been

---

A longtime patient of mine insisted, despite my pleas to the contrary, on taking a full complement of all vitamins plus several herbs in mega dosages. He contributed his excellent health to this potpourri of brightly colored pills. When he was diagnosed with peptic ulcer disease, he went into a depression and blamed the antihypertensive pills I had prescribed for him. I do not know whether his stomach ulcer was caused by the "vitamin salad," but I urged him to at least hold off on some pills while we were trying to heal his stomach ailment. It took all my powers of persuasion to make him lay off his beloved vitamin pills for several weeks. Incidentally, he did not come back to see me ever again.

associated with "increased all-cause mortality" in dosages higher than 400 IU per day.[8]

OLDER ADULTS, NUTRITION, DISEASE, WEIGHT, AND MEDICATIONS: AN UNPALATABLE RECIPE

Older adults are not automatically at risk of nutritional deficiencies, nor are there any nutritional disorders seen only in older adults.

Undernutrition refers to clinically important weight loss of 4–5 percent of a person's total body weight over a period of 6–12 months.[9]

Undernutrition is a common and at times poorly recognized problem in older adults. Why this happens is not an easy question to answer, and it requires some careful distinction between normal changes and disease states common with age. On one hand, normal changes in the aging body include a loss of smell and taste sensations, especially for salty foods, making the food less palatable. On the other hand, there are many diseases that significantly affect a person's ability to eat and maintain a proper diet. Let's consider the scope of the problem.

First, neurologic diseases, such as Parkinson's disease, strokes, and dementias, can make eating difficult because of tremors, swallowing difficulties, loss of appetite, and, in the case of dementia, understanding the need to eat. Cancer in general is often associated with weight loss, particularly malignancies that affect the gastrointestinal system, like cancers of the stomach, pancreas, and colon (or large bowel).

Gastric reflux disease can cause a person to restrict his or her diet for fear of heartburn. In severe cases, this condition can lead to difficulty swallowing because of serious damage to the esophagus (the tube that connects the mouth and the stomach).

Heart failure and severe chronic pulmonary disease can also make eating very difficult. Heart and lung diseases can make a person short of breath, possibly so much so that the effort needed simply to breathe is exhausting and uses up all the energy a person has. This may result in a person not being able to make up for all his or her caloric needs and losing weight in spite of attempts to eat a sufficient diet.

Diabetes is another major disease that seriously affects a person's diet and nutritional state. Patients need to follow a strict diet to control their blood sugar to avoid damage to blood vessels, kidneys, nerves, and so forth. On top of that, diabetes can also cause the stomach to be sluggish. This results in poor emptying, a feeling of fullness, and sometimes nausea, none of which is conducive to enjoying a nice four-course meal.

Let's not forget the bane of human existence these days with the increasing age of mankind—arthritis. Deformed hands from various types of arthritis make food preparation and handling very difficult. The pain of arthritic changes in the knees or back or any other part of the body often does not help a person enjoy a healthy meal. Certainly pain in general, whether from arthritis or related to neurologic conditions or cancer, is a major contributor to poor appetite, weight loss, and poor quality of health.

Depression, another common and often missed diagnosis in older adults, is also a major contributor to poor appetite. In fact, weight loss is often the reason for the diagnosis. Depression may also be the result of social isolation with many older adults living alone and having to shop and cook for themselves. No wonder the common diet is often tea and toast.[10]

Now think about adding a mixture of medications to the previous recipe for nutritional risk, and the scope of the problem becomes even greater. Many medications, both prescription and over-the-counter, can have adverse effects on nutrition. The list of specific medications is long, but essentially any drug may interfere with the ability to eat a healthy diet. Many commonly used medications and their side effects can lead to nutritional problems. (See Chapter 4 for more detailed information on medications.) Heading the list in the prescription category are several groups of cardiovascular medications used to regulate blood pressure and control cholesterol level. Among them are calcium channel blockers such as amlodipine besylate (Norvasc), which like many other in this group, can cause constipation. Angiotensin-converting enzyme inhibitors like lisinopril (Prinivil) can cause nausea, vomiting, and diarrhea, and the commonly used beta-blockers such as atenolol (Tenormin) can cause nausea and vomiting. Diuretics, commonly referred to as "water pills," such as furosemide (Lasix) may leave patients with anorexia and constipation. Even the popular lipid-lowering medications known as statins like pravastatin (Pravachol) can cause constipation, nausea, and vomiting. And digoxin (Lanoxin), which is derived from the foxglove plant, causes stomach upset in some people. The list continues with nonsteroidal anti-inflammatory drugs (or NSAIDs) such as ibuprofen, which can cause stomach irritation and even ulcers. Antibiotics, which have saved millions of lives, can also create havoc in our gastrointestinal system. Many antibiotics cause stomach upset, and their use and especially overuse can result in diarrhea. In its severest form, *Clostridium difficile* diarrhea (commonly known as "C diff") can be life threatening. One particularly common group of medications that should not be forgotten are the "sleepers," or sleeping aids. This group spans both many prescription medications such as the benzodiazepines like Ativan, Restoril, or Valium, as well as over-the-counter medications. These medications tend to cause sedation and possibly confusion, neither of which promotes a good diet.[11] Diphenhydramine, an over-the-counter antihistamine well known as Benadryl, is commonly used as a sleep aid alone or in combination with, for example, Tylenol as Tylenol PM. It has many side effects, including significant sedation, confusion, and constipation.

Up to this point, we have concentrated on undernutrition, or the lack of an adequate diet, which leads to unintentional weight loss. The opposite of undernutrition is overnutrition, which leads to obesity. Obesity as it is defined in children and middle-aged adults refers to weight and body mass index (BMI). However, this formula cannot simply be used in older adults because the weight of an older adult reflects less muscle mass and more fat tissue. This is because the ratio of these two tissues changes with age.[10] (See Chapter 1 for more information on normal changes of the body with age.)

Body mass index (BMI) is calculated by weight (in kgs) divided by height (in meters squared), or weight (in lbs) divided by height (in inches squared) times 704.5.

Overnutrition refers to overweight and in severe cases to obesity. The National Heart, Lung and Blood Institute defines overweight as having a BMI between 25 and 29.9, and obesity as having a BMI of 30 or above.[10]

What do we really know about the health risks of older adults who are overweight? The short answer is not too much. However, we do know that many Americans age 65 and older are overweight and that, for the population as a whole, being overweight is associated with many health problems, including diabetes, high blood pressure, heart disease, stroke, high cholesterol, osteoarthritis, and sleep apnea. Some cancers, such as prostate, breast, uterine, and colon cancers, have also been related to being overweight. Even so, the current evidence is not clear cut. Several studies have indicated that being overweight in people 65 and older does not increase the risk of death, while other studies have found some relationship.[12]

People with sleep apnea (*apnea* from the Greek meaning "without breath) tend to stop breathing repeatedly in their sleep. For more information, visit the American Sleep Apnea Association at www.sleepapnea.org.[13]

We also know that older adults who are significantly overweight often complain of pain in their hips, knees, or back as a result of the extra weight and osteoarthritis. This compromises mobility and the ability to exercise, often resulting in a less active lifestyle. This, in turn, can lead to falls, a loss of strength and potentially frailty. Being overweight also affects the control of hypertension, diabetes, and cholesterol levels, and it can make skin care and nursing care in general more difficult. So even though we don't have all the answers about overnutrition in older adults, it is best to avoid being overweight in older age.

VITAMINS AND THEIR FALL FROM FAME

A careful look at the medical literature over the last few years makes it clear that our obsessive love for vitamins has faded quite a bit. A July 2008 article in the *American Journal of Public Health* openly challenges the Older American Act Nutrition Program, which suggests a multivitamin-mineral supplement to be used in addition to meals. The authors feel that these supplement recommendations are not a "one-size-fits-all quick fix." They say that multivitamin-mineral supplements "do not contain calories, proteins, essential fatty acids, or fiber, nor do they adequately address nutritional gaps of some vitamins and minerals," and conclude that there is "insufficient evidence of their benefits and safety," especially in older adults with chronic medical conditions requiring multiple medications.[14] A May 2006 article in the *Journal of Evidence* report/technology assessment by the United States agencies for Health Care Policy and Research and Healthcare Research and Quality found that the "heterogeneity in the study population limits generalization to the United States population." In other words, the vast difference among older adults makes it difficult to formulate general recommendations with regard to use of multivitamin-mineral supplements.[15]

To summarize, taking multivitamin-mineral supplements may not be as good as we once thought and may even have some detrimental effects on health. But what about specific vitamins? Surely we know that certain vitamins are essential to good health—consider the example of vitamin C and scurvy. But this does not mean that taking extra vitamins will prevent or help heal certain chronic diseases. We've already seen the demise of vitamin E as a cure for almost anything. The January 2007 issue of the *Archives of Internal Medicine* published a review of trials of cognitively intact and impaired older adults taking vitamin B_6, B_{12}, and folic acid supplements. The conclusion was that there is no evidence of benefit to support the use of these supplements to improve cognitive function or prevent cognitive decline.[16] And finally, folic acid in combination with vitamins B_6 and B_{12} failed to have any effect on cancer risk in women.[17]

Other vitamins haven't fared any better lately. Beta-carotene and vitamins A, C, and E have failed to be useful in the prevention of several diseases, including cardiovascular disease in men.[18,19] The lack of evidence for use of vitamin C and selenium in prevention of diseases has been a big letdown for the antioxidant supplement craze. "Pill-happy America" is waking up to a new reality that the morning cereal of multivitamins, mineral pills, and antioxidants is really not doing us any good. Instead, it is costing us millions of our hard-earned money, while making millions for a sometimes questionable industry. We need to stop believing that a pill in the morning will make up for the evening hamburger and fries and the bedtime snack of ice cream and chips.

HERBAL SUPPLEMENTS: VOODOO OR TRUTH?

Plants have been used for thousands of years for medicinal purposes, and more than 120 medications used today are derived from plant species. Beginning in the 1960s and especially in the 1990s, more and more Americans are using herbal supplements. Two events have been credited with the dramatic rise in popularity of herbal supplements. In 1994, Congress, in its sometimes uncertain and strange wisdom, passed the Dietary Supplement Health and Education Act (DSHEA), allowing manufacturers to sell herbal supplements without requiring documentation of either safety or efficacy. This came about as a result of a well-organized campaign by both consumers and manufacturers against the FDA's attempt to develop strict rules and regulations for herbal products. In addition, a *British Medical Journal* article on the use of St. John's wort for the treatment of depression raised a lot of interest among the public and healthcare advocates.[20] A 2002 National Health Interview Survey showed that 18.9 percent of adults in the United States had used natural products in the previous year. Echinacea, ginseng, *Ginkgo biloba*, and garlic were among the favorite products.[21]

Eventually, increasing concern about the usefulness and possible side effects of herbs and their potential interactions with prescription medications resulted in a call to reason and a demand to reform the DSHEA. And finally in 1998, the National Institute of Health upgraded the Office of Alternative Medicine (formed in 1992) to the National Center for Complementary and Alternative Medicine to carefully study and document the usefulness and safety of herbal medicine products. As a result, we now have a reliable source for information on herbal products.[3]

Still, a major problem remains with herbal products, and that is the lack of standardization of the complex substances in each supplement. There are also concerns about purity of the supplements, which may contain harmful contaminants.[21]

Although I am not fundamentally against using herbs for medicinal purposes, I strongly urge you to use the three guidelines listed in the sidebar below.

Three things to remember:

1. Evaluate the herbs you're thinking of using before buying some expensive supplement. Do your research as carefully as if you were planning on buying a new car. It is your health that is at stake.
2. Make sure to inform your doctor of any herbs you are taking. Do not be shy or embarrassed. It is important for your doctor to know, especially in case of potential interactions with other medications.
3. Don't believe everything you read. Don't be fooled into spending your money and risking your health.

A HEALTHY DIET IS LIKE A PUZZLE

Now that you know what not to eat, what should you eat? It helps to think of a healthy diet as a complex puzzle. When all the pieces are put together correctly, they form a food pyramid. This "puzzle" has been rearranged and updated several times since its first debut in 1990. Walter Willett, MD, in his book "Eat, Drink, and be Healthy" notes that the "USDA (U.S. Department of Agriculture) pyramid was wrong. It was built on shaky scientific ground. . . . and scores of large and small research projects have chipped away at its foundation."[22] To understand these rearrangements and improvements on the food pyramid, we need to know more about the individual puzzle pieces.

Let's take a look at the separate pieces—carbohydrates, fats and cholesterol, protein, and fruits and vegetables—before we look at the big picture.

Carbohydrates: Some but Not Others

Carbohydrates are a very important part of our diet, providing an excellent source of energy for the body. They are found in a wide variety of foods, including vegetables, fruits, and whole grains. Carbohydrates are made up of sugar molecules that form chains to make starches and fibers. An unfortunate misconception in the recent past has been the notion that carbohydrates are bad and make you gain weight. The truth is that there are some carbohydrates we should avoid, but not all are "bad."

When we eat carbohydrates, our digestive system breaks them down into the sugar molecules that cross into the bloodstream. With the help of a hormone called insulin, these sugars are transported into the cells to supply the cells with energy. If our body does not have enough insulin or the insulin is not working properly, we end up with abnormally high blood sugar levels, a disease referred to as diabetes mellitus. High blood sugar levels damage small arteries, which can lead to damage in the kidneys, eyes, and even small nerves in the feet and hands. Sometimes the blood sugar levels can be controlled by eating a careful diet; other times diet isn't enough and medications are needed. Eating a careful diet is even more important in older adults with type II diabetes (formerly referred to as late-onset diabetes). Why is this so important? Because some carbohydrates make the blood sugar rise very quickly when they are digested. These are the so-called "bad" carbohydrates, or carbohydrates that have a high glycemic index (*glycemic* refers to glucose, or sugar); they are found in white breads, cereals, and potatoes. On the other hand, carbohydrates that have a low glycemic index are digested more slowly; as a result, the blood sugar does not rise quickly and can be more easily regulated. Examples include grainy breads, nuts, and pasta.[23]

For more information and a more detailed list of foods, each with its respective glycemic index, take a look at www.glycemicindex.com. In summary then, we want to eat more of the carbohydrates with a low glycemic index and less with a high index.

Fats and Cholesterol: The Good and the Bad

Another recent misconception about this puzzle piece has caused major confusion and a thriving food industry. The thought was to eat very little fat and cholesterol; hence, the low-fat diet craziness. Not only is it simply wrong and a gross oversimplification, but it also has not helped prevent many diseases, especially obesity. It is not the total amount of fat we eat, but rather the type that is important. The good types are the mono- and polyunsaturated fats; the bad types are the unsaturated and trans-fatty acids. I must admit neither sounds very appetizing to me.

Let's not forget the omega-3 fatty acids that stare at you from almost every aisle of your corner pharmacy and grocery store. Our bodies cannot make this type of polyunsaturated fat. We can get this good type of fat by eating fish and some salad dressings, but most of us just do not get enough of it on a daily basis. So, we often end up taking it as one of those brightly colored pills, a cash cow for the supplement industry.[24, 25]

And then there is cholesterol, a "soft, waxy substance found among fats circulating in your bloodstream and in all of your body's cells"[26] that can create many problems if too much builds up on the inside of your arteries. The cholesterol in our bloodstream is primarily affected by the types of fats we eat. The reason is that unlike carbohydrates, which can pass into the bloodstream directly from the gut, fats need to be packaged in carrier molecules called lipoproteins to be transported in the bloodstream. This is because fats on their own are not soluble in water (or blood). These carrier molecules, which doctors sometimes seem to be obsessed with, are the high-density lipoproteins (HDL) and low-density lipoproteins (LDL) that we have all heard so much about. The HDLs pick up cholesterol and transport it to the liver for recycling. This is good—they "clean up." The LDLs essentially do the reverse, that is, they carry cholesterol from the liver and distribute it to the rest of the body. This is not so good. If we have too many LDLs, fats will be deposited in plaques on the walls of the arteries, clogging them up and interrupting the blood flow, potentially leading to heart attacks or strokes. This is why you want high HDL levels and low LDL levels. Triglycerides are another way to transport fats and, in general, are good unless there are way too many.

We can influence our levels of these carrier molecules by eating less of the bad type of fats and more of the good type. As mentioned before, the good type of fats are the mono- and polyunsaturated fats found in vegetable oils, nuts, and various seeds. The bad types are the saturated fats, which are "bad" in part because our body can make them and doesn't need an extra supply. These saturated fats are found in dairy products, fish, and meats.[24] You can find detailed information on cholesterol and fats at www.americanheart.org.

You may ask, if there are so many problems with fats, then why eat them at all? First, it would be impossible to avoid eating fats completely because nearly all foods contain some amount of fat. Second, bodies need some fat because it is an important part of cell membranes and an excellent source of energy. We could not live without it. Third, it is a great form of energy storage, although most of us do not think of bigger hips and "love handles" in this way. Plus, it would be ridiculous for me to suggest that you stop eating all your favorite tasty foods—no more wine and cheese parties, no more ice cream on hot summer nights, and no more hamburgers on July 4. But you should not overdo on the "bad" fats and make sure to eat as much as possible of the "good" ones. In fact, a Dutch study, the OmniHeart trial, showed that choosing unsaturated fats more often and lowering the carbohydrates in the diet, "lowers blood pressure, improves lipid levels, and reduces the estimated cardiovascular risk."[27] The fats to avoid like the plague are the trans-fatty acids. They are usually found in fast foods, baked goods, and the goodies in vending machines, and they literally boost the levels of LDL in our blood.[24] Trans-fatty acids are getting easier to avoid because, fortunately, they have been banned in restaurants in many U.S. cities. Try to say goodbye to the regular helpings of french fries and make them a treat for a special occasion, like your birthday.

One more thing before we leave fats behind. There are people who seem to be able to eat as much of the "forbidden foods" as they wish and their cholesterol levels are always fine, while others who deprive themselves of all the goodies still have high cholesterol levels. Genetics has a lot to do with it, and it's just the luck of the draw.

The Protein Secret

Think of proteins as the puzzle pieces that are hardest to find but that end up being one of the most important ones for a complete, good, and healthy diet. Proteins are made up of amino acids, some of which are referred to as "essential" amino acids because our body cannot make them and so we need to get them from our diet. A great source of these essential amino acids is meat, while vegetables lack them.[28] Therefore, we should scrap all the vegetables and eat only meat. Just joking!

The era of proteins arrived when the high-protein, low-carbohydrate Atkins diet stunned the American Heart Association with its traditional, beloved low-fat, high-carbohydrate diet, in that the Atkins diet worked equally well for people trying to lose weight.[29] The good news is that it is very easy to get enough of all the necessary proteins by eating a well-balanced diet of vegetables, dairy products, and meats.

Your Mother Was Right about Fruits and Vegetables

The rule of thumb about fruits and veggies is simply to eat as many as you can as often as possible. It is becoming increasingly obvious that there is a good correlation between eating fruits and vegetables and lowering the risk of heart disease and stroke. The now 14-year-old Harvard-based Nurse's Health Study has made this clear.[30,31] Blood pressure is also positively affected by a diet high in fruits and vegetables.[32] Unfortunately, the correlation between a diet high in fruits and vegetables and cancer is not as clear, and further studies are needed.

So how much of your diet should be fruits and vegetables? The old and truly confusing recommendation was "five a day." Fortunately, the new recommendations are more precise, with a recommended amount of 2.5 to 6.5 cups a day.[30]

THE BIG PICTURE AT LAST

Looking at history always helps us understand the present, and thanks to the Egyptian pharaohs, we can think of a healthy diet in the form of a

Three things to remember:

1. Losing weight unintentionally is not a normal part of normal aging. Please contact your physician if you lose weight unintentionally.
2. Gaining weight excessively is also not a normal part of aging and can cause many medical problems. Please ask for help in managing those extra pounds.
3. Be aware that side effects of many medications can interfere with eating a healthy diet.

pyramid. The idea behind the pyramid shape as it relates to diet is that we should eat more foods represented at the bottom of the pyramid and less of the goodies at the top. Unfortunately, like in real history, some pyramids did not survive and fell apart over time. To continue the comparison and as mentioned earlier, the original United States Department of Agriculture (USDA) pyramid from 1990 had to be renovated. Unfortunately, the updated 2005 version was not as helpful as intended, in part because research had outrun the renovation efforts. As a result, nongovernment agencies have helped out, and we now have two new pyramids: the "Healthy Eating Pyramid" from the Department of Nutrition, Harvard School of Public Health[33] (www.hsph. harvard.edu) and the "Modified MyPyramid," a combined effort of Tufts University and the Jean Mayer USDA Human Nutrition Research Center on Aging at Tufts University.[34] Each has its unique style and way of showing what is important for a healthy diet and lifestyle. Let's take a closer look at each of these pyramids.

Healthy Eating Pyramid (Department of Nutrition, Harvard School of Public Health)

The lower part of this pyramid (see Figure 5.1) shows that a healthy diet should consist of regular consumption of whole grains, vegetables, fruits, and olive or canola and other vegetable oils. Fish, poultry, and eggs are also important. Nuts, beans, and seeds provide important minerals and proteins, and also make for an interesting salad. The recommendations with regard to eggs are not more than three times a week, especially in people with heart disease and diabetes. Dairy products in "level 4" provide calcium and vitamin D. Try to avoid the high-fat cheeses and opt for low-fat milk and yogurt instead. Most older adults still need some calcium and vitamin D supplementation because they cannot get enough from these foods alone.

At the top of the pyramid are all the very tasty foods we all like that should be eaten more sparingly. This does not mean you can never enjoy your favorite goodies, but they should not be on your daily food plan. Another consideration is wine and alcohol in general. Small amounts may be fine but excessive amounts are not. And you should always ask your doctor if there is a problem with drinking alcohol and any medications you are taking.

Figure 5.1
Healthy Eating Pyramid

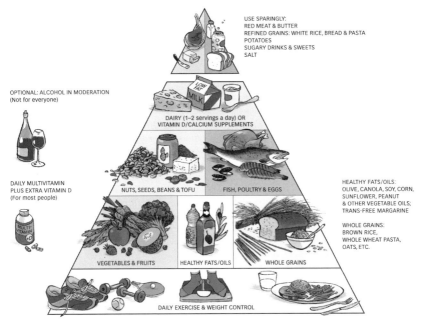

USE SPARINGLY:
RED MEAT & BUTTER
REFINED GRAINS: WHITE RICE, BREAD & PASTA
POTATOES
SUGARY DRINKS & SWEETS
SALT

OPTIONAL: ALCOHOL IN MODERATION
(Not for everyone)

DAIRY (1–2 servings a day) OR
VITAMIN D/CALCIUM SUPPLEMENTS

DAILY MULTIVITAMIN
PLUS EXTRA VITAMIN D
(For most people)

NUTS, SEEDS, BEANS & TOFU

FISH, POULTRY & EGGS

HEALTHY FATS/OILS:
OLIVE, CANOLA, SOY, CORN,
SUNFLOWER, PEANUT
& OTHER VEGETABLE OILS;
TRANS-FREE MARGARINE

WHOLE GRAINS:
BROWN RICE,
WHOLE WHEAT PASTA,
OATS, ETC.

VEGETABLES & FRUITS

HEALTHY FATS/OILS

WHOLE GRAINS

DAILY EXERCISE & WEIGHT CONTROL

Copyright © 2008. For more information about The Healthy Eating Pyramid, please see the Nutrition Source, Department of Nutrition, Harvard School of Public Health, http://www.thenutritionsource.org, and Eat, Drink, and Be Healthy, by Walter C. Willett, M.D., and Patricia J. Skerrett (2005), Free Press/Simon & Schuster, Inc.

Modified MyPyramid from Tufts University[34]

The Modified MyPyramid (see Figure 5.2) has some other important recommendations that are especially useful for older adults. There are depictions of frozen vegetables and fruits in resealable bags, which "are particularly good choices for older individuals, because they allow for easy apportioning of single or double servings and minimize pre-preparation." I like the everyday usefulness of this representation. Like the Harvard Healthy Eating Pyramid, the Tufts Pyramid points out the need to drink plenty of liquids every day. I recommend a minimum of five eight-ounce glasses of fluids of your choice, other than alcohol and soda. Because of a less active thirst mechanism, many older adults do not drink enough fluids. However, again a word of caution: individuals with heart or kidney disease may need to watch their fluid intake. Please talk to your doctor about this.

Both pyramids also point out that some individuals may need supplemental vitamins because of their overall medical condition. However, Dr Alice Lichtenstein, DSc, Director of the Cardiovascular Nutrition Laboratory at the Jean Mayer USDA Human Nutrition Research Center on Aging at Tufts,

Figure 5.2
Modified MyPyramid for Older Adults

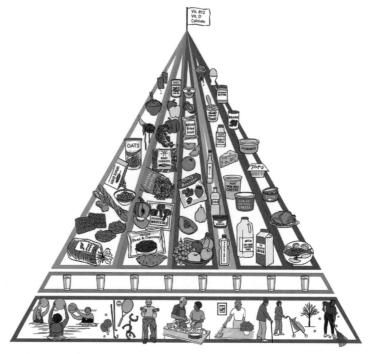

Copyright © 2007 Tufts University. Reprinted with permission from Lichtenstein AH, Rasmussen H, Yu WW, Epstein SR, Russell RM. Modified MyPyramid for Older Adults. *J Nutr.* 2008; 138:78–82.

A Quick Word About Salt

It has been known for some time that older adults and African Americans are more sensitive to the amount of salt in their diet than other groups of people. Salt intake has also been associated with high blood pressure, and reducing salt intake lowers blood pressure not only in people who suffer from hypertension but also in those who have normal blood pressure. In fact, Dietary Approaches to Stop Hypertension, known as the DASH diet, can lower blood pressure within two weeks. There are two wonderful things about this diet. First, it is made up of regular foods—complex carbohydrates, fruits, vegetables, and low-fat dairy products—that you can buy in any grocery store. Second, if sodium is limited to only 1500 mg/day along with the DASH diet, blood pressure can be lowered to the same extent as by the commonly used medication hydrochlorothiazide. In other words, you could literally eat your blood pressure down and you may no longer need to take the drug.[32]

stresses that "we continue to emphasize that the majority, if not all, nutrients an older adult consumes should come from food rather than supplements."[34]

You may have noticed that neither food pyramid shows the amount of each food group you should be eating on a daily basis. This is deliberately done to help you focus on quality of food and combining the different groups for a healthy meal. You may also wonder why I have not mentioned the depiction of activities and exercise in the bases of both pyramids. A healthy lifestyle is more than just eating healthy foods and requires regular exercise. This will be the focus of the next chapter. So off to a good workout!

Three things to remember:

1. It is much better to get all your essential nutrients from food sources, rather than from supplements.
2. Food should be enjoyed!
3. A healthy diet is only part of a healthy lifestyle—don't forget the exercise.

REFERENCES

1. Michael Pollan, "Unhappy Meals: Eat Food, Not Too Much, Mostly Plants," *New York Times Magazine*, http://www.nytimes.com/2007/01/28/magazine/28nutritionism.t.htm.
2. U.S. Geological Survey, "Toxic Substances Hydrology Program: Nutrients," http://toxics.usgs.gov/definitions/nutrients.html.
3. National Center for Complementary and Alternative Medicine, "Get the Facts: Herbal Supplements—Consider Safety, Too," National Institute of Health, http://nccam.nih.gov/health/supplement-safety.
4. The Free Dictionary, "Scurvey," http://encyclopedia2.thefreedictionary.com/Scurvey.
5. Andrew Czeizel and Istvan Dudas, "Prevention of the First Occurrence of Neural-Tube Defects by Periconceptional Vitamin Supplementation," *New England Journal of Medicine* 327 (1992): 1832.
6. "Pathogenesis of Osteoporosis," ed. Lawrence Raisz, in UpToDate.com, http://www.uptodate.com.
7. William Kannel et al., "Factors of Risk in the Development of Cardiovascular Disease: Six-Year Follow-Up Experience," *Annals of Internal Medicine* 55 (1961): 33.
8. Edgar Miller III et al., "Meta-Analysis: High-Dose Vitamin E Supplementation May Increase All-Cause Mortality," *Annals of Internal Medicine* 142 (2005): 37.
9. Jeffrey Wallace, "Involuntary Weight Loss in Older Outpatients: Incidence and Clinical Significance," *Journal of the American Geriatrics Society* 43 (1995): 329.
10. "Geriatric Nutrition: Nutritional Issues in Older Adults," ed. Christine Richie, in UpToDate.com, http://www.utdol.com.
11. *Physicians' Desk Reference*, 63rd ed. (Montvale, NJ: Physicians' Desk Reference, Inc., 2008).
12. Paula Diehr et al., "Weight, Mortality, Years of Healthy Life, and Active Life Expectancy in Older Adults," *Journal of the American Geriatrics Society* 56 (2008): 76.
13. American Sleep Apnea Association at www.sleepapnea.org, "Sleep Apnea Information," http://www.sleepapnea.org/info/index.html?gclid=CLrEtt-K85YCFQkcHgodqE2WYg.
14. Melissa Marra and Nancy Wellman, "Multivitamin-Mineral Supplements in the Older American Act Nutrition Program: Not a One-Size-Fits-All Quick Fix," *American Journal of Public Health* 98 (2008): 1171.

15. Han-Yao Huang et al., "Multivitamin/Mineral Supplements and Prevention of Chronic Disease: The Johns Hopkins University Evidence-Based Practice Center, Baltimore, MD," *Evidence Report/Technology Assessment* 139 (2006), http://www.ahrq.gov/downloads/pub/evidence/pdf/multivit/multivit.pdf.

16. Ethan Balk et al., "Vitamin B_6, B_{12}, and Folic Acid Supplementation and Cognitive Function," *Archives of Internal Medicine* 167 (2007): 21.

17. Shumin Zhang et al., "Effect of Combined Folic Acid, Vitamin B_6, and Vitamin B_{12} on Cancer Risk in Women: A Randomized Trial," *Journal of the American Medical Association* 300 (2008): 2012.

18. Goran Bjelakovic et al., "Mortality in Randomized Trials of Antioxidant Supplements for Primary and Secondary Prevention," *Journal of the American Medical Association* 297 (2007): 842.

19. Howard Sesso et al., "Vitamins E and C in the Prevention of Cardiovascular Disease in Men," *Journal of the American Medical Association* 300 (2008): 2123.

20. Klaus Linde et al., "St. John's Wort for Depression: An Overview and Meta-Analysis of Randomized Clinical Trials," *British Medical Journal* 313 (1996): 253.

21. "Overview of Herbal Medicine," ed. Robert Saper, in UpToDate.com, http://www.utdol.com.

22. Walter Willet, *Eat, Drink, and Be Healthy* (New York: Free Press, 2005), 11.

23. Harvard School of Public Health, "The Nutrition Source. Carbohydrates: Good Carbs Guide the Way," http://www.hsph.harvard.edu/nutritionsource/what-should-you-eat/carbohydrates-full-story/index.html#introduction.

24. Harvard School of Public Health, "The Nutrition Source. Fats and Cholesterol: Out with the Bad, In with the Good," http://www.hsph.harvard.edu/nutrition-source/what-should-you-eat/fats-full-story/index.html#introduction.

25. Harvard School of Public Health, "The Nutrition Source. Ask the Expert: Omega-3 Fatty Acids," http://www.hsph.harvard.edu/nutritionsource/questions/omega-3/index.html#introduction.

26. HeartHub for Patients, "Cholesterol," http://www.hearthub.org/hc-cholesterol.htm.

27. Paul Elliott et al., "Results of the OmniHeart Randomized Trial," *Journal of the American Medical Association* 294 (2005): 2455.

28. Harvard School of Public Health, "The Nutrition Source. Protein: Moving Closer to Center Stage," http://www.hsph.harvard.edu/nutritionsource/what-should-you-eat/protein-full-story/index.html#introduction.

29. Christopher Gardner et al., "Comparison of the Atkins, Zone, Ornish, and LEARN Diets for Change in Weight and Related Risk Factors among Overweight Premenopausal Women," *Journal of the American Medical Association* 297 (2007): 969.

30. Harvard School of Public Health, "The Nutrition Source. Vegetables and Fruits: Get Plenty Every Day," http://www.hsph.harvard.edu/nutritionsource/what-should-you-eat/vegetables-full-story/index.html#introduction.

31. Hsin-Chia Hung et al., "Fruit and Vegetable Intake and Risk of Major Chronic Disease," *Journal of the National Cancer Institute* 96 (2004): 1577.

32. Lawrence Apple et al., "A Clinical Trial of the Effects of Dietary Patterns on Blood Pressure," *New England Journal of Medicine* 336 (1997): 1117.

33. Harvard School of Public Health, "The Nutrition Source. Food Pyramids: What Should You Really Eat?" Harvard School of Public Health, http:www.hsph.harvard.edu/nutritionsource/what-should-you-eat/pyramid-full-story/index.html.

34. Alice Lichtenstein et al.," Modified MyPyramid for Older Adults," *Journal of Nutrition* 138 (2008): 78.

6

EXERCISE AND OLDER ADULTS

Okay, I know what you're thinking. "I'm not going to some fancy gym and make a fool of myself wrestling with those machines and trying to heave those shiny weights in front of big mirrors with unintelligible rock music blaring in the background, with younger members staring and laughing at me. I'm too old for this! Besides, I have some medical problems, and my arthritis especially doesn't allow me to do this in the first place."

I hear you loud and clear. But let's see if we can give you a new way to think about exercising, because the benefits are tremendous and the hazards are far less than you think—and definitely less than the potential side effects of all those pills you're probably taking. There are a lot of misconceptions about exercise in general, and I admit that reading many of the guidelines about exercise seems to require a master's degree in exercise physiology. It may also put you to sleep! But understanding some basic concepts about exercise will have you dreaming about METS, minutes, moderate-intensity aerobic physical activity, and muscle-strengthening activities in no time.

When we talk about exercise and older adults, we're not talking about training for the next Boston marathon or an Olympic event. Exercise encompasses a wide variety of physical activities. Let's first define a number of terms used to describe exercise to avoid adding to any confusion.

EXERCISE 101

Different types of exercises, done in the right mix or combination, "promote endurance, strength, balance, and flexibility." An important type of exercise for older adults is *strengthening exercise*, or resistance training, which builds muscle mass and counteracts the age-related decrease in skeletal muscle. These exercises cause muscles to contract against an external resistance such as weights or large elastic bands. Your own body weight can also suffice. *Aerobic exercise*, or endurance exercise, increases your heart and breathing rates and thereby improves your heart and lungs. A third type of exercise—and one

---

Physical activity is defined as "bodily movement produced by contraction of skeletal muscle that increases energy expenditure above the basal level."

Exercise is best defined as "physical activity that is planned, structured, repetitive, and purposeful in that the main objective is improvement or maintenance . . . of physical fitness.

Physical fitness refers to the "ability to carry out daily tasks with vigor and alertness, without undue fatigue, and with ample energy to enjoy leisure time pursuits and meet unforeseen emergencies."[1]

---

that is particularly important for older adults—is *balance training*. Balance exercises are intended to improve balance and gait so that the risk of falls and consequent major disabilities is reduced. Last, but also very important, are *flexibility exercises*. Exercises that improve flexibility help prevent injuries and falls. More about all these different exercises and specific examples are discussed later in this chapter.[2]

MEASURING EXERCISE

We now need some numbers and measurements to make recommendations and to properly categorize different activities. This gets more difficult. The scientific community uses certain units of measurements that make so little sense to the average lay person they may as well be written in a foreign language. For example, the current recommendation for the total weekly physical activity for adults ranges from 500 to 1000 MET-minutes. So, what does that mean? MET stands for metabolic equivalent, a unit that describes the energy expenditure of a specific activity. If you reread the definition of physical activity, this may start to make some sense. Our bodies use energy whenever we do something. Even when you are sitting in a chair, your body contracts a number of muscles and so uses energy. Therefore, it makes sense that 1 MET is defined as the amount of energy used by our bodies at rest. A 10-MET activity means that our bodies must use 10 times as much energy as we would use if our bodies were at rest.

We can also measure physical activity by the time we spend doing the activity. So, the next time you go out ballroom dancing for three hours and enjoy those waltzes, sambas, and tangos, your body is using energy in a 3-MET activity, which for 3 hours (180 minutes) makes for a total of 540 MET-minutes of activity. Another way of looking at it is to invite your partner out for 3 MET-hours of physical activity (but I take no responsibility for your partner's reaction to such a romantic invitation).[3]

Now, how did we get from exercise to ballroom dancing, and how do we know how much energy our bodies use when we dance the tango? Fortunately, research has provided us with the MET equivalents of common daily activities. Remember that because we define exercise as a physical activity that is structured, repetitive, and purposeful, any daily activity counts as a form of exercise. These activities include housework chores (e.g., vacuuming, washing dishes, putting away groceries, making the beds, etc.) to more enjoyable pursuits such as gardening and outdoor sports, including walking, hiking, jogging, bicycling, fishing, golfing, and swimming. All count toward the weekly recommended amount of 500–1000 MET-minutes of exercise.

Three things to remember:

1. You need to do a combination of strengthening, aerobic, balance, and flexibility exercises.
2. Being physically active counts as exercise.
3. Exercise can and should be fun!

THE BENEFITS OF REGULAR EXERCISE—IT'S NOT ALL ABOUT BIG MUSCLES

Are you starting to think about exercise a little differently now? Wait until you hear about the many benefits of regular exercise. You may want to get up right now to go play a round of golf or even start washing those dishes!

In a study published in 1994 in the *New England Journal of Medicine*, residents at the Hebrew Rehabilitation Center for the Aged showed improvement in their mobility with a resistance training program using small weights. If this is possible for these nursing-home residents, think about the potential improvement in gait and overall well-being that less frail seniors can achieve.[4,5] You might be surprised to hear that even as little exercise as walking a mile a week can have demonstrable benefits.[6] Exercise has many other benefits besides helping you walk better and safer. There is now good evidence that exercise is beneficial for people with cardiovascular disease. This includes older adults who have had a heart attack or who suffer from angina or even from mild heart failure. The heart itself is made of muscle, and exercise will make the heart stronger. Exercise is one of the main treatments for peripheral vascular disease, which is poor blood flow, primarily in the legs, that causes pain after walking a certain distance. Exercise is equally good for the lungs. People with chronic lung disease benefit from exercises of their arms and legs, which often are part of a comprehensive pulmonary rehabilitation program.

Exercise also improves control of blood sugar in people with diabetes, and it helps strengthen the bones in those with osteoporosis. An exercise program is as important as diet for losing weight, reducing cholesterol, and controlling blood pressure. The aches and pains, and especially the stiffness, of arthritic joints can be helped and often markedly improved by appropriate exercise. Gone are the days when doctors told patients suffering from bad osteoarthritis to rest as much as possible—we know now that it's all about movement.[2] And that's not it. We seem to be only at the beginning of recognizing even

broader beneficial effects of regular exercise. There is evidence in the literature that physical activity can potentially decrease the risk of certain cancers,
such as colon, breast, and prostate cancer.

Finally, exercise makes you feel good. Regular exercise can help people
with depression, and there is some evidence to suggest that it may improve
mental function in people suffering from memory problems, such as those
with Alzheimer's disease.[7]

I first met Hank one morning after my workout. Hank was not your average gym
type. He walked with some difficulty and was clearly suffering from a devastating disease. I soon found out that he'd first walked into this gym with a walker three years
ago, despite advice from several physicians to stay home and in his own words, "don't
do anything."

Hank, now in his mid-fifties, started having trouble some 20 years ago, when he
woke up night after night with headaches. Tylenol helped initially, but soon he was
getting hardly any sleep. Tests done at a headache clinic revealed no answers, and
Hank was put on muscle relaxants that made him so drowsy he had to be intubated
and placed on a ventilator for life support. Fortunately, Hank's wife managed to have
him transferred to a tertiary medical center in Boston, where he was diagnosed with a
rare type of muscular dystrophy, a progressive muscle-degenerating disorder that
results in the inability to walk and, ultimately, death because of an inability to breathe.
Hank's life seemed to have stopped as he was condemned to live at home with ramps,
a wheelchair, a walker, and a nighttime ventilator.

This all changed one day when Hank met Dr. Alfred Slonim, a physician in New
York who is an expert in treating his patients by using exercises. Before his life-saving
visit with Dr. Slonim, Hank spent some days with his wife in Aruba. He remembered
this otherwise beautiful place as the low point in his life. He described to me how he
had fallen seven times and could no longer get up by himself. It seemed ridiculous for
Dr Slonim to ask Hank to get on a treadmill and to walk and lift weights to strengthen
his arms and shoulders. But with Hank's positive, "can-do" attitude, he did it! Hank
now drives to the Global Fitness gym and works out several times a week with Kevin
Ewing, a personal trainer who carefully watches him do his strengthening exercises.

I left the gym that morning with a wonderful feeling, equally intrigued and, I admit,
envious of this extraordinary man.

WHAT TYPE AND HOW MUCH EXERCISE SHOULD I DO?

Good question, and, as usual, there is not one simple answer that fits all.
Older adults are very heterogeneous, a concept that is explained in more
detail in Chapter 2, "Geriatric Medicine versus the Anti-Aging Movement."
Because of this great variability among older adults, it is impossible to provide recommendations that would be suitable for all. Instead, an approach
that is more specific and tailored to the needs of each individual is necessary.

One thing that is true for all is that every older adult should be physically
active every day. People who remain active as they age and do not develop a

major medical problem have few if any restrictions. In fact, two of my patients ran the Boston Marathon last year! Now, older adults who have a sedentary lifestyle or who have not exercised regularly, perhaps in part because of some chronic medical condition, should not jump up, rush to the nearest mall, buy some fancy gym clothes, and join the early morning joggers in the nearby park. It is important to start slowly and gradually build up an exercise program. In addition, before starting any exercise program, older adults should discuss their plans with their doctors and ask about possible restrictions and the need for any pre-exercise evaluations. This is especially important for older adults who suffer from any of the following medical problems:[8]

- rapid or irregular heart beat with occasional palpitations
- chest pains and shortness of breath requiring intermittent use of nitroglycerin tablets
- known aortic stenosis or abdominal aortic aneurysm
- severe crippling or worsening lung disease
- leg pains from poor circulation
- hernias
- foot problems, especially nonhealing ulcers
- history of falls or of gait and balance problems
- poor eyesight or recent eye surgery

However, having any of these conditions does *not* mean that you are condemned to a homebound existence in front of the television watching sports day in and day out (although some of you may like that idea). Physical activity remains important and doable for older adults who have any of the medical conditions in this list, but it needs to be done under close medical supervision and with certain restrictions.

Three things to remember:

1. Let your doctor know about your exercise plans or routine.
2. Always start new exercises slowly and build up gradually.
3. Exercising regularly counts more than the amount of time you spend doing it.

At Last, Exercise Recommendations and Examples

According to the 2008 physical activity guidelines for an active, happy, and healthier life by the U.S. Department of Health and Human Services, older adults should do at least "150 minutes (2 hours and 30 minutes) of moderate-intensity aerobic physical activity or an equivalent amount (75 minutes or 1 hour and 15 minutes) of vigorous-intensity activity per week. Older adults can also do an equivalent amount of activity by combining moderate- and vigorous-intensity activity."[3] The guidelines go on to say "no matter what its purpose, walking the dog, taking a dance or exercise class, or bicycling to the store, aerobic activity of all types count." So, the only question now is what exactly is meant by moderate- and vigorous-intensity activities? Remember those METs we mentioned earlier? Moderate-intensity activity uses 3–6 METs, while vigorous-intensity activity uses more than 6 METs. This works out to be between 500 and 1000 MET-minutes a week for the average person.

If you have always been fit and active, unless you have a new medical problem that keeps you from doing your regular exercises or sports, there is no reason why you cannot continue doing what you enjoy as you get older. If you do have a new medical condition, such as a recent hip or knee replacement or a new heart condition, there is no reason to despair. You can still participate in many daily activities while you're recovering until you can get back to your routine exercises.

If you have been leading a more sedentary lifestyle or are simply not the outdoorsy type, many activities other than sports can give you the recommended amount and intensity of physical activity to help you feel good and active on a daily basis. Please remember though if you have any chronic medical condition, make sure to first ask your doctor about the amount and intensity of physical activity you can and should be doing.

Everyday Activities

So, let's see how active you are just by going about your everyday life without doing specific exercises. Table 6.1 shows the number of METs associated with typical routine activities.

In a typical day of housework, you may do 20 minutes of vacuuming (20 times 3.5 = 70 MET-minutes) and 1 hour of cooking and cleaning up (60 times 2.5 = 150 MET-minutes), for a total of 220 MET-minutes. If the next day, you work in the garden for 2 hours (120 times 3.5 = 420 MET-minutes), your total comes to 640 MET-minutes, already over half of the recommended weekly amount of 500–1000 MET-minutes.

If you walk each morning for 30 minutes (30 times 3 = 90-MET minutes), in a week's time, you will earn 630 MET-minutes for your physical bank account. Good news for you golfers: a two-hour game of golf with the guys (120 times 4.5 = 540 MET-minutes) is actually more physical activity than working in the garden.

You probably didn't know how physically active you already are during a week of well-deserved retirement. And yes, you are allowed to sit down in front of the television and watch your favorite sport show, but this will earn you only 1 METs and even less than that if you fall asleep. Still, not bad for doing nothing!

If you are up for it at the end of the day, sexual activity will not only help you sleep better at night but will also credit your account with 1.5 METs. Thought you might want to know this.[9]

Table 6.1
METs Associated with Typical Routine Activities

Activity	METs
Sweeping the floors	3.3
Vacuuming or mopping	3.5
Cooking and cleaning up	2.5
Sweeping the garage floor and sidewalk	4
Watching a grandchild	3
Caregiving for a spouse or friend	4
Mowing the lawn (push mower only)	5.5
Gardening in general	4
Weeding	4.5
Trimming shrubs	3.5
Stacking wood	5
Shoveling snow	6
Walking (take the dog, it's good for both of you)	3
Playing golf (no carts)	4.5
Biking	4
Swimming	7
Skiing	7
Jogging	7 or more
Tennis	7 or more
Watching television	1
Sexual activity	1.5

The Rest of the Mix

So far, we have discussed only aerobic activities. You'll recall though that the recommendations are based on a mix of aerobic, muscle strengthening, balance, and flexibility exercises. Many simple muscle-strengthening and balance exercises can be done at home with no special equipment. No fancy sports club required! Remember that exercising safely includes both a warm-up period before and a cool-down period after. A warm-up can consist of doing a strengthening exercise slowly and using less weight; the cool-down may simply be gradually slowing down the pace of an activity.

Several examples of exercises that you can easily do at home are described next. It's okay to start slowly, but try to build up gradually so that you can repeat each exercise 10 times.

- Wall push-ups: Lean against a wall with your hand and slowly lower your body toward the wall and push away again.
- Chair squats: Sit in a chair, preferably one with arm rests. Slowly rise to a standing position, and then slowly lower yourself back into the chair. Use your arms and the arm rests if needed.
- Bicep curls: Hold a small weight (cans of food or small water bottles will work) in each hand. Slowly bend your arms at the elbows to 90 degrees and lower them again. Keep your elbows at your sides.
- Shoulder shrugs: Hold your arms straight at your sides with a small weight in each hand. Slowly shrug your shoulders as high as you can and let them down again.
- Plantar flexion exercises: These exercises will help strengthen your legs. Stand behind a chair or at a table for stability and slowly stand up on your toes. You can alternate this with standing on your heels.
- Knee and hip flexion: These two simple exercises will also help strengthen your legs and improve balance. Keep standing at the table or behind a chair. Use ankle weights if you have them. Bend one knee as far as you can so that your foot lifts up behind you. Alternate this knee flexion with a hip flexion, in which you bend your knee toward your chest as far as you can. Then, repeat both on the other side.
- Heel-to-toe walk: This is the ultimate balance exercise, and you can do it anywhere. Place one foot directly in front of the other, with the toes of one foot touching the heel of the other. Try it first holding on to something (or someone); as your balance improves, you'll be able to do it by yourself.

For a more in-depth description of these and other types of exercises, see the National Institute on Aging Exercise Guide.[10]

MOTIVATION

As is so often the case in life, routine kills motivation. What makes someone want to exercise day after day? I'm sure you have many excuses why you cannot exercise today. It's important to remember that many of the benefits of exercise come from exercising regularly. This does not mean you need to do the same exercises all the time. Add some variety—maybe you can walk on some days and swim on others. A lovely spring day might beckon a hike in a nearby park, while a gym might be a better option during the rough winter weather. Another way to encourage yourself to exercise is to join other people doing their exercises. Walking with a larger group, or even one family member or friend, makes it much more interesting and fun.[10] Many assisted-living facilities have exercise groups that the residents can join. You are likely to make new friends!

Many people find that working with a personal trainer can also be very motivating. These fitness professionals can help you get started on a program that's right for you and monitor your progress and personal makeover over time. If you want to work out in a gym, professional trainers are especially helpful in teaching you how to use all the shiny machines properly and avoid injury. The National Institute on Aging recommends organizations, such as the American College of Sports Medicine (ACSM), that train and certify professionals to work specifically with older adults. You can contact your health plan or local hospital and ask for an ACSM-certified trainer.[11]

REFERENCES

1. "Overview of the Benefits and Risks of Exercise," ed. Douglas M. Peterson, in UpToDate, http://www.utdol.com/online.
2. David M. Buchner, "Physical Activity," in *Geriatrics Review Syllabus*, ed. Peter Pompei and John B. Murphy (New York: American Geriatrics Society, 2006), CD-ROM version.
3. Physical Activity Guidelines Writing Group, "2008 Physical Activity Guidelines for Americans: Be Active, Healthy, and Happy!" U.S. Department of Health and Human Services, http://www.health.gov/paguidelines/pdf/paguide.pdf.
4. Maria A. Fiatarone et al., "Exercise Training and Nutritional Supplementation for Physical Frailty in Very Elderly People," *New England Journal of Medicine* 330 (1994): 1769.
5. Julie J. Keysor, "Does Late-Life Physical Activity Prevent or Minimize Disablement? A Critical Review of the Scientific Evidence," *American Journal of Preventive Medicine* 25 (2003): 129.
6. Marianne E. Miller et al., "Physical Activity, Functional Limitations, and Disability in Older Adults," *Journal of the American Geriatrics Society*, 48 (2000): 1264.
7. Robert J. Neid and Barry Franklin, "Promoting and Prescribing Exercise for the Elderly," *American Family Physician* 65 (2002): 419.
8. National Institute on Aging, "AgePage. Exercise and Physical Activity: Getting Fit for Life," U.S. Department of Health and Human Services, National Institute of Health, 2007, http://www.nia.nih.gov/HealthInformation/Publications/exercise.htm.
9. Barbara E. Ainsworth et al., "Compendium of Physical Activities: An Update of Activity Codes and MET Intensities," *Medicine and Science in Sports and Exercise* 32 (2000): S498.
10. National Institute on Aging Panel of Experts on the Topic of Exercise for Older Adults, "Exercise and Physical Activity: Your Everyday Guide from the National Institute on Aging," U.S. Department of Health and Human Services, National Institute of Health, 2009, http://www.nia.nih.gov/HealthInformation/Publications/exerciseGuide.
11. Exercise: A Guide from the National Institute on Aging, "Chapter 3: How to Keep Going," http://www.nia.nih.gov/HealthInformation/Publications/ExerciseGuide/chapter03.htm.

7

THE AGING BRAIN

WHAT LITTLE WE KNOW

Our brain, this three-pound package of neurons, is considered our most vital organ. It is responsible for operating both the involuntary nervous system, which controls our heart rate and breathing, and the voluntary nervous system, which allows us to walk and talk. Considering that the brain is the control center for our entire body, it is strange that we seem to know more about the surface of Mars than we do about how the brain functions and ages.

The brain is your most powerful organ, yet it weighs only about three pounds. It is nourished by one of your body's richest networks of blood vessels. With its billions of cells, the brain uses about 20 percent of the oxygen and fuel your blood carries. The real work of your brain goes on in individual nerve cells. Signals that form memories and thoughts move through an individual nerve cell as tiny electrical charges.[1]

Here's what we do know about the result of the aging process on the brain:

- Ventricles (the spaces in the brain that contain fluid) tend to get larger.
- The grooves on the surface of the brain (called sulci) get wider.
- The size (and hence volume) of the brain gets smaller.
- Certain diseases, such as the dementia related to Alzheimer's disease and Parkinson's disease, are more common with advancing age.

However, we also know that despite these changes, the brain of an older person continues to function normally. Older adults can and do learn new information every bit as well as their younger counterparts, but sometimes the learning process tends to be slower than it is in younger adults. Getting old does not mean you'll "lose your marbles," just that some of them may roll a little slower.[2]

Consider an accountant who used to be able to add columns of numbers in his head without having to think about it, but now finds he is much slower and unsure. Or the businessman who prided himself on remembering the names of his customers, but now finds it difficult to put a name to a familiar face.

SHRUNKEN BRAIN AND FALLS—A RECIPE FOR DISASTER

The fact that the brain shrinks with age is important in that there is more room for the brain to move within the skull. This is the reason why physicians are so concerned about older people falling and hitting their heads. Because of the increased movement of the brain, small blood vessels may rupture and result in a "slow bleed." The medical term for this is a subdural hemorrhage (*subdural* means below the dura, which is the outer covering of the brain, and hemorrhage refers to bleeding). As the bleeding continues, pressure builds up under the skull and pushes against the brain, which results in confusion and, in severe cases, death.[3]

Early on in my training, I saw an elderly woman who had slipped in her kitchen and had bumped her head against the cabinet. She had only a barely noticeable bruise and counted herself lucky for not breaking a bone. She also never mentioned her mishap to her family, who found her several days later confused and very sleepy. A CT scan in the emergency room showed a large bleed pushing against her brain.

From the case example above, it is clear that when any elderly patient receives even a minor bump to the head, the first thing to do is call the doctor. This is especially the case when the person is taking medications that thin the blood, such as warfarin (Coumadin) and aspirin—two medications commonly taken by older patients.

Three things to remember about your head and brain:

1. Do not simply accept memory difficulties as part of normal aging.
2. Report any head injury, even a minor bump, to your physician.
3. Protect your head when cycling, skiing, or participating in other sports, and wear your seatbelt when driving. Remember, your head is the only one you have!

DEMENTIA—A BOOK WITH SEVEN SEALS

The diagnosis of dementia is feared by the public, still a puzzle to many physicians, and ignored by the health care system. What exactly is dementia, this medical problem that affects 2 to 4 million people in the United States and costs our health care system $100 billion a year? To put this number into perspective, it is about a quarter of the 2007 U.S. Department of Defense budget and five times as much as the United Nations and all its agencies spend all year.[4,5]

The word *dementia* is derived from Latin, with *de* meaning "away" and *mentia* meaning "mind." In other words, dementia is a condition in which a person's mental capacities have gone away. Dementia is the most common reason for mental decline in older age. It is a neurologic, *not* a psychiatric, disease that results in a gradual and irreversible loss of memory and other brain functions. The brain function declines enough that a person's daily life is affected. If the person has no difficulties with daily functions, then he or she does not have dementia, although the diagnosis may be mild cognitive impairment, which we now know can be a "pre-dementia." The brain has several different functions, and problems with these different functions are seen as:

- difficulties with language, which is called aphasia
- loss of the ability to recognize familiar objects and persons, which is called agnosia
- difficulties with purposeful learned movements, which is called apraxia
- difficulties with planning, abstract thinking, starting an action or inhibiting an inappropriate action, which is referred to as executive dysfunction

---

An excellent example was a patient I took care of for several years. I remember to this day when she brought her husband to me for the first time. She had just heard that he had "misbehaved" toward his female aide, and she was in tears because the aide had quit her job. It all started several years earlier with his memory problem slowly worsening. He forgot to return calls from friends and family, he didn't pay the bills, and he made a mess of the taxes one spring. He started to become upset if people did not understand him because he spoke "funny." Shortly after that, he got lost while driving to the bank. When he was no longer able to shower by himself, his wife knew that she needed help at home. And now, this more serious problem had arisen—he apparently had touched the aide inappropriately.

The Many Types of Dementia—More Confusion

Just as there are many different types of automobiles (e.g., cars, trucks, SUVs), there are several different types of dementia.

The major dementia syndromes are:[6]

Alzheimer's disease
Vascular dementia
Dementia with Lewy bodies
Parkinson's disease with dementia
Frontotemporal dementia
Reversible dementias

About 50 to 80 percent of people suffering from a dementia have Alzheimer's disease. Other types of dementing illnesses include dementia caused by multiple small strokes, which is called vascular dementia. This is particularly common in African Americans and in people who have high blood pressure or diabetes.[7] People who have Parkinson's disease have a six times greater risk of becoming demented than people who do not.[8]

A 72-year-old man was brought to my clinic by his wife because she was concerned he might have Alzheimer's disease. He did not want to go out anymore, complained about walking, stopped answering the phone, and looked very depressed. A trial of an antidepressant medication did not help. It turned out that he had Parkinson's disease and some mild memory problems. His voice had become very low, and it was difficult for him to speak on the phone because he was constantly being asked to repeat himself. He was embarrassed by the way he walked and by the comments of his friends and family.

Other important types of dementia have features that are similar to those of Parkinson's disease. For example, some people have gait problems, body stiffness, and slowness, but they do not have Parkinson's disease per se. The most common type of dementia that can look like other types is Lewy body dementia. Strong visual hallucinations, which typically occur only in the later stages of Alzheimer's disease, can appear early on in Lewy body dementia.[9]

An important group of dementias is referred to as frontotemporal dementia. This type of dementia usually begins at a much younger age (35–75 years) than does Alzheimer's disease (60–85 years). The clinical features are also different in that patients have slow, progressive behavioral disturbances, especially inappropriate social behavior, something that typically happens later in the course of Alzheimer's disease. Because of their younger age, these patients may mistakenly be thought to have a psychiatric disorder, which delays the correct diagnosis.[10] Another important group of dementias is referred to as potentially reversible. The term *potentially* means that not all patients improve, even if the underlying cause is removed or treated. These dementias include:

- medication-induced dementias
- alcohol-related dementias
- metabolic disorders (vitamin deficiencies, or thyroid, kidney, or liver disease)
- depression
- cancer, infections, and subdural hematomas
- normal-pressure hydrocephalus

In the largest single study of 1,000 consecutive patients referred to a university hospital memory clinic, 13 percent had a reversible cause for their memory problems. Medications (28 percent), depression (26 percent), and metabolic conditions (16 percent) were identified as causes (in order of frequency).[11]

In normal-pressure hydrocephalus, the ventricles, which are fluid-filled spaces in the brain, enlarge. Patients have three main problems: difficulty walking and falls, memory problems, and urinary incontinence. Because these conditions do not always occur together, the diagnosis can be difficult to make. A correct diagnosis is important because these patients can be helped by surgery in which a drain is placed from the brain into the abdomen. This drain acts as a shunt (called a ventriculo-peritoneal shunt), and it lets the excess fluid drain out of the brain into the abdomen where the body can absorb it. If surgery is done early in the disease, the chance of recovery, including the ability to walk, is excellent.[12]

Shortly after my fellowship, a woman was brought to the office by her son and daughter-in-law for a second opinion regarding her Alzheimer's disease. She lived in a downstairs apartment in her son's house, and her family was more concerned with her fear of falling than with her memory problems. This once-avid walker was now homebound and increasingly isolated. She would not even walk up the stairs for dinner. She continued to read the paper daily and otherwise was able to take care of herself. As it turned out, the woman did not have Alzheimer's disease, but normal-pressure hydrocephalus. On careful questioning, she admitted to having occasional bladder accidents, and because of that, together with her difficulty in walking, she preferred staying at home. After a successful surgery for hydrocephalus, her walking improved to some degree, but unfortunately her bladder problems persisted.

Three things to remember:

1. Make sure to discuss any concerns about your memory with your doctor.
2. Do not accept difficulties in walking as part of normal aging. See your doctor as soon as possible.
3. Listen to what others say about you, especially if they say your looks have changed or you appear to be walking differently.

MCI—MORE CONFUSION ABOUT MEMORY PROBLEMS

Mild cognitive impairment (MCI) is like adding insult to injury. It refers to a state somewhere between having normal memory abilities and dementia. Patients complain about memory problems but have no difficulties with everyday living or other brain functions.[13]

Several subtypes of this disease are now recognized, one of which is considered a pre-stage to Alzheimer's disease.[14,15] However, the exact definition of MCI remains imprecise and the diagnosis difficult. Although there continues to be controversy among researchers in the field, MCI is clearly a distinct disease that needs to be taken seriously and further investigated.

ALZHEIMER'S DISEASE—THE DREADED "A-WORD"

It all started one hundred years ago in 1906 when the German physician Alois Alzheimer observed and treated a 50-year-old woman whom he recognized to exhibit unusual memory and behavioral problems. After her death, he examined her brain and discovered small areas that looked abnormal. "It is evident that we are dealing with a peculiar, little-known disease in the woman's brain."[16] What Alzheimer saw was what we refer to today as plaques and tangles. Plaques consist of a protein called *amyloid* that is clumped together with dead and dying brain cells. Tangles are made of another protein called *tau*, which accumulates inside the nerve cells and ultimately destroys them. We can think of this as the brain being damaged by inadequate "garbage collection," which results in the protein deposits. As more and more cells die and spill out neurotransmitters (chemicals that are responsible for nerve cells communicating with each other), the function of the brain is gradually disrupted. This process occurs over several years.

From Obscurity to the World Stage

With the 1994 announcement that President Ronald Regan suffered from Alzheimer's disease, it suddenly became known worldwide, starting a multimillion dollar research effort to find a cure. Although a cure remains elusive, our much improved understanding of the disease and its societal effects allows us to better care for patients. According to Alzheimer's Disease International, 24 million people worldwide were diagnosed with Alzheimer's disease in 2001, a number projected to increase to 81 million in 2040. Alzheimer's disease does not recognize borders, races, or religious affiliations. Princess Yasmin Aga Khan, the president of Alzheimer's Disease International, so poignantly points out that "dementia indiscriminately takes loved ones away and places a great burden of care on family members. . . . I know this through experience with my mother, the beautiful actress Rita Hayworth, who had dementia."[17]

The Inevitable Progression

One of the best descriptions of this disease I have heard and refer to frequently is by Paul Raia, PhD, Director of Patient Care for the Alzheimer's Association of Massachusetts. He describes the disease starting in the temporal lobe behind the ear in a part of the brain called the hippocampus. "The hippocampus . . . can be seen as a computer chip." Its function is to record new information and send it on to other parts of the brain where it is processed and stored for future use. In contrast, previously stored information (i.e., long-term memory) is not affected, so patients can remember what happened years and decades ago but can no longer remember what happened yesterday. The disease then progresses to affect the rearmost part of the brain, which includes the lobe that controls vision (the occipital lobe). As a result, patients begin to have difficulty recognizing familiar faces and places. This is a reason why some patients get lost easily and start confusing or not recognizing loved ones. The disease then progresses to affect another lobe on the top of the brain (the parietal lobe), which is responsible for disrupting our motor functions. Patients start to have problems buttoning shirts, holding utensils, or with changes in their gait. Once the disease reaches the front of the brain (the frontal lobe), it affects judgment; the ability to reason and make informed decisions slips away. This area of the brain also influences personality, and personality changes can range from hostility and agitation to marked apathy. Personality changes are especially difficult for loved ones to deal with. One distraught wife once told me, "I am a widow with a living spouse. I lost my husband years ago already." The disease then moves into the depth of the brain and affects swallowing, breathing, heart rate, and temperature control, leaving patients bed bound and mute.

The Confusion about the Causes

There are two types of Alzheimer's disease. A rare, early onset form occurs in patients 40 to 60 years old. The more common, late-onset form occurs after age 60. Both types have a genetic predisposition, and ongoing research is discovering more and more genes that are linked to the disease.[18]

The strongest risk factor for Alzheimer's disease is age. The older a person is, the greater the chance of developing the disease.[19] According to some studies, 40 to 50 percent of people who are 85 years old have some degree of a dementing illness. A family history of the disease, especially in first-degree relatives, is another risk factor unless the relative developed Alzheimer's disease very late in life (eighty-five and older). This is well documented in African-Americans.[20] One type of mild cognitive impairment (discussed before) can increase the risk, as well as anything that causes atherosclerosis. High cholesterol, diabetes mellitus, hypertension, and smoking have been linked to the development of dementia.[21] However, the exact mechanisms are not always fully understood. The same is true of lifestyle and activity. Some observational studies have suggested that having greater social involvement and participating in more physical and mental activities reduce the risk of developing dementia.

DIAGNOSIS—SLOW AND LABORIOUS

There is no single blood test or x-ray that can be used to quickly and conveniently diagnose Alzheimer's disease. A definitive diagnosis is still possible only after death by an autopsy examination of the brain. However, clinical diagnosis is now quite accurate, and we are gaining a better understanding of the disease process. The "old fashioned approach" of a good history and physical exam takes time and involves the patient, the caregiver(s), and the doctor.[22]

Unfortunately, the amount of time needed is rarely available during a standard 10-minute primary care office visit. This is one reason why diagnosis is often not made until late in the disease. Other reasons may include the attitude of physicians or of the caregivers, who may see changes in their loved ones as part of normal aging and inadvertently help to cover up these signs.

Physician attitudes that are barriers to the proper diagnosis and subsequent treatment include "the failure to recognize and respond to the symptoms of dementia," "a perceived lack of need to determine a specific diagnosis," "limited time," and " negative attitudes toward the importance of assessment and diagnosis."[23]

The following "red flags" are helpful to look for in making the diagnosis of a dementia:

- finding the correct word
- asking the same questions over again
- insisting nothing is wrong
- leaving chores unfinished
- difficulties with paying bills, handling money, and driving

---

Three things to remember:

1. Find a physician who is knowledgeable and interested in caring for patients with dementia.
2. Establish an accurate diagnosis first.
3. Make sure caregivers are supported and become a "partner in care."

TREATMENT YES, CURE NO

The mainstay of treatment remains symptomatic. We treat behavioral disturbances and make appropriate changes in the patient's environment to support the ability to live as independently as possible. Treatment also means supporting caregivers in their often unexpected and underappreciated roles.

Medications are available to help patients maintain function and to treat behavioral disturbances. Because the death of nerve cells causes a loss of neurotransmitters, using these medications can be thought of as plugging small leaks in an engine that is slowly losing oil but otherwise still working well. The medications that provide the "oil" work by blocking the breakdown of an important neurotransmitter called acetylcholine, thereby maintaining the level of acetylcholine in the brain.[24] Four medications in this category, which are called cholinesterase inhibitors, are currently approved by the U.S. Food and Drug Administration (FDA):

1. donepezil (Aricept)
2. tacrine (Cognex)

3. rivastigmine (Exelon)
4. galantamine (Razadyne)

Another medication used in the treatment of patients suffering from dementia is memantine (Namenda). Memantine is considered a disease-modifying and neuroprotective agent that may slow down the progression of the disease.[25] It is often used in combination with one of the previous medications.

Studies have shown that patients respond very differently to the cholinesterase inhibitors, with as many as 50 percent showing no benefit from the medications while others have a good response.[26] This is a good reason to try some of these medications and hope for the best.

Other medications that were once popular are no longer recommended for treatment because they have not had any meaningful effect on the disease. These include estrogen, selegeline, vitamin C, and vitamin E. There is also no evidence to support the use of nonsteroidal anti-inflammatory drugs (NSAIDs) such as ibuprofen, naproxen, or indomethacin. NSAIDs also have side effects, including irritation of and bleeding from the stomach or bowels, raising blood pressure, and damaging the kidneys, which can be very serious especially when these drugs are taken over long periods of time. Another over-the-counter medication that is no longer recommended is *Ginkgo biloba.* Its efficacy is questionable, and problems with the exact herbal contents have been found.

Is Prevention Possible?

The short answer is we don't know. Many studies have been done over the years, but they show conflicting results. The best recommendations are the following:

- Vitamin E is no longer recommended, in part because it is not effective and, more importantly, it carries significant risks.[27]
- *Ginkgo biloba* may have some effect.[28]
- Estrogen replacement is also not recommended.[29]
- There is some evidence that NSAIDs are protective, but the risk of heart disease cannot be ignored, so these medications are not recommended for prevention.[30]
- The jury is still out on lipid-lowering medications at this time.[31]
- With respect to diet, there is no one diet that has been shown to prevent dementia.
- Physical exercise and keeping socially and mentally engaged all seem to be beneficial. Although these activities cannot prevent the onset of dementia, they can possibly delay its development.[32]

To understand better what people should do to help maintain their brain function as best as possible, I asked Dr. Margie E. Lachman, Chair of the

Department of Psychology at Brandeis University. Dr. Lachman is involved in studies of people with normal memory function. She lists six important ways that appear to help maintain a person's memory abilities:

1. A higher education is very beneficial, but regardless of whether you have a college or graduate school education, engaging in regular stimulating cognitive activities is helpful. Working crossword puzzles, solving Sudoku grids, and playing challenging games like bridge all help maintain better cognitive function. In fact, learning new things and stretching the mind seem to be most advantageous.
2. Having a sense of control of one's life seems to be important in helping to maintain cognitive function. It is speculated that people who are in control of their lives tend to have better adaptive strategies when faced with challenges. They seem to have better ways of remembering things.
3. Social engagement is increasingly thought to be very important. Good relationships appear to be vital for a proper functioning mind. Please see Chapter 15 for a more detailed discussion of the importance of social connections.
4. Regularly participating in challenging cognitive activities (as noted before) should be part of your daily routine.
5. Physical activity is equally important. Both aerobic and resistance training seems to have a positive effect on the brain. There is more on the types of exercises and other benefits for your health in Chapter 6.
6. Very important is reducing stress in your life. Yoga, meditation, and other ways of stress reduction seem to be beneficial. A walk in the park, smelling the roses, or just enjoying good music is more important now than ever.

All of these activities by themselves appear to have a protective effect on the brain's memory ability. But even more important is that the beneficial effect on the brain is enhanced when you combine all these activities on a regular basis. In other words, the more the better!

REFERENCES

1. Alzheimer's Association, "Inside the Brain: An Interactive Tour," Alzheimer's Association, http://www.alz.org/alzheimers_disease_4719.asp.
2. Henry Nielsen, Annette Lolk, and Per Kragh-Sorensen, "Age-Associated Memory Impairment: Pathological Memory Decline or Normal Aging?" *Scandinavian Journal of Psychology* 39 (1998): 33.
3. Helmut Maxeiner and Michael Wolff, "Pure Subdural Hematomas: A Postmortem Analysis of Their Form and Bleeding Points," *Neurosurgery* 50 (2002): 503.
4. Office of Management and Budget, "The President's Budget: Department of Defense 2007," http://www.whitehouse.gov/omb/budget/fy2007/defense.html.
5. Global Policy Forum, "UN Finance (General Analysis on UN Finance)," http://www.globalpolicy.org/un_finance.html.
6. David S. Knopman et al., "Essentials of the Proper Diagnosis of Mild Cognitive Impairment, Dementia, and Major Subtypes of Dementia," *Mayo Clinic Proceedings* 78 (2003): 1290.

7. John C. Morris, "Dementia Update 2003,"*Alzheimer Disease and Associated Disorders* 17 (2003): 245.
8. Dag Aarsland et al., "Risk of Dementia in Parkinson's Disease. A Community-Based, Perspective Study," *Neurology* 56 (2001): 730.
9. Ian G. McKeith et al., "Consensus Guidelines for the Clinical and Pathologic Diagnosis of Dementia with Lewy Bodies (DLB): Report of the Consortium on DLB International Workshop," *Neurology* 47 (1996): 1113.
10. Guy M. McKhann et al., "Clinical and Pathological Diagnosis of Frontotemporal Dementia: Report of the Work Group on Frontotemporal Dementia and Pick's Disease," *Archives of Neurology* 58 (2001): 1803.
11. Anne-Mette Hejl, Peter Hogh, and Gunhild Waldemer, "Potentially Reversible Conditions in 1000 Consecutive Memory Clinic Patients," *Journal of Neurology, Neurosurgery and Psychiatry* 73 (2002): 390.
12. Joachim K. Krauss and Bern Halve, "Normal Pressure Hydrocephalus: Survey on Contemporary Diagnostic Algorithms and Therapeutic Decision-Making in Clinical Practice," *Acta Neurochirurgica* (Wien) 146 (2004): 379.
13. Ronald C. Peterson et al., "Mild Cognitive Impairment: Clinical Characterization and Outcome," *Archives of Neurology* 56(1999): 303.
14. John C. Morris et al., "Mild Cognitive Impairment Represents Early-Stage Alzheimer's Disease," *Archives of Neurology* 58 (2001): 397.
15. Ronald C. Petersen et al., "Practice Parameter: Early Detection of Dementia: Mild Cognitive Impairment (An Evidence-Based Review). Report of the Quality Standards Subcommittee of the American Academy of Neurology," *Neurology* 56 (2001): 1133.
16. Daniel Kuhn, *Alzheimer's Early Stages* (Almeda, CA: Hunter House, 1999), 8.
17. Alzheimer's Disease International, "Annual Report 2005–2006," Alzheimer's Disease International, http://www.alz.co.uk/adi/pdf/annrep06.pdf.
18. Nicole Schupf, "Earlier Onset of Alzheimer's Disease in Men with Down Syndrome," *Neurology* 50 (1998): 991.
19. Martha M. Corrada et al., "Prevalence of Dementia after Age 80: Results from the 90+ Study," *Neurology* 71 (2008): 337.
20. Robert C. Green et al., "Risk of Dementia among White and African American Relatives of Patients with Alzheimer's Disease," *Journal of the American Medical Association* 287 (2002): 329.
21. Rachel A. Whitmer et al., "Midlife Cardiovascular Risk Factors and Risk of Dementia in Late Life," *Neurology* 25 (2005): 277.
22. Guy McKhann et al., "Clinical Diagnosis of Alzheimer's Disease: Report of the NINCDS-ADRDA Work Group under the Auspices of the Department of Health and Human Services Task Force on Alzheimer's Disease," *Neurology* 34 (1984): 939.
23. Linda Boise et al., "Diagnosing Dementia: Perspective of Primary Care Physicians," *Gerontologist* 4 (1999): 457.
24. Peter J. Whitehouse et al., "Alzheimer's Disease and Senile Dementia: Loss of Neurons in the Basal Forebrain," *Science* 215 (1982): 1237.
25. Barry Reisberg et al., "A 24-Week Open Label Extension Study of Memantine in Moderate to Severe Alzheimer Disease," *Archives of Neurology* 63 (2006): 49.
26. Christopher M. Clark and Jason H. T. Karlawish, "Alzheimer's Disease: Current Concepts and Emerging Diagnostic and Therapeutic Strategies," *Annals of Internal Medicine* 138 (2003): 400.

27. Goran Bjelakovic et al., "Mortality in Randomized Trial of Antioxidant Supplements for Primary and Secondary Prevention Systemic Review and Meta-analysis," *Journal of the American Medical Association* 297 (2007): 842.

28. Jacqueline Birks and John Grimley Evans, "*Ginkgo biloba* for Cognitive Impairment and Dementia," *Cochrane Database of Systematic Reviews* 18 (2007): CD003120.

29. Stephen R. Rapp et al., "Effect of Estrogen plus Progestin on Global Cognitive Function in Postmenopausal Women: The Women's Health Initiative Memory Study: A Randomized Controlled Trial," *Journal of the American Medical Association* 289 (2003): 2663.

30. Paul S. Aisen et al., "Effects of Rofecoxib or Naproxen vs Placebo on Alzheimer Disease Progression: A Randomized Controlled Trial," *Journal of the American Medical Association* 289 (2003): 2819.

31. Larry D. Sparks et al., "Atorvastatin for the Treatment of Mild to Moderate Alzheimer Disease: Preliminary Results," *Archives of Neurology* 62 (2005): 753.

32. Nicola Lautenschlager et al., "Effect of Physical Activity on Cognitive Function in Older Adults at Risk for Alzheimer Disease," *Journal of the American Medical Association* 300 (2008): 1027.

8

HEALTH MAINTENANCE

Despite the great technological advances of the twentieth century, our bodies remain a far better "machine" than anything man has ever built. Nature remains ahead of us even though we may think otherwise. A lifetime of 80 years, for example, translates into 400,000 hours of walking, talking, eating, and interacting with other people. Our heart beats and pumps blood through our bodies on average 3.4 billion times during our lifetime. Our bodies are always "switched on," even when we are sleeping. It's no wonder that over time certain parts start to wear out and don't work as well, and sometimes break down altogether.

Now, compare our bodies to the cars we drive these days. Yes, some are quite fancy and perform very well. But without good care and regular maintenance, even the best-built cars will eventually break down. That is the reason why we regularly, albeit sometimes begrudgingly, pay for oil changes, brake repairs, and new tires. Even if we follow the factory-recommended maintenance schedule (has anyone ever honestly done that?), our cars would never last for 80 years or more. Although our bodies do not require regular oil changes, we do need to have occasional maintenance work done to make sure we keep running on all cylinders. It starts at birth, followed by almost monthly visits to our medical mechanics for the first year. In our twenties, thirties, and even forties, we often think we are invincible and tend to get by without visiting our doctors other than our favorite dentist. But there is no question that our choice of lifestyle will have an impact on our health as we travel down the road of aging. Once we hit that magic age of 50, regular health maintenance is once again on our mind because of the risk of developing chronic conditions like heart disease, cancer, or stroke.

POINTS ABOUT PREVENTION

The best way to deal with any disease is to prevent it completely, or to catch it early when there is a good chance of stopping it from getting worse.

Health Maintenance

An excellent and comprehensive definition of what a "health maintenance evaluation" encompasses can be found on the Palo Alto Medical Foundation Web site.[1] The medical visit should include the following:

- identifying risk factors in one's personal and family health history
- a focused exam as appropriate
- obtaining needed screening tests at right intervals
- encouraging people to choose healthy lifestyles to maximize their health

Most importantly, the "checkup can occur during an office visit devoted to health maintenance or may be covered during an office visit for other concerns."

Even if a disease cannot be cured, identifying the problem and treating it is important to keep it under control and to minimize its effect on your life.

Primary prevention refers to preventing diseases in the first place. Immunizations are the ultimate form of primary prevention. Getting a flu shot every year (unless you are truly allergic) is one of the best ways of avoiding the potentially deadly influenza infection. By the way, you will *not* get the influenza infection after the shot. And no, it will not protect you from the common cold viruses that float around us everywhere we go. From a public health standpoint, the more of us who are vaccinated, the greater the chance to stop the virus from spreading and causing thousands of deaths among older adults each year (this buildup of immunity in a population is called "herd immunity"). One of the best disease prevention practices is to throw out those cigarettes and quit smoking before it ruins your lungs, heart, and arteries. By the way, a December 2008 article in the *Journal of the American Medical Association* reports a very conclusive connection between smoking and colon cancer. So there you have yet another good reason to quit and save yourself some money at the same time.[2] Secondary prevention refers to detecting a disease in its very early stage if at all possible and treating it before it progresses too far. Yearly mammograms to look for early breast cancers are an example of this. Screening for osteoporosis by methods that can identify brittle bones is another good example, because with early detection, treatment can be started and the progression of the disease slowed or even stopped.

Geriatricians are experts in tertiary prevention, which seeks to identify and treat existing diseases that cannot be cured anymore but nevertheless can be managed to slow their progression and to improve the patient's quality of life. Two excellent examples of this are gait and balance disturbance and memory deficits. Although we cannot reverse the effects of a prior stroke and get that leg working properly again, recognizing the importance of a gait difficulty and ordering physical therapy and appropriate exercises can improve balance and walking ability and with it reduce the chance of a fall. Similarly, recognizing early on that there is a memory problem, trying out some of the available medications and then making sure the patient and the caregiver are supported does not cure the dementia, but it will improve the patient's life and well-being.

No Warranties

It is not all up to your doctor to keep you as healthy as possible. You have to do your fair share in maintaining your health. Imagine if your parents were given a manual shortly after having a baby, similar to the thick, cumbersome owner's manual you receive (and never read) when you buy a new car. It might look something like Table 8.1.

Table 8.1
Owner's Manual

Human Being—*Homo sapiens*

1928 model

Copyright The Creator Corp. All rights reserved.

This manual includes the latest information on (check one) male___ female___

Date of delivery: _____

Warranty information: Unfortunately, no warranty is available on this Human Being. Sorry, no refunds. In general, the average life expectancy for a female model is approximately 80.8 years, and that for a male model is approximately 75.7 years (www.cdc.gov).

Service and care: Your medical mechanic best knows the body of this Human Being. Please consult him or her with all your service needs. Follow the outlined maintenance schedule carefully to ensure the best possible health.

Scheduled Maintenance:

Months	Check when complete	Years	Check when complete
1		2	
2		3	
3		5	
6		7	
9		9	
12		11	
18		13	
		15	
		17	

At 18 years, please give this manual to the Human Being to continue following his or her medical mechanic's recommendations. Please note that certain models may require different services because of their health condition and/or family history. Good luck!

Allow me to skip a few pages now and go right to age 65 and older to see what the current recommendations for health maintenance entail.

AGE 65 AND OLDER

Medicare, under its expanded Part B services, now greets all "new members" with an "initial preventive physical examination," which is referred to as the "Welcome to Medicare" visit. In effect, this is a wonderful opportunity for you. Please, please take advantage of this. Your health care provider (e.g., physician, nurse practitioner, physician assistant, etc.) can use this visit to provide patient education, counsel you on your risk factors for various conditions, screen for potential risk factors, and perform an extensive physical examination. According to the Web site of the Centers for Medicare and Medicaid Services, the visit should include the following:[3]

1. A review of an individual's medical and social history with attention to modifiable risk factors.
2. A review of an individual's potential risk factors for depression.
3. A review of the individual's functional ability and level of safety.
4. A physical examination to include an individual's height, weight, blood pressure, visual acuity, and measurement of body mass index.
5. End-of-life planning.
6. Education, counseling, and referral based on the results of the review and evaluation services described in the previous five components.
7. Education, counseling, and referral, including a brief written plan such as a checklist for obtaining the appropriate screening and/or other Medicare Part B preventive services.

Let's look at this initial visit in more detail by sitting in on a virtual visit with me as the doctor seeing a new patient. We'll assume that there are no urgent medical issues that need to be taken care of first. Now imagine that a geriatric fellow, a medical resident, a volunteer, and a medical student are all cramped into the corner of our exam room, and a nurse practitioner is at the computer. I'll start by asking the patient about his or her past medical history. In particular, I'm looking for certain diseases or conditions that need to be carefully addressed so as to avoid further progression or complications that could result from untreated or "undertreated" diseases. Among others high on my list are the following medical conditions:

Past Medical History

High Blood Pressure

High blood pressure, or hypertension, is tremendously common among older adults. Believe it or not, hypertension can be detected only by actually measuring blood pressure. Because hypertension is painless and not "felt," it's referred to as "the silent killer." Continuously high pressure in the arteries damages them on the inside. Over time, plaques that are made up mostly of cholesterol and other fats form on the inside walls of the arteries; this is referred to as atherosclerosis or hardening of the arteries. These plaques act like roadblocks or highway maintenance crews on the roads, and they tend to disrupt and at times completely block the flow of blood. If this unfortunate scenario happens in one of the arteries that supplies the heart muscle itself (the coronary arteries), the result at best is angina (a "cramp" in the heart muscle) or at worst a myocardial infarct (a heart attack). If this happens in one of the arteries that supplies blood to the brain, the result is a cerebral vascular accident (a stroke). If the blood flow is poor in our legs, the result is called intermittent claudication (from the Latin *claudere*, meaning to hobble or limp).

Older adults have a particular blood pressure pattern referred to as isolated systolic hypertension, meaning that the "upper" blood pressure reading is too high. Many studies have shown that reducing the "upper" reading results in fewer strokes and heart attacks.[4,5] Blood pressure can be lowered by exercise, weight loss, a careful diet low in sodium, and, of course, by medication.

Coronary Artery Disease

The heart pumps blood around the body, but it also needs its own blood supply, which is provided by small arteries that encircle the heart like a crown (in fact, *coronary* means "crown shaped"). The heart's pumping action happens by the different chambers of the heart contracting in a coordinated pattern. Because the heart is busy pumping the blood all the time, the heart muscle itself can get its blood only during short relaxation periods (which are called diastole). Any blockage in the blood supply, as described previously, can eventually lead to problems. Asking about symptoms of angina, for example, chest pain or pressure while walking or becoming short of breath, can help establish if the coronary arteries have any significant blockage. Important risk factors for coronary artery disease include hypertension, high cholesterol levels, diabetes, and smoking.

Diabetes Mellitus

The word *diabetes mellitus* stems both from the ancient Greek word *diabainein*, meaning "to pass through," and from the Latin word *mellitus*, meaning "sweetened with honey."[6] In ancient times, these poor patients were noted to have excessive amounts of urine that tasted very sweet. Fortunately, diagnostic methods have improved, and physicians these days do not have to taste urine! What happens in diabetes mellitus is that a hormone called insulin, which is made by the pancreas, is either lacking altogether or not working properly. Insulin makes sure that the sugar released into our blood from eating that tasty chocolate bar is absorbed by our body cells and used for energy. Without insulin, instead of the sugar in the blood being absorbed, it is excreted in the urine by the kidneys, and our body loses all that energy. This in turn causes breakdown of fat and protein to make up for all the lost energy. It's like leaving all the windows in your house wide open in the middle of winter, and having to burn the furniture for heat because the furnace can't keep up. Not only would you risk burning down the house, but you'd also ruin the interior. The high blood sugar concentration (called hyperglycemia) causes other problems like atherosclerosis (described earlier) of the blood vessels. This can cause coronary artery disease, kidney failure, blindness, and even nerve damage. Clearly, early detection and treatment of diabetes mellitus with proper diet, medication, and/or insulin injections are good things to do.

High Cholesterol

While doctors at times looked frantically for all sorts of risk factors for atherosclerosis and especially for coronary artery disease in older patients, we tended to be less concerned about high cholesterol levels in older adults. This has changed dramatically now that studies have shown that treatment with statins, which are medications that lower cholesterol (e.g., Zocor or Lipitor), do in fact reduce the risk of heart attacks and strokes in older patients.[7]

Cognition

Cognition refers to brain function, including memory. With increasing age, our memory often becomes less robust, and, unfortunately, some older adults develop a dementia (see Chapter 7). At age 85, the prevalence of dementia is around 50 percent, a number that cannot be ignored. The ongoing controversy about screening older adults for memory problems is of such extent and scope that by comparison Washington politics look boring. The U.S. Preventive Services Task Force (USPSTF for short) and the American Academy of Neurology do not support screening of patients who have no symptoms.[8] The problem we are therefore left with is that by the time a dementia like Alzheimer's disease is diagnosed, the disease has usually progressed significantly and valuable time for interventions has been lost. Even more of a concern is the fact that older adults with unrecognized memory problems are at risk of sudden changes in mental status (referred to as delirium) when they get seriously ill or are admitted to a hospital, even if only for an elective procedure.

Possible memory problems are not all that difficult to detect. Health care providers can get a sense of a person's memory by simply asking questions about the ability to perform instrumental activities of daily living (IADLs), such as driving, managing money or a household, and maintaining a social life, or about the simple activities of daily living (ADLs), such as bathing,

Shortly after finishing my fellowship, I was asked to see a 68-year-old lady who developed acute confusion after having a successful knee replacement surgery. Four weeks earlier, this active woman had been in the office with her husband and had insisted on having her knee fixed right away so that she could once again play a proper game of golf. She was after all quite an accomplished golfer. To make a long story short, she had developed what is referred to as postoperative delirium. There are many causes of this, but it is important to know if there has been a history of memory problems before surgery. When her husband was questioned, he had noticed that she'd been having some difficulty with driving, managing her checkbook, and keeping track of her golf scores. She was also easily frustrated with everything and everyone. This had all been blamed on her wretched knee and the accompanying incessant pain, when in fact, these symptoms were early subtle signs of a dementia.

dressing, and grooming. Red flags that may point toward some memory problems include a person repeatedly asking the same questions, being easily overwhelmed by simple tasks, and leaving chores undone. If there is a concern, then further evaluation should be done.

Depression

It is depressing news indeed to note that many older adults have undiagnosed depression. Suicide rates are much higher in older adults, and especially in white men older than 85. Doctors and caregivers often miss this devastating disease because it presents itself in many different ways, including disturbed sleep, memory problems, and overall lack of energy.[9] Screening patients is highly recommended and can easily be done with a simple question like, "Over the past two weeks, have you felt down, depressed, or hopeless?"[10] If there is any indication that an older adult is suffering from depression, a consult with a geriatric psychiatrist can be of great help to establish whether the patient needs support or medications or both. Chronic pain is also an important cause of depressive symptoms and must always be considered.

Chronic Pain

The Joint Commission on Hospital Accreditation considers pain the fifth vital sign besides body temperature, blood pressure, pulse rate, and respiratory rate. There is no question that pain affects a person's well-being and quality of life. It is not always obvious if a patient is in pain; many older patients suffer from a dementia or have had a stroke and therefore cannot always clearly report their pain. This underscores the fact that health care providers need to regularly assess their patients for possible pain.

Some people think that having some aches and pains is just what happens when we get older. Nothing could be more wrong and unfortunate. Sometimes, pain is intermittent, and because of this, many older adults do not seek medical attention as often as they should. Pain also presents itself in different ways, which makes it difficult to describe and treat. Neuropathic pain refers to pain from a nerve injury, and it is often burning and chronic in nature. Examples of this type of pain are the pain from shingles (called post-herpetic neuralgia), the pain from carpal tunnel syndrome, and some pains from cancer. A different type of pain, nociceptive pain, refers to pain from nociceptors, which are nerves that sense damage to a body part. This pain is often acute, sharp, and stabbing. Examples include bone fractures, bruises, burns, and the pain from arthritis. There is no need to suffer from pain. There are many pain clinics and physicians who specialize in the treatment of all types of pain.

Gait and Balance Difficulties or a History of Falling

Approximately one in three older adults who live in the community fall each year.[11] Among those older adults who sustain a hip fracture, 25 to 75 percent will unfortunately not fully recover.[12] The estimated cost of all fall-related injuries among adults 65 years and older was an amazing $12.6 billion in 1995, with much higher costs these days.[13]

There are many things that can be done to reduce the risk of falls and even prevent older adults from falling in the first place. I cannot stress enough that avoiding a fall is most important, because the next fall can be the one that results in a hip fracture. If you have fallen, you should also review all your medications with your physician, especially medications for heart conditions or high blood pressure, antidepressants, and sleeping pills. Over-the-counter cold remedies are also a major cause of falls because of their sedating side effect.

Beyond looking at all the medications you are taking, falling should prompt a careful review for any neurologic problems like Parkinson's disease, musculoskeletal diseases like arthritis in the knees or hips, heart disease, and even common problems such as poor eyesight or inner ear diseases. Getting treatment for any disease minimizes the risk of falling.

Even more can be done to help prevent or avoid falls. For example, a home safety evaluation by physical and occupational therapists can be very helpful to identify and eliminate falling hazards in the home environment. Perhaps a prescription for physical exercise is needed. Or, even better, some gait and balance training because studies have shown that falls are reduced 10 percent by exercise and 17 percent by balance training.[14]

Three things to remember:
Never forget to tell your doctor about these three conditions (if you are a patient or a caregiver of a patient):

1. Depression
2. Pain
3. Falls

Family History

After reviewing a patient's past medical history, I ask about the family medical history. Many diseases in relatives, particularly in first-degree relatives, may put a person at risk of developing the same problem. The best way to avoid this "bad genetic luck" is to choose your parents wisely. Of course, this is impossible, and the best way to play with the cards we were dealt is to think prevention. Heart attacks, high blood pressure, and an abnormal bulging or ballooning of the large artery in our abdomen (called abdominal aortic aneurysm) are examples of diseases that can run in families.[15,16,17] In the case of an aneurysm, an ultrasound examination of the abdomen, as is done in expectant mothers, can detect this early on. In fact, the "Welcome to Medicare" visit recommends that all patients at risk have an ultrasound examination. Diabetes and dementia are other examples of diseases that run in families.[18,19] Osteoporosis is another disease that can literally creep up on you. Knowing the risk factors and your family history just might save you pain and your bones a fracture. A number of cancers also occur repeatedly in family members, which gives true meaning to the word *prevention*. Cancer of the large bowel, prostate cancer in men, and ovarian cancer and of course breast cancer in women are the main players.[20,21,22]

Colon Cancer

Colon and rectal cancer, also called colorectal cancer or cancer of the large bowel, is common and, if not detected early, can be fatal. Almost 50,000 Americans die each year from colon cancer.[23] The first sign may be pain in the abdomen or a change in bowel habits. Sometimes, symptoms are more dramatic, and bleeding may occur. If colon cancer is not detected, it can grow large enough to obstruct the bowel and spread through the bowel wall and ultimately to the rest of the body. The best way to diagnosis this cancer is with a colonoscopy, in which a flexible tube is introduced through the anus to examine the large bowel. The recommendations for screening for this disease depend on your age, family history, and your overall health, and the guidelines are always changing. I suggest you discuss this with your doctor. Other diagnostic options include the old-fashioned barium enema, in which barium is introduced into the colon through the anus and then multiple x-rays are taken, and the newer CT colonography, which is computerized tomography of the abdomen after a contrast medium has been swallowed. No one likes the unpleasant bowel "clean out" that needs to be done before these procedures, but it is definitely better than having the cancer. For treatment, the cancerous part of the bowel needs to be removed surgically, and if the cancer has spread outside the bowel, chemotherapy is needed as well.

Prostate Cancer

Prostate cancer is the second most common cancer in men, right after skin cancer. Many men and their doctors don't know that it is present because in most cases it is very slow growing and never extends beyond the prostate. Autopsy studies have shown that 30 percent of men younger than 80 and 60 percent of men older than 80 have some cancer cells in their prostate.[24] In the past, prostate cancer was often detected by a rectal examination, in which the doctor felt for any irregularities on the surface of the prostate. However, by the time the cancer can be felt this way, it is usually already quite big and may already have spread beyond the prostate. These days it can also be detected by a blood test that measures a substance called prostate-specific antigen (or PSA).[25] Regardless, this does not mean that the dreaded, and often joked about, digital rectal exam is no longer required. Unfortunately, the diagnosis is still not straightforward because another common condition of the prostate, benign prostatic hypertrophy (BPH), can also cause the PSA to increase. BPH can also have the same symptoms that cancer does, which confuses the picture even more. These symptoms include needing to urinate suddenly and frequently and having difficulty in starting urination. An ultrasound examination of the prostate can help differentiate between these two conditions, and sometimes a biopsy of a suspicious area in the prostate gland is needed for diagnosis. Treatment can include surgery and/or radiation and chemotherapy. I would urge you to discuss any screening for this disease with your doctor.

Ovarian Cancer

Ovarian cancer is the second most common gynecological cancer, with approximately 20,000 women diagnosed each year.[23] Most cancers develop in women younger than 65 years old, but unfortunately increasing age does not protect women. Like many other cancers, the early symptoms of ovarian cancer are often vague. Who doesn't complain of bloating once in a while? Frequent urination and urgency to urinate may feel like a simple bladder infection. But pelvic and abdominal pain, especially if they occur on a daily basis, should prompt a woman to seek medical advice. If not detected early, ovarian cancer often spreads, or metastasizes, beyond the ovaries.[26] A regular pelvic examination performed by an experienced physician may detect an enlarged ovary. Ultrasound examination is one of the best ways to look for any abnormalities.[27] CT and magnetic resonance imaging (MRI) scans may be necessary, especially if surgery becomes necessary. Chemotherapy is usually a part of the treatment.

Cervical Cancer

Most recommendations nowadays suggest that regular Pap (i.e., Papanicolau) smears are no longer necessary for women who have had at least three normal exams in the last 10 years and are 65 or older. A previous hysterectomy (removal of the uterus, or womb) for a noncancerous cause is also considered a reason to stop regular Pap smears.[28] Again, I strongly suggest that you talk to your physician about screening, especially if you have had any abnormal exam findings in the past.

Breast Cancer

A staggering one-half of all breast cancers each year are in women 65 years and older.[23] Getting older not only puts women at risk of this cancer but also has often unfortunately meant they receive less than optimal therapy.[29] And despite the fact that breast cancer is less aggressive in older women, the death rate tends to be higher.[30,31] The reasons for this are likely a result of undertreatment and late diagnosis of the cancer.[32] There is a wide array of treatment choices, ranging from medications and different types of surgical approaches to radiation after surgery and various combinations of all of these. Regular self-examination of the breasts, feeling for any lumps, and yearly mammograms are the best way to screen for this disease. It is not clear how long older women should have these regular exams, so again, I suggest an open discussion with your physician.

Osteoporosis

According to the National Osteoporosis Foundation, "Osteoporosis is a condition in which the bones become weak and can break from a minor fall or, in serious cases, from a simple action such as a sneeze." Of the 44 million Americans affected, over half are older than 50. And you may be surprised to learn that osteoporosis does not discriminate between the sexes. Although 80 percent of osteoporosis patients are women, men also suffer from this disease. Osteoporosis also affects all ethnicities. Like hypertension, it is painless, and most people don't know they have osteoporosis until they have their first fracture. The risk factors are plentiful and include having a family history of the disease, being thin and small, older, and especially being female. A diet low in calcium and vitamin D does not help the situation, and a lifestyle of smoking, drinking large amounts of alcohol, and inactivity almost guarantees you an osteoporotic fracture. Certain medications, especially anticonvulsant medications taken to decrease seizures, increase the risk, too.[33]

Social History

After taking a family medical history, I'll ask the patient questions about his or her everyday life and challenges. This social history includes the patient's living arrangements, his or her ability to do everyday activities (IADLs and ADLs, see previous discussion), and whether the patient receives help from caregivers. The more a patient relies on a caregiver, the more I am concerned about the caregiver's health. Caregiver distress and burden are well-recognized problems that ultimately impact the health of the older patient. It is therefore important to support the caregiver in his or her ability to care for the older patient. The health of the caregiver and the health of the older patient cannot be separated. Just like pediatricians, who work with both the child and the mother, geriatricians work with "two" patients as well.

This brings us to the sad topic of abuse and mistreatment of older adults. According to the National Center for Victims of Crime, "13 percent of elder abuse involved caregiver neglect; 8% centered on emotional, psychological, or verbal abuse, and 10% involved financial exploitation."[34] These are indeed shocking statistics, and only early detection remains the best means of prevention.

Another very important part of the social history are those devilish habits of ours like smoking and alcohol use. The problems with alcohol and the older body have already been discussed in Chapter 5 on nutrition. Here I simply want to remind you that careful consumption is highly recommended, being especially aware of how too many glasses can easily affect your other medical conditions and interact with your pills. On the other hand, smoking is an absolute no-no. If there is one thing and one thing only that you can do to improve your health and quality of life, it is to throw those cigarettes into the trash. There is absolutely not one good reason to smoke, but there are many good reasons not to. I have talked about many health problems related to smoking throughout this book, not to mention the expense, plus it makes you, your clothes, your car, and your house smell bad, too.

Another hot topic that nearly always evokes a lot of emotions is the driving ability of an older adult. For most of us, so much of our daily life depends on having that driver's license. Losing it certainly changes one's life and often the lives of other family members as well.

This is a case I will not forget. A patient of mine with worsening Parkinson's disease was well aware of his increasing difficulties in safely driving his car around town to buy groceries, do the banking, and take his wife to her weekly hairdresser appointment. His son and daughter-in-law insisted that he relinquish his driver's license. However, he refused to stop driving, even after he almost hit a pedestrian. He made it quite clear to me that if he could no longer drive, he and his wife would need to move from their beloved home. He also threatened me with a lawsuit if I was to continue to insist that he should stop driving. It was not one of my best days.

According to the Centers for Disease Control and Prevention, "Drivers aged 80 and older have higher crash death rates per mile driven than all but teen drivers, and most traffic fatalities involving older drivers occurred during the daytime (79%) and on weekdays (73%); 73% of the crashes involved another vehicle. The age-related decreases in vision, cognitive functions, and physical impairments may affect some older adults' driving ability."[35]

There is no doubt that the vast majority of older adults can safely drive. But there is also no reason to ignore the facts that certain diseases, such as Parkinson's disease, make a person less able to drive. Many resources are now available that can help an older adult determine if he or she is still able to drive safely.[36]

And while we are talking about safety, poor hearing and eyesight, both banes of increasing age, put an older adult at higher risk of being involved in an accident. And one more thing: seat belts do work and save lives. They do not make you drown or burn in your car. So for goodness sake, wear them!

The social history is also the place and time to discuss nutrition and exercise. For an in-depth discussion of both these topics, please see Chapters 5 and 6.

Three things to remember:

1. The best thing you can do for your health is to stop smoking.
2. Remember that alcohol affects you differently when you are older.
3. If you or anybody else has any doubt about your driving ability, please have it evaluated before you are involved in an accident, injuring yourself and/or someone else.

Medication Review

One of the most important parts of every medical visit is a careful review of all your medications, including prescription, over-the-counter, and any supplements you are taking as well. Please refer to Chapter 4 for further information and an in-depth discussion of medications and their use in older adults. An easy way to do this is simply to bring all the medications you are taking with you to your visit with your physician. At the very least, have an updated list ready for your doctor to review. Both your physician and your health will thank you.

Physical Exam

Finally, it's time that I perform a physical exam of the patient. I usually ask the patient to get up from the chair without using the hands to push off, and then to walk to the examination table. I watch my patients carefully to see if they have any difficulties standing up and how they walk. I start by examining the head and neck, including the mouth for any dental problems and the ears for any wax buildup. A comprehensive eye exam is not possible in the office. I will check the neck for any thyroid gland enlargement. Using a stethoscope, I'll listen to the heart and lungs and also to the arteries in the neck, which sometimes make a characteristic sound called a bruit when they are narrowed by atherosclerosis. I'll examine the abdomen for anything abnormal such as a mass or an enlarged liver or spleen. Sometimes a rectal exam and an examination of genitalia are necessary. I'll also make sure to take a good look at the patient's joints, and especially the feet for any sores or problems with toenails. Let's go back to the car analogy for a moment. Think of the feet as being the tires of the body. There is no use in keeping the engine and the rest of the car in good working condition while skimping on tires. A flat tire or blowout stops the car from going at all. The same is true for poor foot care, because ingrown nails or nonhealing sores have a serious effect on mobility, increase the risk of falls, and can even lead to life-threatening infections. A neurologic exam and a close look at the skin for any suspicious-looking moles or other blemishes conclude the physical exam.

Blood Tests

Basic blood tests include a complete blood count, which includes a count and microscopic examination of both the red blood cells and white blood cells in the body, and measurements of electrolytes, as well as kidney and liver function. In addition, I usually order a thyroid function test and, depending on the patient, a lipid profile to check cholesterol levels.

Preventive Measures

Now the real work begins, with a discussion about the many important preventive measures and the best schedule for each individual patient:[37]

1. Annual influenza (flu) vaccination
2. Pneumococcal vaccine once after age 65
3. One-time vaccination with the *Herpes zoster* (shingles) vaccine
4. Tetanus-diphtheria vaccine booster every 10 years
5. Screening mammography, usually every year
6. Screening colonoscopy every 10 years (may vary according to patient's condition and family history)
7. Yearly fecal evaluation for occult blood (can be done at the same time as the annual prostate exam in men or at home using small fecal cards).
8. Pap smears after 65 can be discontinued if a woman has had three consecutive normal smears in the last 10 years or if she has had a hysterectomy for a reason other than cancer, but Pap smears should still be considered if there is a family history of ovarian cancer.
9. Screening bone mineral density exam beginning at 65. Repeat examinations usually depend on the patient's medical condition. No set schedule is recommended.
10. One-time screening ultrasound examination to look for an abdominal aortic aneurysm in men, especially those who have a significant family history or a history of smoking (not as clearly established for women).
11. Comprehensive blood tests, including a lipid profile (for cholesterol) and yearly thyroid function tests
12. A baseline electrocardiogram (ECG) if there is any indication of heart disease.
13. Screening for depression even without any indication at least once a year
14. Various memory screens if there is any suspicion of a memory problem or concern by the patient or caregiver

Other regular evaluations should include vision and hearing tests. Keep those senses up to speed!

I usually like to finish a visit with the sensitive topic of advance directives and a health care proxy. For a more detailed discussion of these important topics, see Chapter 16, "On Being Prepared."

Advance directives are written instructions in which you clearly state your wishes about your health care in the event that you can no longer make these decisions for yourself.

A **health care proxy** is a document in which you authorize a specific person to make decisions on your behalf if you become incapable of doing so.

If you are not exhausted after all this, I am—and I still need to see a few more patients!

REFERENCES

1. Palo Alto Medical Foundation, "Health Maintenance Evaluation-Replacing the 'Annual Physical,'" Palo Alto Health Foundation, http://www.pamf.org/preventive/healtheval.html.

2. Edoardo Botteri et al., "Smoking and Colorectal Cancer: A Meta-Analysis," *Journal of the American Medical Association* 300 (2008): 2765.

3. U.S. Department of Health and Human Services, "Welcome to Medicare Visit," Centers for Medicare and Medicaid Services, http://www.cms.hhs.gov/WelcometomedicareExam.

4. Aram Chobian et al., "The Seventh Report of the Joint National Committee on Prevention, Detection, Evaluation, and Treatment of High Blood Pressure," *Journal of the American Medical Association* 289 (2003): 2560.

5. Francois Gueyffier et al., "Antihypertensive Drugs in Very Old People: A Subgroup Meta-Analysis of Randomized Controlled Trials," *Lancet* 353 (1999): 793.

6. Encyclopedia Britannica, "Diabetes Mellitus—Causes and Types," http://www.britannica.com/EBchecked/topic/160921/diabetes-mellitus.

7. Caroline Roberts, Eliseo Guallar, and Annabelle Rodriguez, "Efficacy and Safety of Statin Monotherapy in Older Adults: A Meta-Analysis," *Journal of Gerontology: Medical Sciences* 62A (2007): 879.

8. David Knopman et al., "Practice Parameter: Diagnosis of Dementia (an Evidence-Based Review)—Report of the Quality Standards Subcommittee of the American Academy of Neurology," *Neurology* 56 (2001): 1143.

9. Joseph Gallo et al., "Depression without Sadness: Functional Outcomes of Non-dysphoric Depression in Later Life," *Journal of the American Geriatrics Society* 45 (1997): 570.

10. Gene Nakajima and Neil Wenger, "Quality Indicators for Care of Depression in Vulnerable Elders," *Journal of the American Geriatrics Society* 55 (2007): S302.

11. John Campbell, Michael Borrie, and George Spears, "Risk Factors for Falls in a Community-Based Prospective Study of People 70 Years and Older," *Journal of Gerontology: Medical Sciences* 44 (1989): M112.

12. Lawrence Rubenstein and Karen Josephson, "Falls and Their Prevention in Elderly People: What Does the Evidence Show?" *Medical Clinics of North America* 90 (2006): 807.

13. Mary King and Mary Tinetti, "Falls in Community-Dwelling Older Persons," *Journal of the American Geriatrics Society* 43 (1995): 1146.
14. Michael Province et al., "The Effects of Exercise on Falls in Elderly Patients. A Preplanned Meta-Analysis of the FICSIT Trials," *Journal of the American Medical Association* 273 (1995): 1341.
15. Howard Sesso et al., "Maternal and Paternal History of Myocardial Infarction and Risk of Cardiovascular Disease in Men and Women," *Circulation* 24 (2001): 393.
16. Frank Lederle et al., "Blood Pressure Change and Risk of Hypertension Associated with Parental Hypertension: The Johns Hopkins Precursors Study," *Archives of Internal Medicine* 168 (2008): 643.
17. Frank Lederle et al., "The Aneurysm Detection and Management Study Screening Program: Validation Cohort and Final Results—Aneurysm Detection and Management Veterans Affairs Cooperative Study Investigators," *Archives of Internal Medicine* 160 (2000): 1425.
18. Haiyan Li et al., "Consequences of a Family History of Type 1 and Type 2 Diabetes on the Phenotype of Patients with Type 2 Diabetes," *Diabetes Care* 23 (2000): 589.
19. Robert Green et al., "Risk of Dementia among White and African American Relatives of Patients with Alzheimer Disease," *Journal of the American Medical Association* 287 (2002): 329.
20. Esther Wei et al., "Comparison of Risk Factors for Colon and Rectal Cancer," *International Journal of Cancer* 108 (2004): 433.
21. Alice Whittemore et al., "Family History and Prostate Cancer Risk in Black, White, and Asian Men in the United States and Canada," *American Journal of Epidemiology* 141 (1995): 732.
22. Joellen Schildkraut and Douglas Thompson, "Familial Ovarian Cancer: A Population-Based Case Study," *American Journal of Epidemiology* 128 (1988): 456.
23. Ahmedin Jemal et al., "Cancer Statistics: CA," *A Cancer Journal for Clinicians* 58 (2008): 71.
24. Victoria Dorr, Stephen Williamson, and Ronald Stephens, "An Evaluation of Prostate-Specific Antigen as a Screening Test for Prostate Cancer," *Archives of Internal Medicine* 152 (1993): 2529.
25. Mathew Cooperberg, Judd Moul, and Peter Carroll, "The Changing Face of Prostate Cancer," *Journal of Clinical Oncology* 23 (2005): 8146.
26. Ram Eitan et al., "The Clinical Significance of Malignant Pleural Effusions in Patients with Optimally Debulked Ovarian Carcinoma," *Cancer* 103 (2005): 1397.
27. Naila Aslam et al., "Prospective Evaluation of Three Different Models for the Pre-Operative Diagnosis of Ovarian Cancer," *British Journal of Obstetrics and Gynecology* 107 (2000): 1347.
28. Katherine Pearce et al., "Cytopathologic Findings on Vaginal Papanicolau Smears after Hysterectomy for Benign Gynecologic Disease," *New England Journal of Medicine* 335 (1996): 1559.
29. Rosella Gennari et al., "Breast Carcinoma in Elderly Women: Features of Disease Presentation, Choice of Local and Systemic Treatments Compared with Younger Postmenopausal Patients," *Cancer* 101 (2004): 1302.
30. Sami Diab, Richard Elledge, and Gary Clark, "Tumor Characteristics and Clinical Outcome of Elderly Women with Breast Cancer," *Journal of the National Cancer Institute* 92 (2000): 550.

31. Jeanne Mandelblatt et al., "Patterns of Breast Carcinoma Treatment in Older Women: Patient Preference and Clinical and Physical Influences," *Cancer* 89 (2000): 561.
32. Christine Bouchard et al., "Undertreatment Strongly Decreases Prognosis of Breast Cancer in Elderly Women," *Journal of Clinical Oncology* 21 (2003): 3580.
33. National Osteoporosis Foundation, "Fast Facts on Osteoporosis," http://www.nof.org/osteoporosis/diseasefacts.htm.
34. The National Center for Victims of Crime, "Elder Victimization," http://www.ncvc.org/ncvc/main.aspx?dbName=DocumentViewer&DocumentID=38713.
35. Department of Health and Human Services, "Older Adult Drivers: Fact Sheet," Centers for Disease Control and Prevention, http://www.cdc.gov/ncipc/factsheets/older.htm.
36. Live Well, Live Long. Health Promotion and Disease Prevention for Older Adults, "Road Map to Driving Wellness," http://www.asaging.org/cdc/module4/home.cfm.
37. "Geriatric Health Maintenance," ed. Mitchell T. Heflin, in UptoDate online, http://www.uptodate.com.

9

Falls—Don't Ignore Those Stumbles and Trips

Remember those first steps of your children and maybe even your grandchildren? How you laughed affectionately at their clumsy attempts to take a few steps before falling onto their padded behinds? This milestone in their development is a joyful moment to remember. In contrast, falls in older adults are no laughing matter. They are serious and a major contributor to the loss of independence.[1] Fortunately, many falls do not result in any significant injuries. But this is precisely the problem. The reason is simple: a person who falls has a 50 percent chance of falling again. Plus, the more a person falls, the greater the risk of developing a "fear of falling."[2] This fear, in turn, makes people more inclined to walk less, therefore becoming deconditioned and weaker. And the weaker a person is, the more likely he or she will fall again. This vicious circle all too often results in the one final fall that results in an emergency room visit and the dreaded hip fracture.

Falls account for a staggering 10 percent of emergency room visits by older adults and 6 percent of urgent hospitalizations.[3]

Unfortunately, hip fractures are only *one* bad outcome of unreported and untreated falls. Others include subdural hematomas (bleeding around the brain) and other fractures and injuries. The ultimate result can be loss of independence in daily activities like dressing, bathing, and using the toilet—often the bitter reality for older adults and their loved ones.[3] This underscores the extreme importance of letting your physician know about any falls, so that he or she can help you avoid the "final" fall and frightening hip fracture.

More Sobering Information on Falls

The incidence of falls increases with age. Thirty to forty percent of older adults living in the community fall each year, and this increases to 50 percent in adults older than age 80. Both men and women suffer from falls.[4]

One of my very first patients after I finished my fellowship fell and broke her hip two weeks after her initial appointment with me. She was a fiercely independent 82-year-old lady who was proud of being able to live alone in her large house in a Boston suburb. I went to visit her in the hospital, feeling dreadful that this happened so shortly after I had seen her in the office. I was quite sure that I'd asked her about falls, and she'd insisted that she had not fallen. When at the bedside I asked her what happened, she started crying and apologized for being dishonest. She then admitted that she had fallen multiple times over the last year but was afraid to tell anyone, including her daughters, because she didn't want to face the possibility of having to leave her house and move to an assisted-living facility. Had I known this, we could have discussed her fears of losing her independence during the office visit, and I could have concentrated on reducing her risk of falls by ordering physical therapy and other appropriate measures. Fortunately, in this case, she was able to return home after an extended rehabilitation stay.

Approximately half of older adults who fall can get up by themselves. The other half need help, and if none is available, they may end up lying on the ground for long times and suffering even more of a decline.[5] It is therefore no surprise that falls are the fifth leading cause of death among older adults.[6]

WHY DO OLDER ADULTS FALL?

There is usually no one single cause why an older adult falls. Most often, many reasons act together to cause a fall. This makes finding the best treatment for an older adult who has fallen a little like trying to find a few important pieces of a big puzzle. Certainly, this can be frustrating for both patient and physician. One useful and informative way to tackle this problem is to think of all the changes in older adults' bodies that reduce the ability to adequately control posture. Dr. Douglas Kiel has summarized this well in his review article "Falls in older persons: Risk factors and patient evaluation" on the UpToDate Web site.[4]

The following changes play an important role in increasing the risk of falls in older adults.

1. The sensory system: A variety of age-related changes in the sensory system can increase the risk of falls. One that nearly all older adults experience is some degree of diminished eyesight such as being near-sighted, having cataracts, or just being less well able to see in the dark. Another change in the sensory system with increasing age is the tendency for certain receptors in our bodies that help us maintain an upright posture to wear out. This, in addition to degenerative changes in structures that help us keep our balance, which are located in the inner part of our ears, may contribute to falls and intermittent dizziness.[4]
2. The muscular system: With age, muscle tissue is increasingly replaced by fat tissue, which results in less function and more disability in older adults.[4]
3. Blood pressure regulation: With advancing age, our bodies find it more difficult to appropriately regulate blood pressure to avoid large drops in pressure

when changing position from lying down to sitting or standing (a condition called orthostatic hypotension). Such a drop in blood pressure compromises the blood flow to the brain and may result in dizziness and fainting (also called syncope). The reasons for this are many, but worn-out blood pressure receptors in blood vessels, the tendency for blood to pool in the digestive tract after a meal (called postprandial hypotension), and a diminished thirst mechanism all play a role in a drop in blood pressure and may lead to falls.[4]

4. Other medical conditions: Certain diseases that are more common in older adults also pose a significant risk of falls. Among these are Parkinson's disease, osteoarthritis of the knees and hips, and memory problems that are severe enough to cause a dementia (see Chapter 7). A prior stroke or any other condition that tends to affect the gait also predisposes to falls.[4]

5. Medications: Medications are likely the most important and relatively easily corrected risk factor for falls (see Chapter 4). Medications that lower blood pressure (antihypertensives), "water pills" (diuretics), and beta blockers (drugs that slow the heart rate) may contribute to an increased risk of falls.[4] Other important medications that have been implicated in increasing the risk of falls are those that affect the brain, including antidepressants, anticonvulsant medications, and especially benzodiazepines, which are Valium-like medications.[7,8] Results of studies looking at whether opioids (morphine-like medications) increase the risk of falls have been conflicting. However, no such confusion exists for alcohol use.[4] There is good evidence that consumption of large amounts of alcohol increases the risk of falls.[9]

FALLS AND THE ENVIRONMENT

Doctors and patients often tend to attribute a fall to an uneven sidewalk, a poorly lit curb, or a flight of old creaky stairs. However, it is rarely that simple, and it does not benefit the patient to blame a fall on purely environmental factors. There is no doubt that a poorly maintained sidewalk can result in a fall, and environmental hazards should absolutely be corrected if possible, but it's important to recognize that environmental hazards tend to "interact with intrinsic risk factors"[4] rather than being the sole cause of a fall. In other words, although younger people may stumble over a patch of uneven pavement, they are far less likely to fall because they do not suffer from arthritis, gait, or balance problems, and are typically not taking any medications that may affect their risk of falling.

WHAT CAN BE DONE ABOUT FALLS?

Contrary to the opinions of many older adults (and sadly some physicians too), a lot *can* be done to improve a person's gait and balance and to reduce his or her risk of falling. Falls are not a normal part of aging. They are unintentional and serve as a marker for frailty and instability. They also point to underlying acute and chronic impairments. Of course, there is no way to miraculously heal the effects of an old stroke that has left a person with a one-sided weakness or to cure the degenerative effects of spinal stenosis that causes weakness in a person's legs. But despite the fact that we cannot cure many conditions that contribute to the risk of falling, we can reduce their severity and thereby reduce the chance of falling. An excellent example is optimizing management of patients with extensive osteoarthritis of the knees. If pain control is maximized and the patient participates in physical therapy, usually gait and balance can be improved to the point of preventing another fall.

What You Should Do If You Fall!

Assuming you did not injure yourself when you fell, here is some advice on what you should tell your primary care physician. First, you must let your doctor know that you had a recent fall, that you are very concerned about it, and that you are asking for ways to avoid another fall. Make sure to mention what you were doing at the time of the fall. Be as exact as possible because this may explain the reason for the fall in the first place. For example, were you getting up out of bed, or standing up from a chair? Were you trying to take something out of an overhead cabinet or closet, or just reaching for something up high? Did you fall while getting up from the table after having had a large meal? Were you reaching down to pick something up from the floor? Were you using the bathroom at the time or trying to get dressed? Did the fall happen shortly after you took any medication, especially any new ones?

In addition to what you were doing when you fell, it is also important to tell your doctor if you experienced anything unusual just before the fall. Did you feel faint or dizzy? Did you experience any palpitations? Did you notice any weakness in your arms or legs? Did you have any difficulty speaking? Did you become unconscious, even if it was only for a short moment? Did you lose control over your bladder or bowels?

Describe as best you can the actual fall. Did you fall straight forward or did you fall backward? And make sure to also tell your doctor if you were unable to get up from the floor after the fall and how long you were lying on the ground while waiting for help.

One other very important piece of information your doctor needs to know is whether you hit your head when you fell down. It doesn't matter if you have no bruise on your face or scalp, or if you had no headache(s) afterward, clearly tell your doctor if you hit your head. As outlined in Chapter 7, "The Aging Brain," any trauma to the head can cause a slow but dangerous bleed

---

I remember very well the case of an older woman who had fallen down a flight of stairs while carrying her groceries in both hands and suffered a hip fracture. After surgery, she experienced profound weakness in both of her arms. When I questioned her specifically about whether she hit her head when she fell, she responded that she had indeed hit her head on the concrete floor at the bottom of the steps. A CT scan showed sure enough that she had not only one, but two subdural hematomas (or "bleeds"), which explained her symptoms.

on top of the brain (a subdural hematoma), and your doctor needs to know if this is a possibility.

What Your Doctor Should Do

With your help, your doctor should now have a very good history of the fall. He or she will now perform a careful examination for any signs that could explain the fall. It is usually very helpful to start by taking your blood pressure both when you are sitting and then again a few minutes after standing up. This is done to see if you have orthostatic hypotension (see previous discussion). Your hearing and vision will be tested, and your heart and lungs thoroughly assessed. A detailed neurologic exam may find an explanation for any weakness you may have noticed in your arms and legs. It is also useful for your doctor to screen for any possible memory problems.

Of course, a careful examination of your joints and muscles is in order to determine if you have any arthritic changes or deformities and to reveal any muscle wasting. A close observation of your ability to stand up from a chair without using your hands to push off and your gait ("get up and go" test) can help establish if you have any significant impairments in gait or balance, or any general weakness, especially in your legs. Your doctor may order some blood tests to check, among other things, whether your blood counts are normal. Depending on the findings of the physical examination and these tests, your doctor may also order some x-rays.

Avoiding Further Falls

As we have already seen, there is not a single cause for a fall in an older adult. Therefore, several interventions are recommended, and they should be done simultaneously:

1. Know what all of your medications are for, and ask your doctor if any changes can be made in your medication regimen to minimize your risk of falls.[10]
2. Commit to an exercise program that is appropriate for your abilities. Ask your physician if he or she can prescribe an individualized exercise program or refer you to a physical therapist. Exercises may be done at home, at senior centers, or in outpatient physical therapy clinics. They often include gait and balance exercises, Tai Chi, and strength and endurance training.[11] (See also Chapter 6, "Exercise and Older Adults," which provides a more in-depth discussion of various types and examples of exercises.) In addition to helping you determine useful exercises, physical therapists are very knowledgeable about the need for and the specific types of assistive devices (e.g., walker or cane) that may improve your stability and reduce your risk of falling.
3. Conduct a thorough home safety evaluation, or ask your physician for a recommendation of someone who can do so for you. If necessary, install sidebars or grab bars in showers and bathrooms, remove or firmly secure

scatter rugs, and remove or redirect any electrical cords that cross walking paths. Look carefully for and correct any other potential hazards. Making sure that lighting in hallways, bathrooms, and stairways is adequate is another simple way to reduce the risk of falling.

4. Take a vitamin D supplement at 700–1000 IU/day. Multiple studies have shown that vitamin D supplementation at this dosage can reduce the risk of falling among older adults.[12]

Three things to remember:

1. Falls are not a normal part of aging.
2. Consider a fall a serious "illness" that needs urgent medical attention.
3. If you have fallen or have a fear of falling, do not be afraid to ask for help. A lot can be done to reduce your risk of another fall.

REFERENCES

1. Mary Tinetti et al., "Shared Risk Factors for Falls, Incontinence, and Functional Dependence," *Journal of the American Medical Association* 273 (1995): 1348.
2. Nicole Austin et al., "Fear of Falling in Older Women: A Longitudinal Study of Incidence, Persistence, and Predictors," *Journal of the American Geriatrics Society* 53 (2001): 1598.
3. Mary Tinetti, "Preventing Falls in Elderly Persons," *New England Journal of Medicine* 348 (2003): 42.
4. "Falls in Older Persons: Risk Factors and Patient Evaluation," ed. Douglas Kiel, http://www.uptodate.com.
5. Mary Tinetti et al., "Predictors and Prognosis of Inability to Get Up after Falls among Elderly," *Journal of the American Medical Association* 269 (1993): 65.
6. "Fatalities and Injuries from Falls among Older Adults—United States, 1993–2003 and 2001–2005," *Morbidity and Mortality Weekly Report* 55 (2006): 1221.
7. Rosanne Leipzig et al., "Drugs and Falls in Older People: A Systematic Review and Meta-Analysis. I: Psychotropic Drugs," *Journal of the American Geriatrics Society* 47 (1999): 30.
8. K. E. Ensrud et al., "Central Nervous System-Active Medications and Risk for Falls in Older Women," *Journal of the American Geriatrics Society* 50 (2002): 3303.
9. Peggy Cawthon et al., "Alcohol Intake and Its Relationship with Bone Mineral Density, Falls, and Fracture Risk in Older Men," *Journal of the American Geriatrics Society* 45 (2006): 1649.
10. Sabrina Pit et al., "A Quality Use of Medicines Program for General Practitioners and Older People: A Cluster Randomized Control Trial," *Medical Journal of Australia* 187 (2007): 23.
11. Lesley Gillespie et al., "Interventions for Preventing Falls in Older People Living in the Community," *Cochrane Database of Systematic Reviews* 2 (2009): CD007146.
12. Heike Bischoff et al., "Fall Prevention with Supplemental and Active Forms of Vitamin D: A Meta-Analysis of Randomised Controlled Trials," *British Medical Journal* 339 (2009): 3692.

10

DEPRESSION AND ANXIETY— A SAD STATE OF AFFAIRS

When does feeling "blue" end and depression start? The answer is not as straightforward as we would like. This is undoubtedly one reason why depression is often not diagnosed and therefore undertreated or not treated at all. Depression is much more widespread among older adults than is apparent. People may not admit to being depressed for fear of being labeled "weak" or "crazy" or because they feel ashamed that they've "let this happen to them."[1] Nothing is further from the truth than those common misperceptions. First, you should know that depression is not a normal consequence of aging. Depression is a chronic medical illness and a "serious health concern leading to unnecessary suffering."[2] As such, it needs to be thought of not unlike other medical conditions such as diabetes or hypertension. Some people may experience only one episode of depression, while others are less lucky and have repeat bouts of depression.[3]

CAUSES OF DEPRESSION

Most researchers and experts in the field of mental health agree that there is no one single cause for depression but rather a possible combination of the following:

- Biochemical—There appear to be "physical changes" in the brains of patients suffering from depression. Certain chemicals in the brain, called neurotransmitters, seem to play a part in this.
- Genes—Studies of families that have a high occurrence of depression seem to indicate that the cause of depression can have an underlying genetic component.
- Environment—Life situations that are particularly challenging and "difficult to cope with" can also be a culprit.[3]

Older adults are no strangers to challenging life events such as bereavement, retirement, moving from their home to an assisted-living facility or nursing home, or illness that results in a loss of physical and even cognitive function.[4] Older adults who have suffered a previous episode of depression at a younger age have a higher risk of late-life depression than those who have never experienced depression before. This suggests, as already mentioned, that there is indeed a possible family or genetic factor at play.[5]

OLD VERSUS YOUNG

While younger adults tend to complain about experiencing a depressed mood, older adults tend to have a "preoccupation with physical health concerns rather than with feelings of sadness."[6] Common complaints include a change in appetite, difficulty sleeping and feeling tired during the day, being irritable or even agitated at times, and having difficulty with concentration. Of course, sadness and feeling worthless can also be present at times and even, frighteningly, thoughts of suicide.[1]

ILLNESS AND DEPRESSION

Some illnesses put older adults at an increased risk of experiencing a depression. Among these conditions are heart attacks and strokes.[7,8] In both cases, depression significantly increases the risk of death in these patients. Another illness clearly associated with a higher risk of depression is memory problems. In fact, depression may be a first sign of a dementia such as Alzheimer's disease.[6]

Other dementias, especially the dementia of Parkinson's disease, have also been associated with depression. It is therefore no wonder that symptoms of depression can easily be confused with common medical conditions such as Alzheimer's disease, arthritis, cancer, heart disease, Parkinson's disease, stroke, and thyroid disorders.[1]

Not too long ago, a colleague of mine asked me to see a patient whose wife noticed that he was becoming increasingly withdrawn and less social. He stopped going to the men's club and avoided leaving the house as much as possible. His wife was convinced that he was depressed, and asked for help. His primary care physician started him on an antidepressant medication, and sure enough his spirits improved and he became more active again. It soon became evident that he was having some memory troubles, and on a trip to visit his friends, he became lost for 24 hours, driving around in circles. The police finally found him at a gas station when the attendant called to say that a man was trying to buy gasoline for his car without money. What had happened? His depression initially masked the underlying problem of dementia, which became apparent only after the depression was treated. Unfortunately, this is not an uncommon scenario.

THE MANY FACES OF DEPRESSION

As if depression in and of itself isn't bad enough, there is more than one type of depression. A consultation with a psychiatrist is often needed to make the correct diagnosis.

Major Depression

A so-called major depression is diagnosed when a person experiences five or more of the following symptoms on a day-to-day basis for a minimum of two weeks. One of these complaints must be either a "depressed mood" or a "loss of interest or pleasure in nearly all activities." The others can be four or more of the following:

1. experiencing a change in appetite or weight
2. having some difficulty sleeping
3. being agitated
4. having a lack of energy and fatigue
5. feeling worthless or having feelings of guilt
6. having difficulty concentrating and making decisions, having "recurrent thoughts of death or suicidal ideation" and even some plans or attempts of suicide[2]

Although this is called a major depression, it does not mean to imply that other types of depression are not serious.

Dysthymia

Dysthymia is a Greek word meaning "bad state of mind or ill humor." It refers to a depressed mood "most of the time for at least two years, along with at least two of the following symptoms: poor appetite or overeating, insomnia or excessive sleep, low energy or fatigue, low self-esteem, poor concentration or indecisiveness, and hopelessness."[9] Dysthymia and major depression have some symptoms in common, but older adults with major depression in addition to the previous complaints also feel "anhedonia (inability to feel pleasure) and psychomotor symptoms (chiefly lethargy or agitation)."[9] Dysthymia should not be taken lightly. It needs to be addressed and treated appropriately, especially because more than 50 percent of people with dysthymia will also develop a major depression.

Subsyndromal Depression

Subsyndromal depression is yet another type of depression that is seen especially in older adults but fits the category of neither major depression nor dysthymia. Again, one might be fooled by the name thinking it suggests a low level of depression, but subsyndromal depression is equally important to recognize and treat because it represents a significant risk of developing a major depression and is associated with overall poor health.[10]

More Types of Depression

One type of depression that is of particular concern is called delusional depression. These people experience, among other symptoms, paranoid ideas such as feeling persecuted. This type of depression is often associated with significant memory impairment.[2]

There are even more types of depression, but a detailed description of all of them is beyond the scope of this chapter. The point is to be aware and seek treatment if you experience any symptoms of depression.

DETECTION AND SCREENING

It is clear that we should all be vigilant about detecting depression as early as possible. In fact, a number of effective screening questionnaires are available that can quickly be administered in a primary care office. They are reliable and have been shown to identify those older adults who suffer from depression or are at risk of developing a depression.

The short Geriatric Depression Scale is a self-report questionnaire that has been studied extensively and is used frequently.[11] It consists of the following five questions:

1. Are you basically satisfied with your life?
2. Do you often get bored?
3. Do you feel helpless?
4. Do you prefer to stay at home rather than going out and doing things?
5. Do you feel pretty worthless the way you are now?

An answer of "no" to question 1 or "yes" to questions 2 through 5 suggests a possible diagnosis of depression.[11] It is important to remember that this is only a screening questionnaire, and so it does not definitively make the diagnosis. An appropriate assessment, which I believe should include a consultation with a psychiatrist, should follow to make the final diagnosis.

An even shorter questionnaire consists of two simple questions, and a "yes" answer to both makes it very likely that a person is suffering from depression. These questions are:

1. "During the past month, have you been bothered by feeling down, depressed or hopeless?"
2. "During the past month, have you been bothered by little interest or pleasure in doing things?"[12]

WHAT SHOULD A MEDICAL WORK-UP START WITH?

First of all, it is necessary to ensure there is not a medical condition that may cause a person to be depressed and that needs urgent treatment. A good history and medical examination will be helpful in detecting such conditions as chronic untreated or undertreated pain, heart disease, and even possible undetected cancers or an unrecognized memory problem. Next follows a careful medication review because some commonly used medications may be causing depressive symptoms. Among these are some cardiovascular medications like the beta-blockers, angiotensin-converting enzyme (ACE) inhibitors, and some calcium channel blockers. Older blood pressure medications like reserpine and alpha-methyldopa have been especially implicated. Other drugs that cause depressive symptoms are corticosteroids and mefloquine used for malaria prophylaxis.[13,14] Appropriate x-rays or other imaging tests may be indicated, and some routine blood tests should be ordered to check for anemia (low blood count), abnormal kidney or liver function, and thyroid disease.[1]

Suicide and the Older Adult

One important part of the initial evaluation of a person with possible depression is to establish if there is a suicide risk. Data from 2005 showed that there was a suicide by an older adult every 100 minutes, or 14.5 suicides a day in the United States. These shocking statistics add up to more than 5,000 older adults dying of suicide a year.[15] Studies have shown that most older adults who commit suicide have in fact "visited a physician within a month before death."[16]

Non-Hispanic white men who are 85 and older are "the most likely to die by suicide."[16] Older adults with a prior attempt of suicide, those who are widowed or otherwise socially isolated, and those who are suffering from inadequately treated pain are at high risk of suicide.[2] The warning signs for possible suicide attempt of an older person are "statements about death and suicide, reading material about death and suicide, increased alcohol or prescription drug use, failure to take care of self or follow medical orders, stockpiling medications, sudden interest in firearms, social withdrawal or elaborate good-byes, rush to complete or revise a will, and overt suicide threats." Unfortunately, many older adults will not do or show any of these actions or make comments about possible suicide attempts.[17] Many will exhibit only symptoms that are similar to those of a person experiencing a depression, like feeling hopeless or sad and finding no pleasure in any activities.

There really is no reason for older adults to have to resort to suicide. Our extensive health care system offers many resources, including hospice care for those with end-of-life care needs, pain specialists and pain clinics for those suffering from chronic pain, and social workers who can help and offer advice with difficult social and family situations. Good geriatric and psychiatric care is also available at most major academic medical centers.

If you are in crisis or know of someone who may need help right away, please call the National Suicide Prevention Lifeline at 1-800-273-TALK (8255). All calls are confidential. Calls are toll-free and available 24 hours a day, 7 days a week.

TREATMENT OPTIONS

Several options are available, and I suggest that a geriatric psychiatrist is involved in the actual treatment and follow-up alongside the primary care physician. Treatment is best thought of in several stages, with the initial focus on the acute treatment of the depression, followed by a course of treatment to avoid any immediate relapse and later a "maintenance treatment to prevent a future recurrence."[6] Psychotherapy, pharmacotherapy with antidepressant medications, and electroconvulsive therapy all have been shown to be effective in the treatment of depression in older adults.[6] Studies have shown that psychotherapy and medications are similar in their effects and depending on the type of depression and the patient's possible medication contraindications and other medical conditions, they may be used together for improved effectiveness.[18,19]

Pharmacotherapy or Medication

Many different types of medications are available. Some that have been used in the past are still very effective but have significantly more side effects than the newer types of medications. There is no doubt that medications can significantly improve the quality of life of depressed older adults, but they need to be given in lower dosages and monitored carefully.[1]

Again, a full discussion of all currently FDA-approved medications for depression is beyond the scope of this chapter, but a few of the most commonly used ones are listed here:

1. Selective serotonin-reuptake inhibitors (known as SSRIs) are often used as first-line treatments. Examples include fluoxetine (Prozac), sertraline (Zoloft), paroxetine (Paxil), fluvoxamine (Luvox), citalopram (Celexa), and escitalopram (Lexapro).[1]
2. Serotonin-norepinephrine reuptake inhibitors (known as SNRIs) are also commonly used. Examples of these medications include venlafaxine (Effexor), duloxetine (Cymbalta), and mirtazapine (Remeron).[1]
3. Tricyclic antidepressants are used less commonly because of side effects, particularly affecting the heart.[1]

It may take a couple of months before the full therapeutic effect is achieved, but many older adults often feel some improvement in their mood and energy long before.

Psychotherapy

This involves "talking through problems" with different mental health experts like psychotherapists, psychiatrists, or therapists. These sessions can be conducted as group sessions, or with just the individual alone or with family members or a spouse present.[1,2] During these sessions, patients learn more about themselves and especially their condition. They learn new coping skills and how to manage stressful situations. Sessions are usually held once a week for an hour, and depending on the type of condition a person has, may continue for a few months to a year or longer.[20]

Electroconvulsive Therapy (ECT)

The thought of this type of treatment can send shivers down one's spine. I remember the husband of one of my patients telling me that he would not even consider having his wife undergo such medieval torture-like treatment. The poor reputation of ECT is undeserved these days. The fact is that it can be very useful in patients who do not improve on medications. The idea behind ECT is that electric currents are passed through the brain and trigger a brief seizure. This seems to cause changes in brain chemistry and result in an improvement in symptoms of some mental illnesses.

ECT today is quite different from the days before anesthesia was used and patients received large electric shocks. Nowadays, the entire procedure takes only 10–15 minutes and is done on an outpatient basis. A short-acting anesthetic agent and a muscle relaxant are given intravenously before a small electrical shock is administered. The patient does not feel anything, and there are no violent movements—just small twitches of the hands or feet. Side effects are typically minor. The most common is that patients may experience some confusion after awakening, which can last for a few hours. Some memory loss is possible during longer treatment periods, but a persistent memory loss is very rare. Some patients may experience high blood pressure and a fast heart rate. Therefore, patients with heart disease or hypertension should consult with their primary care physician and may also need to see a cardiologist. Despite these side effects, ECT is very helpful for some patients with just a few treatment sessions.[21]

Unfortunately, depression does not always come by itself. Many older adults also suffer from anxiety disorders, which are often overlooked and which could worsen the depression.[22,23]

Anxiety—the Overlooked Disease

As much as older adults are no strangers to stressful situations that may predispose them to developing depression, they are also at high risk of developing anxiety "when they feel that their physical and mental capacities are diminishing and they are losing their autonomy."[23] In fact, anxiety is the most common mental disorder affecting older adults, with one in 10 people older than 60 experiencing some form of anxiety.[24]

What Is an Anxiety Disorder?

Anxiety is a normal part of life. We all have experienced some form of anxiety in our lives, and it is a normal response to and coping mechanism in stressful situations. It becomes a disorder when "there is no threat and/ or if its intensity is far higher than the situation warrants."[25] As a result, some older adults experience a "persistent and intense fear of objects, persons, situations or events that disrupt considerably the person's usual activities."[23]

DIFFERENT TYPES OF ANXIETY

Generalized anxiety is the most common type of anxiety disorder in older adults. Some 7 percent of older adults experience "constant distressing worries" that are difficult to control.[25]

Phobias are another type of anxiety disorder seen in older adults. In this case, a person has a "severe and excessive fear of a person, thing, or event."[25] It is interesting to mention that a person actually knows that his or her fear is excessive and unsupported.[26] As a result, people start to avoid anything that will trigger these intense emotions, which ultimately starts to disrupt their daily lives. An example of a common phobia is agoraphobia, which is a fear of public places that often results in a person's unwillingness to leave his or her residence.

A social phobia causes a person to be afraid of embarrassing himself or herself in public. Some people may actually have difficulty with eating out or using a public restroom.[26] None of these types of phobias are exclusively seen in older adults; many younger adults experience them, too.

A panic disorder is a particularly intense form of anxiety that is usually short lived (some 30 minutes), but people often experience a feeling of sickness, shortness of breath, or even chest pain.[25] This kind of severe anxiety is very distressing to a person and caregivers who witness such an event. People often go to an emergency room when this happens.

Post-traumatic stress disorder is another type of anxiety disorder often seen in older adults. It is the result of having been a witness to or a victim of severe trauma, a life-threatening event, or another very traumatic experience and then intermittently reliving the experience in form of thoughts or dreams. It often results in irritability, increased "startle," and an inability to sleep.[25]

WHAT ARE THE TYPICAL SYMPTOMS OF ANXIETY?

Not unlike symptoms of depression, symptoms of anxiety disorders often present as physical complaints. Older adults commonly report palpitations, nausea, shortness of breath, dizziness, feeling faint and unsteady, abdominal pains, difficulty concentrating, and memory loss. Feeling tired and having difficulty sleeping are also common. Because any one of these symptoms may also be part of some typical disease or a side effect of common medications, it is not surprising that anxiety disorders are difficult to diagnose and often missed completely.[23]

I remember an 88-year-old patient of mine who was a Holocaust survivor. He was the only one to survive from his family. He came to the United States in 1947 with nothing but the clothes he had received in the displaced persons camp in Germany shortly after he and his fellow camp survivors had been liberated by American troops. He started working two jobs, married and had two children, and took yet another job to make the down payment on a house. He worked hard and made sure his children went to college. After he retired and his children had grown and left and his wife had passed away, he was lonely and started to have nightmares of his time in the concentration camp. He became so incapacitated that he needed to be admitted to a psychiatric hospital, where, sadly, he passed away.

HOW ARE ANXIETY DISORDERS TREATED?

Interestingly enough, some of the same medications used for treating depression are also helpful for treating anxiety in older adults. The drugs of choice are the selective serotonin-reuptake inhibitors (SSRIs), such as fluoxetine (Prozac), sertraline (Zoloft), paroxetine (Paxil), and citalopram (Celexa).[25,26] Buspirone (Wellbutrin) is also effective in treating anxiety and agitation particularly in older adults who are suffering from a dementia.[26]

The benzodiazepine medications deserve a word of caution. Common drugs in this class include diazepam (Valium), lorazepam (Ativan), and alprazolam (Xanax). These older anxiolytic medications should be taken only under close supervision by a physician and for a short period of time. They are problematic in older adults and can cause fatigue, memory problems, and falls. They should never be taken when driving. Valium, the longest-acting benzodiazepine, should be avoided altogether because it tends to accumulate in the body (see Chapter 4, "Medications and Older Adults).[25]

Similar to its use in treatment of depression, psychotherapy is also effective in helping many older adults manage their anxiety.[23]

Here is a final word on over-the-counter cold medications. As already pointed out in Chapter 4, cold remedies are stimulants for the nervous system and can thereby increase anxiety. In general, they should not be used by older adults or only after consulting with a physician. The same holds true for alcohol, which some people use at times as a remedy. The truth is that the effect of alcohol is short lived and, in the long run, it worsens both anxiety and depression.[23] The point is that anxiety and depression are serious diseases that need to be treated carefully under the supervision of a physician. Self-remedies do not work and are harmful.

Three things to remember:

1. Do not be ashamed if you feel depressed or anxious. It is not your fault, and is no different from having developed another medical condition like high blood pressure or diabetes.
2. Let your physician know how you feel, and get some help.
3. Medications do work, and it can be very helpful to try them.

REFERENCES

1. Medline Plus, "Depression—Elderly," www.nlm.nih.gov/medlineplus/ency/article/001521.htm.
2. "Diagnosis and Late-Life Depression," ed. Randall Espinoza and Juergen Unuetzer, http://www.utdol.com.
3. Mayo Clinic Staff, "Depression," http://www.mayoclinic.com/health/depression/DS00175.
4. David Steffens et al.," Prevalence of Depression and Its Treatment in an Elderly Population: The Cache County Study," *Archives of General Psychiatry* 57 (2000): 601.
5. Martin Cole and Nandini Dendukuri, "Risk Factors for Depression among Elderly Community Subjects: A Systematic Review and Meta-Analysis," *American Journal of Psychiatry* 160 (2003): 1147.
6. Gary J. Kennedy, "Depression and Other Mood Disorders," in *Geriatric Review Syllabus*, ed. Peter Pompei and John B. Murphy (New York: American Geriatrics Society, 2006), CD-ROM version.
7. Nancy Frasure-Smith et al., "Gender, Depression, and One-Year Prognosis after Myocardial Infarction," *Psychosomatic Medicine* 61 (1999): 26.
8. Ellen Whyte et al., "Depression after Stroke: A Prospective Epidemiological Study," *Journal of the American Geriatrics Society* 52 (2004): 774.
9. Harvard Health Publications, "Dysthymia," http://www.health.harvard.edu/newsweek/Dysthymia.htm.
10. Helen Lavretsky and Anand Kumar, "Clinically Significant Non-Major Depression: Old Concepts, New Insights," *American Journal of Geriatric Psychiatry* 10 (2002): 239.
11. Patrizia Rinaldi et al., "Validation of the Five-Item Geriatric Depression Scale in Elderly Subjects in Three Different Settings," *Journal of the American Geriatrics Society* 51 (2003): 694.
12. Bruce Arroll et al., "Screening for Depression in Primary Care with Two Verbally Asked Questions: Cross-Sectional Study," *British Medical Journal* 327 (2003): 1144.
13. Scott Patten and Corrado Barbui, "Drug-Induced Depression: A Systematic Review to Inform Clinical Practice," *Psychotherapy and Psychosomatics* 73 (2004): 207.
14. Mike Beers and Leigh Passman, "Antihypertensive Medications and Depression," *Drugs* 40 (1990): 792.
15. American Association of Suicideology, "Elderly Suicide Fact Sheet," http://www.211bigbend.com/hotlines/suicide/SuicideandtheElderly.pdf.
16. National Institute of Mental Health, "Older Adults: Depression and Suicide Facts," http://www.nimh.nih.gov/health/publications/older-adults-depression-and-suicide-facts-fact-sheet/index.shtml.
17. Garret Evans and Heidi Radunovich, "Suicide and the Elderly: Warning Signs and How to Help," University of Florida IFAS Extension, http://edis.ifas.ufl.edu/FY101.
18. Martin Pinquart, Paul Duberstein, and Jeffrey Lyness, "Treatments for Later-Life Depressive Conditions: A Meta-Analytic Comparison of Pharmacotherapy and Psychotherapy," *American Journal of Psychiatry* 163 (2006): 1493.
19. Patricia Arean and Beth Cook, "Psychotherapy and Combined Psychotherapy/Pharmacotherapy for Late-Life Depression," *Biological Psychiatry* 52 (2002): 293.

20. Mayo Clinic Staff, "Psychotherapy," http://www.mayoclinic.com/health/psychotherapy/MY00186.
21. Mayo Clinic staff, "Electroconvulsive Therapy," http://www.mayoclinic.com/health/electroconvulsive-therapy/MY00129.
22. Eric Lenze et al., "Comorbid Anxiety Disorders in Depressed Elderly Patients," *American Journal of Psychiatry* 157 (2000): 722.
23. Janel Gauthier, "Anxiety Disorders in the Elderly," http://www.calgaryhealth region.ca/mh/sites/ADRC/pdfs/professional/brochures/ElderlyEn.pdf.
24. Eric Lenze, "Anxiety Common in Elderly, Yet Often Undiagnosed and Under-treated," University of Pittsburgh, School of the Health Sciences Media Relations, http://www.upmc.com/MediaRelations/NewsReleases/2006/Pages/ElderlyAnxiety.aspx.
25. University of Pittsburgh Medical Center, "Late-Life Anxiety Disorders: What You Need to Know," http://www.wpic.pitt.edu/research/depr/anxiety.htm.
26. Erin L. Cassidy and Javaid I. Sheikh, "Anxiety Disorders," in *Geriatric Review Syllabus*, ed. Peter Pompei and John B. Murphy (New York: American Geriatrics Society, 2006), CD-ROM version.

11

INCONTINENCE—THE SECRET DISEASE

Not too many diseases cause patients to suffer in silence, but urinary and bowel incontinence are definitely among the top contenders. What is a normal part of life in the very young becomes a devastating disease at the opposite end of the age spectrum. Both sexes are affected, although urinary incontinence is twice as common in women as in men.[1]

First, everyone should understand that bowel and urinary incontinence are *not* a normal part of aging. Instead, they are a symptom of an underlying disease or changes in the aging body.

WHAT IS URINARY INCONTINENCE?

The best and simplest definition is the "involuntary loss of urine."[1] This refers both to the bothersome and annoying problem of losing a few drops of urine here and there and to the truly devastating condition of losing large amounts of urine.

Urinary incontinence usually results from a variety of different diseases that may occur alone or in combination with each other. The treatment therefore depends very much on an accurate diagnosis of the specific type of incontinence. However, independent of the actual type of incontinence, social isolation, depression, strained relationships, and a loss of quality of life are the usual consequences to the patient.

NORMAL BLADDER FUNCTION

To understand what causes urinary incontinence, we first have to understand how the bladder normally functions. The bladder is really a storage container for excess water and dissolved waste products (urine) that are removed by the kidneys. The kidneys function like a wastewater recycling plant, removing waste products from the blood through an elaborate and very clever filtration process. The urine then flows from the kidneys through two tubes called ureters into the bladder, which is a "balloon–like organ" in the pelvis.[2] Another tube called the urethra connects the bladder to the outside, allowing the urine to leave the body.

For the bladder to properly function, the muscle of the bladder wall (called the detrusor) must remain relaxed to allow urine to be stored, while at the same time two sphincter muscles surrounding the urethra must remain contracted to prevent urine from flowing out. These muscles are controlled by two different nerve systems that work in opposite ways. When we need to void, the bladder muscle contracts, while the two sphincter muscles relax, allowing urine to flow out and leave the body. The bladder itself and the nerves that control it are in turn controlled by specific areas in the brain. If any part of this complicated voiding mechanism is disrupted, whether there is a malfunction in the brain or at the level of the bladder, incontinence is possible.

CONDITIONS THAT CAUSE INCONTINENCE

Damage to the spinal nerves that supply the bladder and sphincter muscles will seriously disrupt the normal voiding mechanism, as will any damage to areas of the brain that control voiding. Multiple sclerosis, strokes, and dementia can all cause this type of brain damage. In women who have had several pregnancies, the pelvic support of the bladder may be weakened and the bladder may change its position; this causes the sphincter muscles to become less effective in closing off the bladder neck, and incontinence is possible. In men, an enlarged prostate gland can obstruct the flow of urine out of the body by squeezing or constricting the urethra. Over time, the bladder muscle can become dysfunctional, resulting in a wide range of problems from having difficulty in voiding, to needing to void frequently, and experiencing urine "dribbling" and incomplete emptying of the bladder.[3]

Another common condition, especially in women, is a urinary tract infection that irritates the bladder and may result in incontinence. Severe constipation may also lead to bladder irritation in both men and women.

Besides "local" factors that affect the bladder directly, other conditions may cause involuntary loss of some urine. Significant obesity can increase the abdominal pressure on the bladder and cause leakage.[4] Incontinence can also result from difficulties in getting to the bathroom on time. Older adults suffering from severe gait and balance problems as a result of arthritis or Parkinson's disease or a previous stroke may also have these difficulties.[2]

THE DIFFERENT TYPES OF INCONTINENCE

Four main types of incontinence occur in both women and men: stress incontinence (primarily in women), urge incontinence, overflow incontinence, and functional incontinence. Of course, the cause of incontinence can be complex, in part because more than one type can occur together, in what is then called mixed incontinence.

Stress Incontinence

Stress incontinence refers to the leakage of small amounts of urine "when increases in intra-abdominal pressure overcome sphincter closure mechanisms in the absence of a bladder contraction."[5] This can occur in both younger and older women and sometime in men who have had their prostate removed. Coughing, sneezing, or lifting something heavy may cause this to happen. It is very important to recognize that this type of incontinence usually leads to the loss of only small amounts of urine at a time. This is very different from urge incontinence, and the two must not be confused.

Urge Incontinence

Urge incontinence refers to the leakage of large amounts of urine. It is the result of overactivity of the bladder muscle (or detrusor). The name is derived from the "sudden need to urinate" and the inability to hold the urine long enough to get to a toilet.[2]

This is the most common form of incontinence experienced by older adults, especially older women. There are a number of different reasons for this overactivity of the bladder. These range from what are called idiopathic changes (meaning we do not know the specific cause) to a local irritation in the bladder caused by an infection, inflammation, a bladder stone, or even a tumor. Another possible reason is a disruption in the nerve connection between the brain and the bladder. In other words, the bladder is desperately trying to tell the brain that it needs to empty, but it does not get any response. A properly functioning brain will tell the bladder to relax and wait until the ladies room is found in the department store. If the connection with the brain is disrupted, the bladder does not get any information "from above," and it will eventually contract and empty itself.

Overflow Incontinence

Overflow incontinence happens when a person continually loses small amounts of urine. The bladder is full, and urine slowly spills over and out. This type of incontinence is much more common in men than in women. The underlying problem is that the bladder is not emptying itself.[5] An example of this is the case of a man who has an enlarged prostate gland that compresses the urethra, thereby obstructing the outflow of urine.

Another reason for overflow incontinence is damage to the nerves that supply either the bladder or the sphincter muscles. Examples are spinal nerve injuries and an advanced stage of diabetes.[5]

Functional Incontinence

Functional incontinence is not the result of any specific bladder or sphincter problem, but rather an inability to get to the toilet in time. Difficulty walking, being bed or chair bound, or even being cognitively confused are all examples of possible reasons for functional incontinence. Sometimes, this type of incontinence is also referred to as transient incontinence, emphasizing that appropriate interventions to improve gait and balance, or treat delirium if it has developed, may resolve the problem altogether. Functional incontinence is probably much more common than we think.[5]

WHAT SHOULD YOU DO IF YOU EXPERIENCE URINARY INCONTINENCE?

The first and most important step is to recognize that incontinence is not a normal part of aging and that there are ways to remedy the problem. Make sure to tell your doctor if you have this problem and let your caregiver know as well.

Your doctor will ask you many questions to try to establish which type of incontinence you are experiencing. So be prepared to answer specific questions about your incontinence and do not be embarrassed by the very personal nature of some of the questions.[5] Your doctor may ultimately send you to see a specialist like a urologist or a gynecologist. These specialists may ask you to keep a daily diary of episodes of incontinence. You will be asked, for example, to write down what you were doing at the time it happened and where you were. This can help identify any factors that aggravate or in fact cause the incontinence.[1]

Your doctor will also ask you about all the medications you are taking. Please make sure to mention *all* medications, including over-the-counter supplements. These may well be exacerbating the problem.

An elderly male patient of mine was once brought to the emergency room because of severe abdominal pain that had slowly gotten worse over a long holiday weekend. His wife and caregiver thought he was constipated and, having always heard me complain to her that her husband was not drinking enough fluids, made sure to keep his water glass filled all weekend long. She also had given him some Benadryl to help him sleep over the last few weeks. What she could not know was that Benadryl can cause the bladder muscle to weaken. Because of his enlarged prostate gland, the weakened bladder muscle could no longer empty the bladder. As a result, his bladder became increasingly distended and started to cause the pain. In the emergency room, a catheter was inserted into his bladder, draining three liters of urine and instantly relieving his pains.

Your doctor or a specialist will usually perform a careful general examination that includes looking for any abnormalities in the vagina in women and a thorough prostate exam in men. A careful neurological exam is often also warranted.[5] Usually blood tests are ordered to look for any electrolyte abnormalities, and blood sugar and calcium levels. The urine is usually tested for any sign of infection. Other important tests that help in making the correct diagnosis include a measurement of the residual urine volume left in the bladder after you have voided. This can be done quickly and without any discomfort by using an ultrasound device. Depending on the results of the examination and laboratory tests, further evaluation may include an ultrasound examination of the kidneys and if necessary a cystoscopy. This is usually performed by an urologist who will insert a small tube with a camera at its end into the bladder to look at the urethra and the bladder wall. Beyond this set of tests there are so-called urodynamic studies that can be done. These tests are not routinely performed and often not necessary to establish the correct diagnosis.[5]

WHAT TREATMENTS ARE AVAILABLE?

To state it clearly from the start, there is no "magic" pill to treat incontinence. Because there are so many different types of incontinence, which also tend to overlap, a variety of approaches is needed. The general recommendation is to try to use the simplest and often least invasive treatment first.[6] A detailed description of all possible treatment options is beyond the scope of this chapter, but the following discussion serves as a general overview.

Lifestyle Changes and Behavioral Therapy

Weight loss and exercise, together with stopping smoking (for smokers) and drinking less caffeinated beverages and alcohol, are helpful for stress incontinence, especially in women who have nighttime episodes of incontinence.[6] Behavioral therapy that includes bladder training and pelvic muscle exercises are often used to treat stress, urge, and mixed incontinence.

Bladder Training

One type of bladder training exercise is simply making frequent bathroom trips to keep the bladder as empty as possible and thereby avoid any accidents. Another type of exercise uses relaxation techniques to better manage urinary urgency. Instead of running to the bathroom, urgency can be decreased by "taking a deep breath and letting [the air] out slowly, contracting the pelvis muscles and/or visualizing the urge as a 'wave' that peaks and then falls."[6] Although this is not easily accomplished and requires a strong will and lots of patience, practice, and time, it can be a very successful and ultimately rewarding way of overcoming an incontinence problem. And it is at least as effective as reaching for the pill box.[7]

Here is a word about older adults with memory problems. Studies have clearly shown that what is called "prompted voiding" is an effective way to ensure that an older adult who is cognitively impaired remains continent. However, this requires the caregiver(s) to regularly prompt the person to toilet and to praise him or her for every successful bathroom trip. This can be a very rewarding treatment option for both the patient and the caregiver, and it helps avoid using medications that can have serious side effects, especially in older adults.[6]

Pelvic Muscle Exercises

Also referred to as Kegel exercises, pelvic muscle exercises can help women overcome stress, urge, and mixed incontinence, and men who are experiencing stress incontinence after surgery for removal of the prostate.[5] These exercises strengthen specific pelvic muscles by repeated contractions. The difficult part is for the individual to correctly identify and work the muscles that need to be strengthened. This requires lots of motivation and perseverance and usually monitoring by a health professional.[8] A good source for a more detailed description of these types of exercises is the Web site of the National Association for Continence at www.nafc.org. The usefulness of electrical devices and magnetic stimulation devices to help with pelvic muscle contractions and the use of "weighted cones" that are inserted into the vagina are not very clear.[8]

Medications

Medications are primarily used to treat urge incontinence as a result of an overactive bladder. These drugs are called anticholinergic agents, and they work by blocking certain receptors in the body (muscarinic receptors). This relaxes the bladder muscle, which in turn reduces the urinary urge and increases bladder capacity. Medications are often used in combination with behavioral therapy, which has been shown to be a very effective way of treating incontinence.[6]

There is really no major difference between the currently available medications, and the decision to use one over another is often based on the side effect profile, the type of other medications the person is taking, as well as the cost of the medication.[6,9]

These medications are quite effective, but unfortunately, they block muscarinic receptors in other parts of the body as well, which causes significant and annoying side effects, including the following:[10]

- Dry mouth as a result of blocking secretions from the salivary glands
- Blurred vision as a result of blocking muscles of the lens of the eye
- Constipation as a result of causing the bowel to slow down
- Fast heart rate
- Drowsiness
- Worsening of cognitive function, especially in older adults with dementia[6]

It is not surprising that some patients cannot tolerate these side effects at all.

A warning to older adults who suffer from poor or sluggish emptying of the stomach (not uncommon in people with diabetes), or who have a particular type of glaucoma called angle-closure glaucoma. In these cases, anticholinergic medications should not be used, or only after consulting with their physician. Furthermore, patients suffering from dementia should also not use these medications if at all possible.[6]

Here is a list of the currently available medications:

- oxybutynin (Ditropan)
- tolterodine (Detrol)
- fesoterodine (Toviaz)
- trospium (Sanctura)
- solifenacin (VesiCare)
- darifenacin (Enablex)

Other Treatment Options

Protective undergarments and pads are helpful for both men and women. Unfortunately, Medicare does not pay for these (only Medicaid). For more detailed information, again a good resource is the Web site of the National Association for Continence at www.nafc.org.

Among other options, surgery has its place; however, this may be helpful only in *selected* older adults suffering from both urge and stress incontinence.[6] For women, pessaries are an alternative to surgery in cases of stress incontinence. Pessaries need to be properly fitted, which is usually done by a gynecologist or urologist.[6]

Finally, a word of caution about catheters as a way to treat incontinence. Catheters are tubes that remain in the bladder and drain the urine into a bag, eliminating the need for the patient to void. They are associated with a very high degree of bladder infections and local trauma and should only be used to treat patients with acute urinary retention, that is, patients who are unable to void. They can, however, be used for very debilitated older adults and those suffering from wounds.[6]

BOWEL INCONTINENCE

So far, we've talked about urinary incontinence, which is devastating in and by itself, but there are older adults who suffer from what may well be even worse. Like urinary incontinence, bowel or anal incontinence is the "accidental loss of solid or liquid stool."[11] It is far more common than one might think, in part because many older adults are literally ashamed of telling their doctor that they have this problem (not dissimilar to the situation with urinary incontinence). In older adults living in the community, 15 percent of older women and 6 to 10 percent of older men suffer silently day in and day out. Some 10 percent of men and women have both urinary and bowel incontinence.[11]

Let's again take a quick look at normal function. Similar to the bladder serving as a storage area for urine, the rectum (end portion of the large bowel) serves as a storage area for feces. It also has two sphincter muscles, an inner and an outer sphincter, that maintain continence. When the rectum fills with stool and expands, nerves send a signal letting us know that we need to move our bowels. When we are ready, those sphincter muscles then relax so that the stool can pass out through the anus.[11]

Incontinence can occur if either the stool consistency is abnormal, as in diarrhea or severe constipation, or if there is damage to nerves either locally or in the brain. Other causes include local trauma and malformations, pelvic floor changes, and cancer and possibly its treatment. For a more detailed description, a helpful Web site is that of the International Foundation for Functional Gastrointestinal Disorders at www.IFFGD.org.

Treatment depends on the underlying cause, which is most commonly as a result of either diarrhea or constipation. Dietary changes and bowel retraining, which help to develop a routine and a regular "predictable schedule for evacuation," are helpful.[11]

KEEP IN MIND

Both urinary and bowel incontinence should be viewed as medical conditions, like heart and lung disorders. The best treatment always starts with the patient acknowledging the problem and letting his or her physician know so that the incontinence can be addressed by using all methods available.

Three things to remember:

1. Bowel and bladder incontinence is not a normal part of aging.
2. Ask for help! Do not be embarrassed.
3. Don't be discouraged or give up if a treatment is not immediately successful.

REFERENCES

1. National Kidney and Urologic Diseases Information Clearinghouse, "Urinary Incontinence in Women," http://www.kidney.niddk.nih.gov/kudiseases/pubs/uiwomen.
2. National Institute on Aging, Age Page, "Urinary Incontinence," http://www.nia.nih.gov/HealthInformation/Publications/urinary.htm.
3. "Lower Urinary Tract Symptoms in Men," ed. Kevin McVary and Rajiiv Sami, http://www.utdol.com.
4. Leslee Subak et al., "Weight Loss to Treat Urinary Incontinence in Overweight and Obese Women," *New England Journal of Medicine* 360 (2009): 481.
5. "Clinical Presentation and Diagnosis of Urinary Incontinence," ed. Catherine DuBeau, http://www.utdol.com.
6. "Treatment of Urinary Incontinence," ed. Catherine DuBeau, http://www.utdol.com.
7. Kathryn Burgio et al., "Behavioral vs. Drug Treatment for Urge Incontinence in Older Women: A Randomized Controlled Trial," *Journal of the American Medical Association* 280 (1998): 1995.

8. Catherine E. DuBeau, "Urinary Incontinence," in *Geriatric Review Syllabus*, ed. Peter Pompei and John B. Murphy (New York: American Geriatrics Society, 2006), CD-ROM version.

9. Christopher Chapple et al., "The Effects of Antimuscarinic Treatments in Overactive Bladder: A Systematic Review and Meta-Analysis," *European Journal of Urology* 48 (2005): 5.

10. Peter Herbison et al., "Effectiveness of Anticholinergic Drugs Compared with Placebo in the Treatment of Overactive Bladder: Systematic Review," *British Medical Journal* 326 (2003): 841.

11. International Foundation for Functional Gastrointestinal Disorders, "About Incontinence," http://www.aboutincontinence.org.

12

HOSPICE AND PALLIATIVE CARE—
BEYOND USUAL MEDICAL CARE

"Hospice is a concept of caring derived from medieval times, symbolizing a place where travelers, pilgrims and the sick, wounded or dying could find rest or comfort."[1] It was not until the 1960s when this concept of care was added to our modern view of medical care. Dame Cicely Saunders, who, as a young nurse had witnessed the suffering and pain of the wounded during World War II in her native England, established in 1967 St. Christopher's Hospice in London.[2] Since then, the philosophy and practice of care provided at St. Christopher's has progressively spread around the world. Inspired by a lecture given by Dr. Saunders at Yale, Florence Wald, former dean of Yale University School of Nursing, together with two physicians founded the first American hospice in Branford, Connecticut, in 1974.[2] The concept of hospice is based on the simple, but at the time almost revolutionary sounding, idea that a dying patient requires care of the "physical, psychological, social and spiritual aspects of suffering.[3]

In other words, it became apparent that there is a need to treat patients beyond the regular medical care provided by traditional medical institutions. "The hospice movement was, in part, a reaction against perceived deficiencies in modern medical care," which often tended to "interfere with humanitarian care and created barriers to comprehensive care of the dying."[3]

Four years after the opening of the first hospice in Connecticut in 1974, a U.S. Department of Health, Education, and Welfare task force report stated that "the hospice movement as a concept for care of the terminally ill and their families is a viable concept and one which holds out a means of providing more humane care for Americans dying of terminal illness while possibly reducing costs. As such, it is the proper subject of federal support."[4] However, it took another eight long years for Congress in 1986 to finally make the Medicare Hospice Benefit permanent and allow states to include a hospice option in their respective Medicaid programs.[4]

Hospice Today

We have come a long way from the early beginnings of hospice care in the United States. Today when we speak of hospice, we are referring to a concept of care rather than to a particular place of care. This concept "affirms life and regards dying as a normal process."[1] Hospice care is based on palliative rather than on curative treatment, closely following the wishes of the patient and his or her family. It stresses quality of life rather than quantity, neither hastens death nor postpones it, and includes the family in the overall care by providing support in both practical and spiritual ways.[1] Another way of saying it is that hospice care focuses "on the dying process and helping individuals who are terminally ill (and their family and friends) pass through this process more comfortably."[5]

Nowadays, hospice care is available in a variety of settings. Patients can choose to have their care at home, in a nursing home, or may possibly be admitted to an inpatient hospice. The latter setting is often very helpful for patients who are functionally debilitated or cognitively impaired. Unfortunately, Medicare and other insurers do not always cover the extra expenses, which then need to be paid by the patient or family.[3]

Who Is Eligible?

To sign up for hospice care under Medicare, a patient must satisfy the following four requirements:

1. The person must be eligible for Medicare Part A (Medicare Hospital Insurance).
2. The person must sign a statement requesting hospice care for his or her illness instead of the regular Medicare benefits.
3. Both the personal physician and the hospice medical director must clearly document that the patient is suffering from a terminal illness and that with all probability life expectancy is six months or less.
4. The hospice providing the care must be a Medicare-approved hospice program.[1]

There are two frequently asked questions about hospice programs that tend to cause concern and confusion on the part of both patients and caregivers. Can a patient decide to leave the hospice program? The answer is yes. If there is an unexpected improvement in the terminal illness, a patient has the right to decline hospice benefits and be able to join the program later on again. The second question pertains to the need for a "do not resuscitate" (DNR) order before joining hospice. Legally speaking, the answer is no. Any patient who is thinking of joining a hospice program should consider whether his or her treatment goals are in line with the hospice philosophy of a palliative rather than a curative approach to care.

WHO BENEFITS FROM HOSPICE CARE?

Certainly, the patient benefits first and foremost from hospice care. But, as noted before, hospice care goes far beyond straight medical care and includes the family, friends, and other caregivers of the patient. An "ideal" patient is one who is suffering from a terminal illness, which is "an illness from which there is little or no chance of recovery and that will most likely cause death in the near future."[5] Although a cure is no longer possible, careful management of discomfort and pain are crucial for the overall comfort of the patient and for the psychological support of the family. Unfortunately, many eligible patients enter hospice much too late because this may be perceived as giving up or losing hope. "The hope that hospice brings is the hope of a quality of life, making the best of each day during the last stages of advanced illness."[6] Of course, choosing to enroll in a hospice care program is a very personal decision, and it depends very much on the person's "philosophy of living and spiritual beliefs."[7]

THE HOSPICE TEAM

The care in all these different settings is provided by an interdisciplinary team. Typically, a registered nurse coordinates the team's efforts in patient care. Depending on the specific needs of the patient, the nurse will visit weekly or more often if necessary. Nurse's aides are a very important part of the team. They assist the family caregiver in the routine care and can at times help with other household chores. However, it is important to mention that most of the patient's personal care, such as dressing, bathing, toileting, and feeding, remain the responsibility of the family caregiver. A medical social worker focuses on the overall needs of the family and provides counseling when necessary. Chaplains are available to "provide a spiritual focus" in the care setting. A hospice team would not be complete if it weren't for the many volunteers who give their time and efforts to support families in this critical time of need. They can be helpful in many ways from simply visiting and sitting with a sick patient to providing respite for a caregiver who needs to leave the house for a few hours.

Each hospice has a medical director who is part of the team and who participates in the regular team meetings. He or she acts as a resource for challenging medical questions and serves as a backup to the nurses. Some medical directors also visit patients at home or in nursing facilities, answer any family questions, and act as a liaison with the referring physicians. Although the medical director can act as the patient's primary physician, patients do not have to give up their primary care physician. Physicians can continue to manage the care of their patients and ask for support from the hospice medical director if needed.[3]

WHAT ELSE DOES THE HOSPICE TEAM DO?

One of the most important aspects of hospice care is to adequately assess and treat symptoms that patients may experience during the course of a terminal illness and at the time of dying. These often include pain, nausea, vomiting, fatigue, difficulty swallowing, constipation, and shortness of breath. A careful assessment is crucial to the quality of life; however, accurate assessments can be difficult, especially if the patient is confused. One of the most effective assessment methods is to ask the patient to rate his or her symptoms on a scale of 1 through 10, with 10 being the worst. Another way is to have the patient rate his or her distress using terms such as "not at all, a little bit, somewhat, quite a bit, very much."[8] In confused patients, the family member who knows the patient best can greatly help the hospice team by evaluating and communicating any symptoms the patient may have but cannot describe.

Besides excellent nursing care, the hospice team provides psychological support to both the patient and the family as well as bereavement care, which usually continues for a year after the death of the patient.[3] The exact nature of the care and support provided will depend on the cultural and religious circumstances of the family and caregivers.

Pain Treatment

Because pain is common at the end of life with many different illnesses, appropriate treatment for pain, avoiding both under- and overtreatment, is an extremely important part of hospice care.[9] Frequent reassessment of the patient by the hospice team is crucial. Among the common diseases that cause pain are cancer, heart failure, stroke, osteoarthritis, and pressure ulcers.[10] Patients suffering from dementia are particularly at risk of experiencing pain.[11]

Pain is usually treated with medications, but nonpharmacological approaches—the use of treatments other than medications—are also very helpful. Examples of approaches that complement the usual medical treatment include acupuncture, massage, electrical nerve stimulation (applied through the skin), and psychological therapies. These techniques may reduce the need for increased dosages or stronger pain medications, thereby limiting side effects while still ensuring good pain relief.[12]

Three main categories of pain medications (analgesics) are commonly used:

1. **Non-opioid analgesics:** These refer to medications such as acetaminophen (Tylenol) and the nonsteroidal anti-inflammatory drugs like ibuprofen. These are usually used for milder pain syndromes. Some of these formulations are now available in topical form, such as lidocaine or diclofenac patches, which make administration easier.
2. **Opioid analgesics:** These are used for moderate to severe pain and include drugs such as morphine, oxycodone, hydromorphone, fentanyl, and methadone. Sometimes, the hospice team will switch between these medications to find the one that provides the best pain control with the least side effects. Common side effects of opioids may include sedation (feeling sleepy), nausea, and constipation. If sedation and nausea do occur, they are usually

temporary in nature. Constipation, however, is a common and persistent side effect that requires the use of bowel medications (e.g., stimulants like Senokot laxatives and stool softeners like docusate sodium) that are usually given prophylactically when opioid treatment is started.

3. **Adjuvant analgesics:** These medications are often used when a patient experiences pain that is resistant to opioid medications. Examples of such pain include pain from nerves (neuropathic) or bone pain when cancer has spread (metastasized) to the bones. Gabapentin (Neurontin) is a medication often used for nerve pain, and steroids or bisphosphonates are often used for bone pain. The latter are usually used for osteoporosis.[10]

Sometimes, despite all the powerful pain medications available, the pain still cannot be adequately treated. In these cases, the only way to offer relief from "unbearable suffering" is to provide what is called "palliative sedation."[13] This is a treatment of last resort and used when death is expected shortly. It is important to know and understand that palliative sedation is *not* euthanasia ("the act or practice of killing or permitting the death of hopelessly sick or injured individuals (as persons or domestic animals) in a relatively painless way for reasons of mercy").[14] Palliative sedation is very different in that its first goal is not to cause death but rather to provide symptom relief.[13]

A 95-year-old patient of mine in a nursing home suffered a devastating stroke that left her paralyzed on her left side and with a significant speech impediment and difficulty swallowing. The family was determined to do everything to make her better. I agreed with them, except that she was no longer able to eat or communicate, and she was literally bedbound. Her living will was clear in that it stated she did not want any artificial ways of life support, including a feeding tube. Because feeding her was near impossible, she rapidly started losing weight and had to be kept hydrated with intravenous fluids. I suggested to the family to seek the advice of and best treatment recommended by hospice for this poor woman. With no uncertainty, I was told that hospice was not an option. "Mother would never have agreed to be 'made to die.'" I was quite upset because I felt the patient was suffering. Divine compassion intervened, and she died peacefully of another stroke within a few hours of that conversation.

The "Double Effect"

I have often heard the concern and fear that hospice care will result in an earlier death of the patient. And I have had patients and their families who decided against using hospice for exactly this reason in particular.

"The principle of double effect is used to justify the administration of medication to relieve pain even though it may lead to the unintended, although foreseen, consequence of hastening death by causing respiratory depression."[15] This concept is often discussed in the care of terminal cancer patients who require significant amounts of analgesic medications for adequate pain control and because of the potential of opioid medications to cause respiratory depression. It is therefore understandable that physicians and nurses are hesitant to administer ever-increasing amounts of these medications to patients for pain relief. There is no doubt that an excessive dose of these medications can indeed result in respiratory depression and death. However, if the dosage is carefully titrated, pain control can be maximized while the patient also develops a tolerance to the respiratory side effects.[15] In fact, "the literature contains little data to support the belief that appropriate use of opioids hastens death in patients dying from cancer and other chronic diseases."[16] So what does this all mean? Because of the fear of possibly hastening death in a terminally ill patient, pain relief is often inadequate and suffering not relieved. It is the right of any human being not to suffer from pain, which can be appropriately relieved by medications. In other words, the double effect points to the overwhelmingly positive effects of palliative treatment, which far outweigh the negative effects.[16]

OPEN-ACCESS CARE

Another aspect of hospice care that has become an increasingly controversial issue is what is called open-access care. In the early days of hospice care, most patients had less than six months to live and almost all were cancer patients. Nowadays, many patients who have a terminal disease such as Alzheimer's disease, end-stage chronic obstructive pulmonary disease, or end-stage heart disease are eligible to sign on and benefit from the excellent care provided by hospice. However, the disease course in these patients is less predictable, with many patients living longer than expected. As a result, many hospices have found themselves in a difficult situation with regard to providing the best and appropriate care while working within the fixed Medicare reimbursement fees. Patients often ask for other medical treatment beyond the financial resources of the hospice.[17]

An example of this kind of catch-22 is the use of blood transfusions. Many hospices regard blood transfusions to be beyond typical care, but transfusions are a palliative treatment option that at times can significantly improve patients' quality of life. As a result, some hospices are trying to "prevent these situations with open-access programs," allowing "people the choice to let go of active treatment (of their disease) with one hand and grab on to the hospice rope until they feel comfortable letting the hand go."[17] Unfortunately, these programs are still an exception to the rule; it is not clear yet if this kind of access to broader care is financially sustainable.

Three things to remember about hospice:

1. It is better to join a hospice program earlier rather than later.
2. Taking advantage of hospice care does not mean that the patient is imminently dying.
3. Hospice care will improve the quality of life for both the patient and the caregiver(s).

REFERENCES

1. Hospice, "The Hospice Concept," http://www.hospicenet.org/html/concept.html.
2. National Hospice Foundation, "The History of Hospice," http://nationalhospice-foundation.org/i4a/pages/index.cfm?pageid=218.
3. "Hospice: Philosophy of Care and Appropriate Utilization," ed. Ruth Langman, http://www.utdol.com.
4. National Hospice and Palliative Care Organization, "History of Hospice Care," http://www.nhpco.org/i4a/pages/index.cfm?pageid=3285.
5. Brian Pace, "JAMA Patient Page on Hospice Care," *Journal of the American Medical Association* 295 (2006).
6. American Cancer Society, "What Is Hospice Care?" http://www.cancer.org/docroot/eto/content/eto_2_5x_what_is_hospice_care.asp?sitearea=mlt.
7. Department of Health and Human Services, Eldercare Locator, Fact Sheets, "Hospice Care," http://www.eldercare.gov/Eldercare.NET/Public/Resources/Fact_Sheets/hospice_care.aspx.
8. "Symptom Assessment at the End of Life," ed. Victor Chang, http://www.utdol.com.
9. Robert Buchanan et al., "Analyses of Nursing Home Residents in Hospice Care Using Minimum Data Set," *Palliative Medicine* 16 (2002): 465.
10. "Pain Management at the End of Life," ed. Kathleen Broglio and Russell Portenoy, http://www.utdol.com.
11. Joseph Shega et al., "Patients Dying with Dementia: Experience at the End of Life and Impact of Hospice Care," *Journal of Pain and Symptom Management* 35 (2008): 499.
12. Cynthia Pan et al., "Complementary and Alternative Medicine in the Management of Pain, Dyspnea, and Nausea and Vomiting Near the End of Life. A Systematic Review," *Journal of Pain and Symptom Management* (20) 2000: 374.
13. Alexander de Graeff and Mervyn Dean, "Palliative Sedation Therapy in the Last Weeks of Life: A Literature Review and Recommendations for Standards," *Journal of Palliative Medicine* 10 (2007): 67.
14. Merriam-Webster On-Line, "Euthanasia," http://www.merriam-webster.com/dictionary/euthanasia.
15. Susan Fohr, "The Double Effect of Pain Medication: Separating Myth from Reality," *Journal of Palliative Medicine* 1 (1998): 315.
16. Richard McMurray et al., Council on Ethical and Judicial Affairs, "Decisions Near the End of Life," *Journal of the American Medical Association* 267 (1992): 2229.
17. Alexi Wright and Ingrid Katz, "Letting Go of the Rope: Aggressive Treatment, Hospice Care, and Open Access," *New England Journal of Medicine* 357 (2007): 324.

13

Some Nuisances of Aging— When to Worry?

A number of annoying "side effects" of aging can make the "golden years" less shiny. Sleep problems and dizziness are often regarded as the most aggravating nuisances of advanced age. This is not to say that these conditions are a normal part of aging, or that every older adult will ultimately experience some or all of these. However, there are well-recognized changes in the sleep patterns of older adults, and many medical conditions may cause dizziness. The difficulty for both older adults and their doctors is the question: When do these nuisances need to be further evaluated for a possible underlying serious medical condition?

Sleep Disturbances, or Another Long Night

Sleep occurs in stages that are numbered from 1 to 4. Stages 1 and 2 are the lighter stages of sleep, while stages 3 and 4 represent the deeper periods of sleep. Starting in early adulthood, these deeper stages of sleep progressively decline to the point that at age 90 and older they are almost nonexistent.[1] Besides this, a number of other changes also occur, but their significance is not all clear. However, what is clear is that older adults often complain of earlier awakening, more disrupted nighttime sleep, more daytime napping, and an earlier bedtime.[1] Simply sleeping less or requiring less sleep does not necessarily mean that something is wrong. A disrupted sleep pattern with some good and bad nights is also not unusual. If, however, these changes in sleep patterns start to disrupt a person's daytime functioning or if the sleep becomes chronically "non-restorative or poor in quality despite adequate opportunity" for a good night's rest, then the diagnosis of insomnia is warranted.

Insomnia

A number of common conditions can result in insomnia. Among them are:[1]

• Heart and lung diseases that cause shortness of breath or intermittent coughing

- Gastroesophageal reflux disease, which becomes worse when lying down
- Excessive nighttime urination as a result of heart failure, urinary disorders, and some common medications
- Chronic pain from arthritis and other pain syndromes
- Depression and anxiety disorders
- Medications that one may not think of as possibly interfering with sleep, such as bronchodilators that have a stimulating effect, or antihypertensive medications (like propranolol) that can cause nightmares.
- Chronic use of sleep medications that can cause a fragmented sleep
- Smoking and excessive alcohol before bedtime

Other important sleep disorders that need to be properly diagnosed and treated are sleep apnea, periodic leg movement during sleep, and restless leg syndrome.

Sleep Apnea

Sleep apnea is a common and often not diagnosed disease in which a person literally stops breathing while asleep, for a few seconds or sometimes longer, several times an hour. There are different types of sleep apnea, depending on the underlying problem. Obstructive sleep apnea is the most common type, and it is caused by, as the name suggests, an obstruction of the normal airflow to the lungs. It is often associated with snoring and being overweight. However, people who are not overweight and who do not snore can still "silently" suffer from this disease. Another type of sleep apnea is called central sleep apnea, because there is a problem in the brain that affects control of the breathing muscles.[2] It is often the bed partner who recognizes the breathing problem, either because of the snoring and/or the absence of breathing. The latter can be quite frightening and the reason for contacting the primary care physician. Both the disrupted sleep and the reduced level of oxygen in the blood (from not breathing) are of concern, and sleep apnea has been suggested as a risk factor for hypertension, heart disease, and dementia.[3] Sleep apnea has also been linked to excessive daytime somnolence, which is especially a problem when driving.

Periodic Leg Movement during Sleep

In this condition, repetitive leg movements can occur every 20–40 seconds and may last all night, surely keeping anyone from enjoying a good night's rest. A bed partner also may be disturbed by these movements and often moves to the living room couch. Periodic leg movement tends to increase with advancing age and can occur together with restless leg syndrome.[1]

Restless Leg Syndrome

This refers to an "uncontrollable urge to move one's leg at night."[1] It frequently happens shortly after getting into bed, and it keeps the person from falling asleep. Many patients notice that getting out of bed helps them. The legs are often described as tingling, itching, cramping, or even as burning and aching. There may be a family history of this syndrome, and it may also involve the arms.[1]

Diagnosis of Sleep Disorders

As with so many other medical conditions, a careful history is most important. If you think you may be experiencing any of the previously described conditions, it will help your doctor if you describe what is happening as accurately as possible. Please avoid the urge to ask for a sleeping pill until any underlying medical conditions are excluded, and other sleep disturbances, especially sleep apnea, have been ruled out as the cause for your insomnia. A definitive diagnosis may not be made until a sleep study is done in a sleep laboratory, where the patient is literally observed and monitored during sleep.

Treatment Options

If no treatable medical conditions can be identified, and there is no evidence of sleep apnea or a leg movement disorder, then general treatment for insomnia can be tried. It's best to start with a nonpharmacological (i.e., no medications) approach before trying a pharmacological approach (i.e., using medication). For the treatment of periodic leg movement during sleep and restless leg syndrome, see the following.

Nonpharmacological Approach

This approach is based on a variety of behavioral therapies, most importantly what is called "sleep hygiene," which "refers to actions that tend to improve and maintain good sleep."[4] Sleep hygiene measures have clearly been shown to lead to better sleep and involve the following recommendations:[5]

- Sleep as much as necessary to feel rested and then get out of bed.
- Maintain a regular sleep schedule.
- Try not to force sleep.
- Avoid caffeinated beverages after lunch.
- Avoid alcohol near bedtime (e.g., late afternoon and evening).
- Avoid smoking, particularly during the evening (and never smoke in bed).
- Do not go to bed hungry.
- Adjust the bedroom environment as needed to decrease stimuli.
- Resolve concerns or worries before bedtime.
- Exercise regularly for at least 20 minutes, preferably more than 4–5 hours before bedtime.[4]

Other types of behavioral therapy include something called stimulus control, which helps to disrupt the notion that "patients with insomnia associate their bed and the bedroom with the fear of not sleeping." Patients are asked not to go to bed until they are sleepy and not to stay in bed longer than 20 minutes if they are awake and cannot fall asleep. Instead, they should get up and "engage in a relaxing activity, such as reading or listening to soothing music."[4]

Relaxation therapy stresses learning how to "relax one muscle at a time until the entire body is relaxed."[4] In a similar approach, cognitive therapy teaches being able to cope with anxiety at night if a person wakes up and cannot fall back to sleep.[4]

Other time-proven activities to improve sleep that have not been scientifically studied include taking a relaxing bath before bed time and participating in some moderate-intensity exercise like a short walk after dinner.

Pharmacological Approach

If you have given all the nonpharmacological measures a good solid trial, and you are still experiencing insomnia, then prudent use of medications may be in order. Medications commonly used to help with sleep problems are the benzodiazepines (like Valium), nonbenzodiazepines (which are a newer class of medications available without a prescription), and other over-the-counter sleep aids.

If a benzodiazepine is used, only the shorter-acting types, such as lorazepam (Ativan) or temazepam (Restoril), should be taken. The intermediate-acting flurazepam (Dalmane) and the long-acting diazepam (Valium) should be avoided especially in older adults. They may cause significant daytime sedation, drowsiness, and mental impairment, all of which may have serious consequences for driving ability and normal daily functioning. Another word of caution about the ultra short-acting triazolam (Halcion): if stopped abruptly, it can cause rebound insomnia. And finally, all of these medications can also lead to allergic reactions. For more information, check the Web site www.drugs.com.[6]

The newer nonbenzodiazepines include the following:

- zolpidem (Ambien), also available in an extended-release version
- zaleplon (Sonata)
- eszopiclone (Lunesta)

All of these medications are marketed for both short- and long-term use. However, they can be habit forming, and the side effects are similar to those of the benzodiazepine medications. Therefore, careful use is recommended.[6] As with any over-the-counter preparation, I strongly suggest that you let your doctor know if you are taking any of these sleep medications.

Other Over-the-Counter Sleep Aids

These include diphenhydramine (Benadryl), either as a separate medication or in combination with acetaminophen (as Tylenol PM) or ibuprofen (as Advil PM). Benadryl is *not* recommended for older adults as a sleep aid. The list of side effects is frightening enough and should keep any older adult awake all night worrying. These include "decreased alertness, diminished cognitive function, delirium, dry mouth, blurred vision, urinary retention, constipation and increased intraocular pressure."[6]

Melatonin is a hormone produced by the brain that regulates other hormones. Despite the advertisements that claim beneficial effect, evidence for the use of melatonin supplements as a treatment for insomnia is sparse except for a subgroup of patients who have low melatonin levels or in the case of a condition called "delayed sleep phase syndrome."[6]

Valerian, an herbal product, does not appear to be of any benefit when it comes to the treatment of insomnia. Instead, it may interfere with other medications and can possibly cause liver damage.[6]

A word about the "nightcap": Alcohol has been used extensively to promote sleep because it tends to decrease the time needed to fall asleep. However, it ultimately causes sleep disturbances as the night goes on, and its potential for dependency and interference with other medications makes it a poor choice as a sleeping aid.[6]

Still Other Medications Used as Sleep Aids

Trazodone (Desyrel) is an antidepressant that is often used as a sleep aid, although it is not approved for this use. The routine use of an antidepressant for the long-term treatment of insomnia in nondepressed older adults is not recommended.[7]

In the past, chloral hydrate was used as a sedative, but it should no longer even be considered for use, especially in older adults.

Treatment of Periodic Limb Movement and Restless Leg Syndrome

According to Dr. Jean K. Matheson, Associate Professor of Neurology, Harvard Medical School and the Neurology Sleep Director of the Sleep Disorder Center, Beth Israel Deaconess Medical Center in Boston, any treatment starts with stopping any drugs that could possibly be exacerbating the symptoms such as antihistamines or any antidepressants such as duloxetine (Cymbalta) and venlafaxine (Effexor). It is also important to screen for and treat any possible causes of neuropathies (i.e., nerve irritation) like B_{12} deficiency and diabetes. The most useful drugs for periodic limb movement and

---

Three things to remember:

1. Medications can cause more harm than good in the treatment of insomnia, especially medications like Benadryl and Valium.
2. Sleeping problems are not a normal part of aging.
3. Make sure to tell your doctor that you are having sleeping problems and try to explain in as much detail as you can what it is that keeps you awake.

restless leg syndrome are pramipexole (Mirapex) and ropinirole (Requip). Gabapentin (Neurontin) is a useful second-line medication.

DIZZINESS—SOMETHING ELSE TO RUIN MY DAY

Dizziness is one of the most common complaints among patients age 50 and older who present to primary care physicians. "Dizziness is more common in advanced age, with 47% of men and 61% of women aged 70 and older affected."[8] However, as with many other medical conditions in older adults, dizziness is *not* a normal part of aging. And, fortunately, in most cases, dizziness is self-limiting and has an overall benign course. So then what makes dizziness so difficult to manage and treat?

- The exact classification of the underlying cause remains difficult.
- Older adults and their physicians tend to think first of serious underlying medical conditions such as heart disease or neurologic causes.
- There may be multiple causes for the dizziness.
- A specific therapy is not always available.[9]

The biggest challenge is that dizziness is a "nonspecific term" used to describe a large variety of personal and individual sensations, which differ among different people.[10] It is therefore very important to give as careful a history as you can to your physician, and do not allow him or her to "put words in your mouth." It is critical to describe the sensation you are feeling as accurately and precisely as possible.[10] The famous physician Dr. William Osler (1849–1919) is often quoted for saying, "Listen to the patient, he is telling you the diagnosis."[11]

Classification of Dizziness

A useful and well-accepted classification distinguishes four types of dizziness: vertigo, presyncope, disequilibrium, and nonspecific dizziness.

Vertigo

When someone has vertigo, there is a sensation of motion. People describe themselves as spinning, whirling, or even falling. At times, however, it seems that the environment around them is what is moving.[8,10] This feeling is usually not constantly present but may instead recur intermittently, provoked by a certain head movement or by coughing or sneezing.[10] Vertigo is either the result of a problem in the balance mechanism in the inner ear or in the nerves that connect the ear to the brain. It is rarely a problem in the brain itself.[12] Examples of vertigo include the following:

- *Benign paroxysmal positional vertigo* means an intermittent sensation of vertigo caused by a change in position such as when you lift your head up from a pillow, simply turn your head, roll over in bed, or bend down. It is called benign because it usually resolves by itself, but the associated nausea, vomiting, and difficulty walking certainly do not feel benign. The cause for all this is not that clear, which adds to the frustration of both the patient and the doctor. Rest and adequate hydration are often the best way to deal with this unpleasant sensation.[13]

- Meniere's disease causes both vertigo with its associated unpleasant consequences as well as a buzzing or ringing in the ear. At times, there may even be some hearing loss. Again, the cause is not clear, but it can become worse over time and needs to be monitored carefully.[12,13]

- Unfortunately, some serious diseases of the brain such as stroke, tumors, and multiple sclerosis can also cause vertigo. Therefore, it is important to let your doctor know if you experience difficulty walking, headaches, double vision or a loss of vision, slurred speech, numbness in the face, or weakness in any limbs. These ominous signs suggest some involvement of the brain and need urgent attention.[10]

Presyncope

This very unpleasant feeling of "nearly blacking out" or "nearly fainting" is often accompanied by feelings of warmness, lightheadedness, sweating, nausea, and even visual blurring. Bystanders may describe the person as becoming pale and ashen. A person may be sitting, standing, or even lying down when this happens.[10]

The underlying problem is a momentary reduced blood flow to the brain, but finding out the actual reason for this lack of blood supply is very difficult. One common cause is the result of sudden low blood pressure (or hypotension), as in the case of orthostatic hypotension, which occurs when a person changes position (e.g., standing or sitting up from a lying position) and blood pressure drops significantly. This can be caused by medications, being dehydrated, or even after having enjoyed a large meal (called postprandial hypotension).

Another cause of presyncope is referred to as a vasovagal attack. This "occurs when the part of your nervous system that regulates heart rate and blood pressure malfunctions in response to a trigger."[14] Triggers can be anything from the sight of blood to heat exhaustion or minor exertion, such as when straining on the toilet.[14] I often warn my patients to be especially careful and avoid straining when visiting the bathroom at night.

The most serious causes of presyncope are related to heart problems such as tight valves or heart rhythm problems.[13] Feeling palpitations or even chest pain before the feeling of fainting warrants an urgent call to the doctor.

Disequilibrium

In disequilibrium, a person may feel unsteady when walking and even at times when standing. There are a number of causes for this lack of balance, including foot problems, peripheral neuropathies (e.g., nerve irritation common in diabetes patients), musculoskeletal disorders, and ear and eye problems. The more of these problems that occur together, the worse the unsteadiness.[10,13] Unfortunately, some specific types of strokes may also result in a lack of balance, and these of course need to be carefully investigated.

A longtime patient of mine suddenly felt very unsteady when walking. He reported four days of not being able to leave his apartment and hanging on to dear life when walking even short distances between the bedroom, kitchen, and bathroom. He was not having any other problems and had no complaint of vertigo. He appeared otherwise well and unchanged. I was struck by his lack of balance and admitted him to the hospital, fearing a stroke. This was indeed the cause for his disequilibrium, and it took quite some time in a rehabilitation facility before he was able to go home again.

Nonspecific Dizziness

Nonspecific dizziness refers to a hodgepodge of many different underlying conditions, ranging from depression, anxiety, panic disorders, and hyperventilation to episodes of low blood sugar, or hypoglycemia. Of course, medications like antidepressants should always be considered as a possible cause.[10]

If you are experiencing any type of dizziness, make sure you keep as safe as possible until you can see your doctor. If you fear that you may fall and injure yourself, please ask for help. Make sure to stay well hydrated, and do **not** drive until your doctor informs you that it is okay for you to do so.[14]

If you are experiencing any heart problems or any of the above mentioned symptoms, which could be caused by a stroke, call 911 *immediately* and ask for help.

Diagnosis of Dizziness

More than three-quarters of cases of dizziness can be properly diagnosed by a good history and a careful physical examination. When talking to your doctor, please describe as precisely as possible the specific sensation of dizziness you are feeling, and whether you experience any nausea, vomiting, ringing in the ears, or other symptoms before or during the episodes of dizziness. Make sure to also mention any triggers that bring about the sensation and exactly what you were doing when you started to feel the dizziness.

A through review of *all* medications, both prescription and over-the-counter medications and supplements, is crucial.

During the examination, your blood pressure will be taken multiple times—when you are lying down and then when you are sitting or standing up—to see if there is a significant drop in blood pressure with the change in position (i.e., orthostatic hypotension). Your doctor will do a thorough heart and lung examination, an abdominal examination, as well as look at your ears and watch carefully for any abnormal eye movements. Musculoskeletal and neurological examinations are also important, and your doctor should also observe you while you are walking (if you can do so safely). Depending on the history and the physical examination, further tests such as blood tests, an electrocardiogram, and radiological examinations such as an MRI may be necessary.[10,13]

Treatment Strategies

Remember that in many cases the dizziness resolves by itself over a period of two weeks.[14] Treating any underlying diseases that can cause dizziness will often also resolve the dizziness. Although a comprehensive review of all treatment options is beyond the scope of this chapter, some treatment options for the common causes of dizziness follow.

In the case of benign paroxysmal positional vertigo, a specific head maneuver (called the Dix-Hallpike maneuver) performed by your doctor or a physical therapist may be all that is needed. This head tilting maneuver can reset the balance mechanism in the inner ear and is often very successful. Patients can also do certain exercises that are variants of this head maneuver by themselves. Medications are not very helpful unless the episodes of vertigo are frequent and recurring.[15]

Meniere's disease may be initially treated by removing fluid from the body using a diuretic medication (i.e., "water" pill) and avoiding extra salt in the diet. Sometimes, a medication called meclizine (Antivert) started at a low dosage once or several times a day can be helpful. There are other types of drugs, but all should be carefully administered, especially in older adults because of their effect on the central nervous system. On occasion, surgery has also been successful.[8,14]

If orthostatic hypotension is the underlying problem, removing or at least adjusting the medication regimen is usually the first step. Maintaining adequate hydration and wearing compression stockings is also helpful. Sometimes medications that can increase the blood pressure need to be used.[8]

An increasingly popular treatment option for patients with vertigo that is not a result of any problem in the brain, especially if it is recurring and other measures have not been successful, is a set of physical exercises collectively referred to as vestibular rehabilitation. These exercises involve balance training, promote activity rather than inactivity, and counteract the fear of falling. Over time, the brain can adapt to a lack of input from malfunctioning balance organs in the inner ear.[16]

In summary, dizziness is truly one of the most frustrating medical conditions for both the patient who experiences it and the doctor who has to

---

Three things to remember:

1. Do not ignore symptoms of dizziness.
2. When describing your symptoms, be as accurate as possible.
3. Medications are usually not the solution to the problem. Time and physical exercises are the mainstay of treatment.

diagnose and treat it. Luckily, most causes are benign and the problem is mostly short lived.

Other Nuisances

There are a number of other medical conditions that many of my patients would consider nuisances of aging. Slowly deteriorating hearing and the progressive loss of vision are a few. Remember that regular screening examinations are important to keep your senses as sharp a possible (see Chapter 8, "Health Maintenance"). Falling and progressive walking difficulties are certainly on the list, and doing some simple exercises for gait and balance cannot be overemphasized (see Chapter 8 and Chapter 6, "Exercise and Older Adults" for more information).

Now that we have covered the nuisances of aging, let's talk about a much more enjoyable topic—sex.

References

1. Cathy A. Alessi, "Sleep Problems," in *Geriatric Review Syllabus,* ed. Peter Pompei and John B. Murphy (New York: American Geriatrics Society, 2006), CD-ROM version.
2. U.S. Department of Health and Human Services, National Institute of Health, "What Is Sleep Apnea?" http://www.nhlbi.nih.gov/health/dci/Diseases/Sleep Apnea/SleepApnea_WhatIs.html.
3. "Sleep Apnea in the Elderly," ed. Steven Feinsilver, in UpToDate.com, http://www.uptodate.com.
4. "Treatment of Insomnia," ed. Michael Bonnet and Donna Arand, in UpToDate.com, http://www.uptodate.com.
5. J. D. Edinger and W.S. Sampson, "A Primary Care 'Friendly' Cognitive Behavioral Insomnia Therapy," *Sleep* 26 (2003): 177.
6. Drug Information Online, "Drugs A to Z," http://drugs.com.
7. Wallace Mendelson, "A Review of the Evidence for the Efficacy and Safety of Trazodone in Insomnia," *Journal of Clinical Psychiatry* 66 (2005): 469.
8. Deborah Eaton and Peter Roland, "Dizziness in the Older Adult, Part 1: Evaluation and General Treatment Strategies," *Geriatrics* 58 (2003): 28.
9. Kurt Kroenke, "Dizziness," in *Geriatric Review Syllabus,* ed. Peter Pompei and John B. Murphy (New York: American Geriatrics Society, 2006), CD-ROM version.
10. "Approach to the Patient with Dizziness," ed. William Branch and Jason Barton, in UpToDate.com, http://www.utdol.com.
11. Mark Silverman, Jack Murray, and Charles Bryan, *The Quotable Osler*, rev. paperback ed. (Philadelphia: American College of Physicians, 2008), 97.
12. Mayo Clinic Staff, "Dizziness," MayoClinic.com, http://www.mayoclinic.com/health/dizziness/DS00435.
13. The AGS Foundation for Health in Aging, "Dizziness," American Geriatrics Society, http://www.healthinaging.org/agingintheknow/chapters_ch_trial.asp?ch=23.

14. Mayo Clinic Staff, "Vasovagal Syncope," MayoClinic.com, http://www.mayoclinic
    .com/health/vasovagal-syncope/DS00806.
15. "Benign Paroxysmal Positional Vertigo," ed. Jason Barton, in UpToDate.com,
    http://www.utdol.com.
16. Lucy Yardley, "Randomized Controlled Trial of Exercise Therapy for Dizziness
    and Vertigo in Primary Care," *British Journal of General Practice* 429 (1998):
    1136.

14

SEXUALITY AND OLDER ADULTS

Old age is all about sex and drugs and rock 'n roll. Okay, maybe I'm exaggerating a little bit, so let's just say old age is all about sex and drugs. Yes, you read that correctly, and for all of you who choose to start reading this book with this chapter (especially all you men), you will be in for a surprise. Although I cannot guarantee you an orgasm, I do promise lots of excitement. Unfortunately, our society and its obsession with youthful looks have contributed to the notion that older adults are not interested in sex, and even worse, unable to enjoy sex, becoming literally asexual.[1] Many older adults and even health care providers think that sexuality is not a lifelong experience and, finding it embarrassing to talk about, avoid the topic altogether. This is exactly how misconceptions and myths thrive, and taboos are maintained.

Adding to the problem is that our health care system has not paid enough attention to sexual dysfunction, especially in older adults and particularly in women. But medications are now playing an increasing role in sexual function for older adults. With the advent of medications for male erectile dysfunction, the interest in both male and female sexual dysfunctions has shifted from mild neglect to a booming million-dollar industry. As a result, sexuality in midlife and beyond is having a comeback.

A lot of fear and anxiety about sexual activity in later life is the result of "lack of knowledge about the normal age-related changes in sexual functioning."[1] The best way to alleviate these fears is to know what is normal and to be expected with age, what is not normal, and ultimately when to seek medical help.

A STUDY OF SEXUALITY OF OLDER ADULTS

The first comprehensive national survey of the sex lives of older adults, conducted by the University of Chicago, was published in the *New England Journal of Medicine* in 2007. The data was based on a face-to-face two-hour interview of 3,005 adults who ranged in age from 57 to 85 years old. One of the most important findings is that most of the respondents thought of sexuality as an important part of their lives. Many men and women remain sexually active well into their seventies and eighties and participate in vaginal intercourse, oral sex, and masturbation; 54 percent of the oldest respondents reported having sex at least twice a month, and 23 percent reported having sex weekly. I wonder if retirement and not having to go to work in the morning have anything to do with this? The survey also showed that physical health was more important than age in determining sexual activity. As health declined, so did frequency of sexual activity, especially in women. Forty-three percent of sexually active women complained of a lack of desire, 39 percent of vaginal dryness, and 34 percent of an inability to climax. Over a third of sexually active men experience erectile dysfunction. One in seven (14 percent) of men reported taking medication to help them improve their sexual function, while only 1 percent of women took any medications for this purpose. Overall, "men and women who rated their health as being poor were less likely to be sexually active" and only "38% of men and 22% of women reported having discussed sex with a physician since the age of 50 years."[2] So, there you have it in black and white. Sex does not suddenly stop with retirement. It is health instead of age that seems to play an important part in determining how active one's sex life is.

SEX—MAYBE MORE THAN YOU THINK

Sex is not only the physical act of intercourse for the sole purpose of procreation. Your own lifetime experiences and expectations are a major part of and determine your sexuality. In other words, the penis and the vagina are not the only important "tools" for sexual enjoyment. Kissing, caressing, and other types of intimate contact together with open and honest communication can be intensely pleasurable and may well cause an orgasm. Similarly, erotic material and masturbation can bring about sexual pleasures.[3] As our bodies change with age, sex may mature, too. Love making at 70 and beyond may not be like the lustful sex you enjoyed when you were in your twenties, but "greater experience, fewer inhibitions, and a deeper understanding of your needs and those of your partner can more than compensate for the consequences of aging."[3] However, before seeing how this happens, it is important to understand what a normal sexual response is.

NORMAL SEXUAL RESPONSE

The sex act is far more complicated than one would expect, although at the same time it is "instinctive" and an "automatic part of human behavior."[4] In both men and women, sex really starts in the brain, where thoughts, memories, images, fantasies, or even a scent can trigger sexual arousal. In women, when the brain increases blood flow to the genitals, the labia and vaginal wall swell, resulting in lengthening and dilation of the vagina. At the same time, small uterine glands produce lubricating secretions that coat the walls of the vagina. The clitoris becomes engorged with blood and increases in length and diameter. Blood flow to the breasts also increases and the nipples harden. During orgasm, the vaginal and uterine muscles contract repeatedly, followed by relaxation and a decrease in blood flow to the genitals. Many women require direct stimulation of the clitoris to experience an orgasm, but for some women sexual satisfaction does not necessarily require an orgasm.[5]

In men, scientists distinguish six stages of sexual activity (men always tend to make things more complicated than women). Male sexual activity also begins in the brain in an area called the hypothalamus, which sends impulses through the spinal cord to nerves in the pelvis. These nerves in turn send chemical signals to the arteries of the penis, which allows more blood to flow into the spongy tissue of the penis, resulting in an erection. An erection is not just a "hydraulic event"; it also depends on a chemical reaction that involves nitric oxide, arteries, and an impossible-to-pronounce chemical called cyclic guanosine monophosphate, or cGMP for short. It is through this cGMP that those erectile dysfunction pills like Cialis, Levitra, and Viagra work. These medications "boost" cGMP levels in the penis. Just before ejaculation, the prostate gland, along with other structures, discharges fluid in preparation for ejaculation, which is propelled via muscular contractions through the male reproductive tract.

At the same time, muscles at the bladder neck contract to avoid the semen flowing back into the bladder. Men usually experience an orgasm during ejaculation. Shortly after ejaculation, the veins in the penis widen, allowing blood to drain out of the penis so that it returns to a flaccid state. Most young men will need about 30 minutes, and older men up to three hours, before they can "respond to sexual stimulation" again.[4]

CHANGES WITH AGE

Normal changes with age need to be clearly distinguished from the effects of illnesses, especially those that are classic "sex killers," including hypertension, atherosclerosis, and diabetes, and of course, certain medications.

When it comes to age-related sexual changes, men and women share a number of similarities. Both sexes tend to suffer from a decrease in desire or libido and fewer sexual thoughts, and both tend to experience less-intense orgasms. Blood flow to the genitals is reduced, and both sexes experience hormonal changes although to a different degree. In women, menopause causes marked hormonal changes that tend to affect the normal sexual response. While lower levels of testosterone probably cause the decrease in libido, lower estrogen levels result in vaginal dryness.[6] The vaginal walls become thinner, and the vagina itself becomes shorter and less able to expand during arousal. Women also experience slower arousal, less blood congestion in the clitoris, and a diminished clitoral sensitivity. There are fewer, and at times painful, uterine contractions, and the body returns more rapidly to an unaroused state.[3] In men, testosterone levels slowly diminish over the years. Men tend to experience less sensitivity in the penis and require more direct stimulation than before. Achieving and maintaining an erection is more difficult. Erections are also not as rigid as before, and the penile tissue becomes less elastic. This should not be confused with erectile dysfunction, which is not a normal age-related change and is discussed in some detail next. A longer time is required to reach an orgasm, the force of the ejaculation is less, and the amount of semen is reduced. As already mentioned, more time is needed for men to become aroused again and to have another erection.[3]

I do admit that all this could give you the impression that sex is no more fun or even possible when you get older, but remember these are all normal changes, and for the vast majority of older adults, they cause no problem in their sex lives. It is your general health that determines how good your sex life is.

SEXUAL DYSFUNCTIONS

As Dr. Altman and his co-author Suki Hanfling mention in a special health report from Harvard Medical School, "sexual dysfunction can be defined as any aspect of your sexual response that causes you or your partner dissatisfaction or distress." The importance here is not the actual problem but rather that "the condition is troubling to the people involved." In other words, if one partner is not concerned by the other's lack of desire, then there is really no problem.[3] Some sexual dysfunctions have more than one underlying medical or even psychological reason. Keeping this in mind, the most common sexual dysfunctions in women are the following.

Sexual Desire Disorder

Women may experience a lack of sexual thoughts and fantasies or experience some anxiety about certain sexual activity. The reason for this may be hormonal changes after menopause, mood disorders like depression, low self-esteem, or even relationship problems.

Sexual Arousal Disorder

This refers to a lack of sexual excitement and includes the absence of vaginal lubrication. Again, hormonal changes, such as estrogen deficiency, play a role, but it may also be caused by reduced blood flow to the genitals as in the case of atherosclerosis. Diabetes also plays a role here. Many common prescription medications, like tranquilizers, beta-blockers, and antihistamines, can also be involved.

Orgasmic Disorder

Some women may find it difficult to reach an orgasm, which can be the result of muscular or nerve damage. Again, medications may be the cause.

Sexual Pain Disorders

This category includes several types of discomfort, among them pain during sexual intercourse (also referred to as dyspareunia) and spasm of the vagina (also called vaginismus), which prevents penetration. Muscular disorders and blood flow problems are other major causes of this type of pain. Psychological factors and previous traumatic experiences like rape also cannot be ignored. The most common cause of pain during sexual intercourse is atrophic vaginitis due to estrogen deficiency. Vaginal or bladder infections can also be a cause.[3,7]

In men, the following disorders are distinguished:

Sexual Desire Disorder

Similar to women, some men suffer from a lack of libido. The older a man is, the more common it is for him to have fewer sexual thoughts or fantasies than he did when he was younger. Some hormonal changes can be blamed for this, but poor health, partner availability (or lack of a partner), and medications also play a role. Although testosterone decreases by about 1 percent per year after age 40, most older men still have adequate amounts for sexual function.[4]

Erectile Dysfunction

ED, as it is called, refers to the inability to achieve or maintain an erection adequate for sexual intercourse. When men get older, the chance of suffering from ED increases, and it does interfere with their sex lives. The most common cause of ED is vascular disease. Blood flow into the penis becomes obstructed as a result of a hardening and narrowing of the arteries (atherosclerosis); as a result, the pressure in the penis is too low for a sufficient erection. The classic risk factors for ED include high blood pressure (hypertension), diabetes, high cholesterol, and smoking. I would say that this is probably the perfect reason to quit smoking. The second most common cause of ED is as a result of damage to nerves. In addition to men who have had a spinal cord injury, men suffering from diabetes, strokes, and Parkinson's disease may have problems with ED. Nerves can also be damaged during prostate operations and other surgeries involving the pelvis. Of course, medications can cause ED through various mechanisms. Antidepressant medications, antipsychotics, and antihypertensive medications, including diuretics ("water pills") are all possible perpetrators. Even some common over-the-counter medications like antihistamines in cold remedies and H_2 blockers used for acid reflux found in abundance in many bathroom cabinets can be the cause for a "flaccid" night. Less common causes of ED are thyroid disease and some hormonal problems. And "psychogenic erectile dysfunction" can result from relationship conflicts, performance anxiety, and even childhood sexual abuse. There is also the "widower's syndrome," in which a man who finds himself in a new relationship "feels guilt as a defense against subconscious unfaithfulness to his deceased spouse."[6]

Ejaculatory Disorders

Ejaculation can be either premature or delayed. Medications such as antidepressants, like those that belong to a class of drugs called selective serotonin reuptake inhibitors, can be the culprits but are often also used as a treatment for delayed ejaculation.[3]

DISEASES THAT CAN CHALLENGE ANYONE'S SEX LIFE

We've already looked at several diseases that can result in sexual dysfunction, either by causing a problem with blood flow or by injuring certain nerves. But there are other medical conditions that can also ruin your sex life.

Heart disease, and especially a recent heart attack, may wreak havoc with any plans for an intimate evening. Many people fear that the exertion of sex may cause another heart attack or, in the case of someone suffering from angina (which refers to chest pain or pressure as a result of poor blood flow to the heart muscle), bring on chest pain. These are legitimate concerns, and you should not be embarrassed or ashamed to openly discuss them with your doctor and your partner. Most patients receive detailed instructions on many activities, including sex, when they leave the hospital after suffering a heart attack. Patients who have undergone cardiac bypass surgery should follow the instructions regarding sex carefully. In the case of angina, in general, if it is well controlled with medications, there should be no problems. If indeed the angina is difficult to control, sex may not be the best type of recreational activity, and an honest and open discussion with your doctors is highly recommended. One thing to note in particular is that men who take medications containing nitrates (for example, nitroglycerin for angina) should not take pills for ED because of a possible life-threatening drop in blood pressure.[3]

Arthritis is another very common condition that can cause real challenges to any attempt at having sex. Pain and stiffness are truly not conducive to an active sex life. Again, an open discussion with your doctor is essential, especially about adequate pain medications. Other suggestions include a trial of different positions, or cushions or wedges that may make intercourse more comfortable. Trial and error and some patience by both partners are what is often needed until the most comfortable and pleasurable position is found. The point is not to give up. Similarly, cancer and the treatment of cancer can pose challenges for both partners, and it should not be ignored. "Nearly half of the women who undergo treatment for breast or gynecological cancers (like uterine or ovarian cancers) have long-term sexual problems."[3] Most men who are treated for prostate cancer will suffer from ED at least for some time after the treatment. Radiation therapy is another culprit. In men, radiation for prostate cancer can result in diminished libido, and women who have undergone pelvic radiation may experience pain during intercourse.[3]

Chemotherapy also poses many challenges to an active sex life. As a patient of mine once told me, feeling washed out and often suffering from nausea was one thing, but hair loss was the straw that broke the camel's back, along with the desire for sex. Again, an open and honest discussion of feelings, fears, and concerns is needed in these situations. Oncologists will be able to provide helpful suggestions.

An often forgotten and more often than not underestimated disease is depression. "Depression can be both the cause and the result of sexual problems."[3] This is a little like the chicken and the egg—which came first is not so easy to establish. However, the effects are clear and can be devastating, especially if it leads to relationship problems. Just to add insult to injury, many commonly used antidepressant medications, such as the selective serotonin reuptake inhibitors (SSRIs) like Prozac, Zoloft, and Paxil, can dampen any sexual desire and make it more difficult to obtain an orgasm. I know I'm repeating myself, but again, the best thing to do is to talk to your doctor about these concerns. You may be able to try another antidepressant that has fewer sexual side effects.

Antidepressants are not the only medications that can put a dent in an active sex life. Besides those already mentioned, other commonly used medications like cholesterol-lowering drugs and drugs for acid reflux, which are usually not thought of as possible "sex killers," can also negatively affect a person's sex life.

BEYOND MEDICAL DISEASE

Everyday life itself can also have a major influence on our sex lives. A strained marital relationship, sexual boredom, and affairs will leave their marks on a couple's sex life. Both men and women can experience so-called "performance anxiety." Men who have had an embarrassing experience with ED may feel inadequate and therefore start to avoid all sexual activity. Women who have experienced some pain during sex may have anxiety and thus tend to avoid sexual encounters.

Sometimes, age itself can sour our sex lives. Normal changes in our bodies, which most of us cannot escape, may become an obstacle to sex. The body with the bulge around the middle or those few extra pounds around the hips may not make us feel very sexy and can ruin an intimate evening.[3] Whatever the reason for the soured sex life, the solution must start with an open and honest discussion between the couple. Any sex therapy, medications, or other help will do little if there is no "talking in the bedroom."

TREATMENT OF SEXUAL DISORDERS

It would be beyond the scope of this chapter to even start to provide a comprehensive overview of the treatment options for the variety of sexual disorders. You may wish to purchase the Special Health Report from Harvard Medical School on "Sexuality in Midlife and Beyond," which I have referenced extensively in this chapter. The review on treatment options is well researched, easy to read and understand, and up-to-date, and it will provide you with an excellent source of information for any discussion with your doctor and with your partner.

Regardless, the important point in the treatment of sexual disorders is that there is much more beyond pills for ED, although they have revolutionized the sex lives of many older adults. There are other ways to help men with erectile problems, ranging from hormones, which can also be useful in boosting libido, to penile bands, vacuum devices, and even injections into the shaft of the penis. Beyond these treatments, there are surgical procedures to improve blood flow and surgical penile implants for problems that are otherwise very difficult to treat. When it comes to women, things get a little more complicated and less high tech. Although those pills for ED in men can also improve blood flow to the genitals in women, unfortunately, they do little to increase libido. Topical medications are available that are rubbed onto the genitals, and there are mechanical devices that are placed over the clitoris to suction blood into it to improve arousal. Vaginal dryness is often improved with a variety of lubricants. Under the careful supervision of a physician, hormones, of which there are many types, can also be used. When it comes to vaginal pain (dyspareunia), treatment tends to get even more complex and ranges from lubricants, antibiotics, and physical therapy to surgery, biofeedback, and sex therapy. Sex therapy is also very helpful to treat orgasm difficulties in both men and women.[3]

REFERENCES

1. Susan Deacon, Victor Minichiello, and David Plummer, "Sexuality and Older People: Revisiting the Assumption," *Educational Gerontology* 497 (1995): 497.
2. Stacey Tessler Lindau et al., "A Study of Sexuality and Health among Older Adults in the United States," *New England Journal of Medicine* 357 (2007): 762.
3. Alan Altman and Suki Hanfling, *Sexuality in Midlife and Beyond* (Boston: Harvard Health Publications, 2007), 4–47.
4. Harvey Simon, "Sexuality and Seniority," *Harvard Men's Health Watch* 13 (2009): 1–3.
5. Barbara Arcos, "Female Sexual Function and Response," *Journal of the American Osteopathic Association* 104, supp. 1 (2004): S16.
6. Angela Gentili and Thomas Mulligan, "Disorders of Sexual Function," in *Geriatric Review Syllabus,* ed. Peter Pompei and John B. Murphy (New York: American Geriatrics Society 2006), CD-ROM version.
7. Jennifer Frank, Patricia Mistretta, and Joshua Will, "Diagnosis and Treatment of Female Sexual Dysfunction," *American Family Physician* 77 (2008): 635.

15

SOCIAL CONNECTEDNESS, SUPPORT THROUGH CAREGIVING, AND SPIRITUALITY

THE IMPORTANCE OF THE THREE S'S

A substantial body of research shows that there is much more to good health than watching your diet and weight, exercising regularly, throwing out those cigarettes, and not overdoing it on the alcohol.[1] A major factor in good health is building and maintaining strong social relationships. Being married has been shown to be "positively related to physical health and longevity." But it is not only married couples whose health benefits from their relationship; for anyone, having strong social relationships and being an active member of a community also promote good health.[2] And it is not only human relationships that provide support—research has shown that support from pets can also contribute to good health.[3] People are highly social animals, and loneliness can break our hearts.

SOCIAL CONNECTIONS ARE KEY

So imagine swapping some of your medications for frequent outings with friends, book club meetings, walking groups, or even a chat at work in the hallway. Social interactions "may contribute to maintaining health and achieving longevity because they are performed on a daily basis and their effects may accumulate over the life course."[4] Even better, when it comes to having friends and acquaintances, the more the merrier. A 2008 study showed that women who had larger social networks had a lower risk of strokes than those with fewer relationships.[5] But best of all, having lots of friends and social interactions also seems to preserve your memory.[6] So what are you waiting for? Pick up the phone and make some plans for the evening. If you really want to be inspired, check out the documentary about the fun-loving senior citizen's choir, the Young @ Heart Chorus, led by tireless director Bob Cilman. Watch it with some friends, and I promise you a wonderful evening and a fun discussion at your next luncheon. Shining through the many vivacious and often hilarious scenes is the moving and inspirational attitude of all the chorus members. It is evident that participating in the choir has given many of its members a new outlook on life and hope for tomorrow. In fact, many seem to have literally reemerged from old age.[7]

Robert J. Waldinger, MD, Associate Professor of Psychiatry, Harvard Medical School, Brigham and Women's Hospital, studies how social factors affect a person's health and well-being. In an interview in the spring of 2009, he referred to the importance of social relationships with people as the "elephant in the examination room." In other words, doctors rarely, if ever, think about this increasingly important topic and rarely, if ever, ask about how relationships and social interactions may affect their patients' health. In addition, Dr. Waldinger says that what's important is not only the number of friends you have or how often you meet with them but also the quality of the social interactions. A close relationship with friends is as important as a close tie to family members, and a good understanding with a niece or nephew can be as beneficial as that with an adult child.

You may ask how it is possible that social isolation is a risk factor "comparable in size to obesity, sedentary lifestyle, and possibly smoking."[8] Research has shown a number of specific positive health effects. For example, Cacioppo and colleagues noted that older adults who were not socially isolated had lower blood pressure readings than their lonely counterparts. Higher blood pressure is thought to be the result of more hormonal and nerve stimulation of the arteries, which causes an increase to the resistance of blood flow and therefore an increase in blood pressure. Another interesting discovery was that feelings of loneliness can actually disrupt sleep. Sleep is regulated in part by hormones, and sleep patterns affect hormonal and other important functions in the body, including control of blood sugar. So a bad night doesn't just make you cranky and tired but literally affects your overall health. In other words, lonely days "will invade the nights" too.[8]

MORE ON MARRIAGE

Marriage, I am sure you will agree, is a special and unique type of social relationship. Studies have shown that it has a significant effect on the health of both partners. Marriage affects not only chronic medical conditions like heart disease and cancer but even something as trivial as the common cold. Married couples tend to have better mental health, and both men and women "are less likely to die in any given period than the unmarried." It is interesting to note that health benefits accumulate over time, and that married people who have never been divorced or widowed enjoy the best health.[9] A good example of this is that having spousal support can improve the management of type 2 diabetes, especially with sticking to an exercise program.[10] Marital status also seems to have a very beneficial effect on the memory abilities of older men[11]—yet another good reason why men need women more than we think!

Unfortunately, the marital relationship may also have its downside. An illness of a spouse can affect the health of the other and even increase the risk of death. The type of illness can also be a stressor. The more a disease interferes with "physical or mental ability . . . the worse the outcome for the partner."[12] A poor marriage can take a toll on both partners, with lots of marital conflict resulting in "a decline in health over time, and this decline is greater at older ages and similar for men and women."[13] This is a serious issue and should not be underestimated; in fact, a low-quality marriage carries a greater health risk than a divorce,[14] and to top it off, "negative aspects of marriage appear to become more consequential for health as individuals age."[15]

SUPPORT THROUGH CAREGIVING

Another unique form of social interaction is caregiving. Caregivers, or *carers* as they are referred to in the United Kingdom, are either specially trained health care professionals or lay people like family members or friends who care for someone who has some cognitive or physical limitations. The care provided by the caregivers enables the patients to remain as independent as possible for as long as possible. These unsung heroes are a lifeline for many older adults, and they usually become the most important person for the ones they care for. Caregiving is not a Monday to Friday, nine-to-five job, with scheduled vacation time and holidays off, but rather a 24/7 job, or even a 36-hour job as Nancy Mace and Peter Rabins suggest in their well-known book *The 36 Hour Day.*[16] There is no standard job description for caregivers, no pension funds, no holiday parties, not even lunch breaks with coworkers. Caregiving is often a very lonely undertaking. A typical day on the job can include everything from personal care (i.e., helping with bathing or dressing) and medication administration to shopping, cleaning, food preparation, doctor visits, and simply being there for a loved one. A caregiver is a "hands-on health provider, care manager, friend, companion, surrogate decision-maker and advocate."[17] I was once told by the wife of one of my patients that caring for her husband was the most challenging task of her entire life and that running a business was nothing in comparison.

The numbers are staggering. Seven million Americans act as caregivers, and 65 percent of older adults who require some form of long-term care rely "exclusively on family and friends to provide assistance," while the remainder "supplement family care with assistance from paid providers."[17,18] With the number of older adults exponentially increasing, the need for more caregivers will grow too. The majority of caregivers are women who provide "informal care to spouses, parents, parents-in-law, friends and neighbors." This has other social and economic implications, because these women often pass up job promotions, take a leave of absence, switch from full-time to part-time employment, or simply quit their jobs.[17]

Caregiving from a Distance

When we speak about caregiving, we usually think of the "informal" caregivers, who are family members providing unpaid care to a loved one. But there is more than one type of caregiving. Very commonly, caregiving is done from a distance. In this situation, family members such as adult children who live out of town or state call regularly, arrange medical appointments, visit on holidays, and spend their vacation time with their loved ones trying to get all the things done that could not otherwise be arranged over the phone. Long-distance caregiving adds another level of complexity to the already challenging caregiving needs such as "maintaining effective communications with the care receiver, managing feelings of guilt and anger over the situation, attempting to balance [their] time with, and away, from the care receiver [and] locating resources in the care receiver's community."[18] It is no wonder that doctors' offices often receive telephone calls requesting an office visit shortly before or immediately after Thanksgiving and Christmas when family members are in town visiting.

Effects on Caregivers

In spite of what appear to be overwhelming challenges and tough working conditions, "nearly 80% of family caregivers are finding the caregiving experience emotionally rewarding, despite initial negative perceptions."[19] In an independent online CaringToday/CVS pharmacy/Family Caregiver Insights Study conducted in the spring of 2007 in which 514 prescreened and qualified adults were interviewed, 69 percent enjoyed the experience and over half felt that the quality of the relationship with the care receiver had improved over time; 37 percent of caregivers felt that the "most immediate need once [they] assumed the role of caregiver [was] establishing life balance among caregiving, family, career and personal needs."[20] Interestingly, the primary concern of 87 percent of caregivers was the need to better understand the medications their loved ones were taking. In particular, the need to understand how drugs interact and to recognize side effects was of great concern to many.[18]

We also cannot ignore the fact that there is a "dark side" of caregiving. Caregiver burden and distress are very common, especially among those who look after a loved one suffering from dementia.

An elderly patient of mine suffered from many debilitating medical conditions and a progressive memory decline. I started to dread her appointments, not because I could do very little for her, but because I could not bear to see her daughter cry at every visit from being overwhelmed by her mother's caregiving needs. Her sisters refused to help take care of the mother or even visit to let her simply get away for a few short hours. About the only thing I could do was hand out facial tissues. It took the professional intervention of a social worker to solve this unfortunate situation.

Being able to provide effective help and support for caregivers requires distinguishing between caregiver burden and caregiver distress. *Caregiver burden* results when the care needs of a loved one continue to increase slowly over time. This is extremely common in those who look after a patient with dementia or Alzheimer's disease because of the slow, progressive nature of these conditions. Caregivers often become unable to keep up with all daily chores, which results in frustration, despair, and the feeling of being overwhelmed. Extra help and some respite is often the solution to this problem. The case example described above is a perfect example of severe caregiver burden.

Caregiver distress results when the condition of a loved one changes suddenly. Confusion or agitation that suddenly gets worse, an inability to walk, and sudden increases in personal care needs are the usual causes. Caregivers often feel a sense of panic about their inability to take care of their loved ones. Prompt medical evaluation for any sudden functional decline and treatment of possible underlying conditions is the best way to help both the patient and the caregiver.

Another serious "side effect" of long-term caregiving is caregiver depression. It is not that the act of caregiving itself results in depression, but that "caregivers often sacrifice their own physical and emotional needs" to provide the best possible care. As a result, "the emotional and physical experiences involved with providing care can strain even the most capable person. The resulting feelings of anger, anxiety, sadness, isolation, exhaustion—and then guilt for having these feelings—can exact a heavy toll."[21] This becomes a concern when caregivers start to exhibit sadness and crying that does not "go away or when those negative feelings are unrelenting." The most important thing to do is not to ignore these feelings but to discuss these with a friend, family member, or a "trained health or mental health professional."[21] Supporting the caregiver by providing hands-on help or allowing the caregiver to take some time away from the daily chores is very helpful. In addition, equally, if not more important, is educating caregivers on improving their skills, recognizing their own limitations, and knowing when to ask for help.

The REACH study, a two-year study that looked at "primary care interventions to alleviate the psychological distress suffered by caregivers of those with Alzheimer's disease," showed that while interventions that "focus only on care recipient behavior" do indeed reduce caregiver distress and burden, but "without addressing caregiving issues, may not be as adequate for reducing caregiver distress."[22] A pioneer in this field is Mary Mittleman, PhD, of NYU Langone Medical Center, who has published extensively on ways of improving caregiving skills, especially for caregivers of dementia patients. In the recent book *The Comfort of Home for Alzheimer's Disease: A Guide for Caregivers*, which Dr. Mittleman coauthored, a detailed plan of how to take care of an individual with Alzheimer's disease is provided, from how to communicate with the patient to choosing the right home-care worker and handling the legal, medical, and financial concerns for the patient.[23] Another useful source of information is the Family Caregiving 101 Web site, which answers the 10 most often heard questions about caregiving.[24]

SPIRITUALITY—THE LAST S

Imagine physicians writing out prescriptions for weekly religious services in a church, synagogue, mosque, or any other house of prayer of your choice. You may find this idea unusual, but research has shown that religion and spirituality have numerous health benefits. Regular attendance at religious services has been shown to lower blood pressure, help with depression, and even strengthen the immune system. People who frequently attend religious services feel better and have better health behaviors, especially not smoking and drinking less alcohol. Best of all, they tend to live longer.[25] Further support comes from research done by Louisiana State University, which found a "13.7-year advantage in longevity for African Americans who attend worship services more than once a week compared with those who never attend.[26]

Research has also shown that people who are spiritual also experience health benefits, regardless of whether they attend regular services in churches or temples. Whereas religion is "generally recognized to be the practical expression of spirituality; the organization, rituals and practice of one's belief," spirituality "is thought to include a system of beliefs that encompasses love, compassion and respect for life." One can be both religious and spiritual. Some individuals may experience "both spirituality and religion very privately within themselves, and/or through social interaction with persons and organizations in an external way.[27]

In 2008, McCauley and colleagues from the Johns Hopkins School of Medicine asked older adults with chronic conditions about their daily spiritual experiences and noted that "increased daily spiritual experiences may be associated with more energy and less depression."[28] Spirituality was also found to be a "significant predictor of psychological well-being" and that spirituality could be a "resource in maintaining psychological well-being." In fact, the more frail a person is, the more important spirituality seems to become.[29] A similar result was found by Dr. Daaleman of the Department of Family Medicine at the University of North Carolina, Chapel Hill, who noted that "geriatric outpatients who report greater spirituality, but not greater religiosity, are more likely to appraise their health as good."[30] Dr. Harold G. Keonig, Professor of Psychiatry and Behavioral Sciences and Co-director of the Center for Spirituality, Theology, and Health at Duke University Medical Center, is a pioneer in the field of religion and health. One of his latest books, *Medicine, Religion, and Health, Where Science and Spirituality Meet*,[31] is an interesting, comprehensive review of how religion affects both mental and physical health.

FINAL ADVICE

So my advice to all you out there in your homes, condos, and apartments is to get out and be among as many people as you can, whether you call them your friends or just acquaintances. Once they retire, most people have some extra time on their hands, and there is no excuse to be inactive. So get off that couch!

How about getting involved in a local volunteer activity? If that's not your cup of tea, what about taking a course at a local community college in art, photography, music, or dancing? You never know what you may become! If you've had enough of classrooms, how about the great outdoors? For the active-minded, nature walks, bike rides, canoeing, and hiking are great fun, especially in groups. A game of golf during midweek without all the weekend golfers on the fairway can be especially relaxing. Or, for a little less action but still exciting activity, try bird watching or garden clubs, which can be quite competitive. Traveling is another great way of enjoying retirement and meeting other people. Traveling isn't just expensive overseas trips; simple excursions by bus with a church group, or by car with friends, to local museums, shows, or other attractions is a great way to spend the day. Retirement is not the time to be sitting alone at home. Get "out and about," and your body and mind will thank you.

REFERENCES

1. George Vaillant and Kenneth Mukamal, "Successful Aging," *American Journal of Psychiatry* 158 (2001): 839.
2. Lisa Berkman, "The Role of Social Relations in Health Promotion," *Psychosomatic Medicine* 57 (1995): 245.
3. June McNichols et al., "Pet Ownership and Human Health: A Brief Review of Evidence and Issues," *British Medical Journal* 331 (2005): 1252.
4. Petra Klumb and Heiner Maier, "Daily Activities and Survival at Older Ages," *Journal of Aging and Health* 19 (2007): 594.
5. Thomas Rutledge et al., "Social Networks and Incident Stroke among Women with Suspected Myocardial Ischemia," *Psychosomatic Medicine* 70 (2008): 282.
6. Dana Glei et al., "Participating in Social Activities Helps Preserve Cognitive Function: An Analysis of a Longitudinal Population-Based Study of the Elderly," *International Journal of Epidemiology* 34 (2005): 864.
7. Young at Heart Chorus, http://www.youngatheartchorus.com.
8. John Cacioppo et al., "Loneliness and Health: Potential Mechanisms," *Psychosomatic Medicine* 64 (2002): 407.
9. Mary E. Hughes and Linda J. White, "Marital Biography and Health at Midlife" (paper presented at the meeting of the Population Association of America, Minneapolis, May 1–3, 2003).
10. Elizabeth A. Beverly and Linda A. Wray, "The Role of Collective Efficacy in Exercise Adherence: A Qualitative Study of Spousal Support and Type 2 Diabetes Management," *Health Education Research* (2008), http://her.oxfordjournals.org/cgi/content/abstract/cyn032v1.
11. Boukje van Gelder et al., "Marital Status and Living Situation during a Five-Year Period Are Associated with a Subsequent Ten-Year Cognitive Decline in Older Men: The FINE Study," *The Journals of Gerontology Series B: Psychological Sciences and Social Sciences* 61 (2006): P213.
12. Nicholas Christakis and Paul Allison, "Mortality after the Hospitalization of a Spouse," *New England Journal of Medicine* 354 (2006): 719.
13. Debra Umberson and Kristi Williams, "Marital Quality, Health, and Aging: Gender Equity," *The Journals of Gerontology Series B: Psychological Sciences and Social Sciences* 60 (2005): S109.

14. Kristi Williams, "Has the Future of Marriage Arrived? A Contemporary Examination of Gender, Marriage, and Psychological Well-Being," *Journal of Health and Social Behavior* 44 (2003): 470.

15. Debra Umberson et al., "You Make Me Sick: Marital Quality and Health over the Life Course," *Journal of Health and Social Behavior* 47 (2006): 1.

16. Nancy Mace and Peter Rabins, *The 36-Hour Day*, 4th ed. (Baltimore: Johns Hopkins University Press, 2006).

17. Family Caregiver Alliance, "Women and Caregiving: Facts and Figures," http://www.caregiver.org/caregiver/jsp/content_node.jsp?nodeid=892.

18. Oregon.gov, "Seniors and People with Physical Disabilities: Caregiving," http://www.oregon.gov/DHS/spwpd/caregiving/home.shtml.

19. National Family Caregiver Association, "*Caring Today* Magazine Survey: 80% Find Caregiving Emotionally Rewarding," http://www.thefamilycaregiver.org/press_room/detail.cfm?num=104.

20. *Caring Today*, "What Caregivers Say," http://www.caringtoday.com/what-caregiver-say.

21. Family Caregiver Alliance, "Caregiving and Depression," http://www.caregiver.org/caregiver/jsp/content_node.jsp?nodeid=393&expandnodeid=480.

22. Robert Burns et al., "Primary Care Interventions for Dementia Caregivers: Two-Year Outcomes from the REACH Study," *The Gerontologist* 43 (2003): 547.

23. Maria M. Meyer et al., *The Comfort of Home for Alzheimer's Disease: A Guide for Caregivers* (Portland: Care Trust Publications, 2007).

24. Family Caregiving 101, "Family Caregiving: It's Not All Up to You," http://www.familycaregiving101.org.

25. William Strawbridge et al., "Frequent Attendance at Religious Services and Mortality over 28 Years," *American Journal of Public Health* 87 (1997): 957.

26. Loren Marks et al., "Religion and Health among African Americans," *Research on Aging* 27 (2005): 447.

27. College of Arts and Sciences at the University of Missouri–Kansas City, "Spirituality and Aging," http://cas.umkc.edu/casww/sa/Spirituality.htm.

28. John McCauley et al., "Daily Spiritual Experiences of Older Adults with and without Arthritis and the Relationship to Health Outcomes," *Arthritis and Rheumatism* 59, no. 1 (2008): 122–128.

29. Sarah Kirby, Peter Coleman, and Dave Daley, "Spirituality and Wellbeing in Frail and Non-Frail Older Adults," *The Journals of Gerontology Series B: Psychological Sciences and Social Sciences* 59B (2004): P123.

30. Timothy Daaleman, Subashan Perera, and Stephanie Studenski, "Religion, Spirituality, and Health Status in Geriatric Outpatients," *Annals of Family Medicine* 2 (2004): 49.

31. Harold G. Keonig, *Medicine, Religion, and Health: Where Science and Spirituality Meet* (West Conshohocken, PA: Templeton Foundation Press, 2008).

16

ON BEING PREPARED

Whether you are retiring completely or winding down slowly, you and your spouse or significant other now have the opportunity to do the many things you may have always dreamed of doing when you finally had more time. Of course, now that you understand the importance of regular exercise, health maintenance, and social connectedness, you should have plenty to do! You may be surprised to find that you are busier than you were before, between the daily household chores, your routine exercise program, the regular doctor visit(s), and your new hobbies and friends.

All of this is good, but there are still a few more things you need to do to be prepared for the changes that often accompany entering a new phase of life. I am not talking about financial planning for retirement (although this is important especially in our times of economic uncertainty), but rather what I call your personal and health planning. There are three important items you need to take care of before your life as a senior citizen can be as carefree and enjoyable as possible.

1. Make sure you have a current last will or testament.
2. Complete your advance care planning.
3. Along with your spouse or significant other, carefully consider where you'd like to live to best enjoy the golden years of life.

For some people, just the thought of a will or advance care planning can send chills up and down their spine, but nevertheless these are important issues that need to be addressed—and the sooner the better. Remember that you do not have to do all the work alone. In fact, I would suggest asking for as much help as possible from experienced professionals. Think over all your options carefully. It is far better and easier to plan ahead than it is to have to rush and make last-minute decisions, sometimes during a health crisis or other undesirable circumstances. I promise you that you will feel so much better once you have made the necessary decisions and the paperwork is done.

LAST WILL AND TESTAMENT

A will or testament is a document that "sets forth the manner in which you want your assets to pass to your heirs."[1] This document must meet certain requirements laid out by the laws of each state. In general, anybody 18 years old or older can write a will as long as the "maker" of the will is of sound mind. Some important points to remember:

1. A will cannot be verbal and must be written. So-called "holographic wills," which are handwritten, may not be accepted in all states. To avoid a lot of potential legal complications, it is always best to type a will.
2. A will must be signed. Some states require a signature on each page, while others do not. There are also certain restrictions as to who can be a witness, which also differ by state.
3. The will must be properly witnessed by at least two individuals according to the laws of each state. In the state of Louisiana, a will must be notarized. In general, notarization of wills is recommended because it makes the document "self-proving" and authenticates it, thereby ensuring that no further requirements will be necessary in "order to get the document admitted to probate court after the death of the maker."[2] If this sounds complicated, wait until you hear what happens if you do not make a will. In this case, a person dies in what is called "intestate." As referred to by the law, this means that all the property of the deceased is "distributed according to a formula fixed by the law." And of course, different states have their own way or formula of handling these situations. The result is nothing short of lots of legal nightmares for the family members who are left behind, regardless of the amount of money or other assets involved. This alone is a very good reason to make a will, even if you are not a millionaire. Remember that you can always change a will by replacing it or by making an amendment called a "codicil," but there will necessarily be new legal requirements. Once you have completed this task, you can sit back and relax because the document is literally "good" forever or until you decide to change it.[3]

Making a will can be a somewhat confusing process, and it's generally a good idea to work with a lawyer who is familiar with and understands the ins and outs of this process. I would also urge you to seek out a lawyer who has some experience in elder law. This can save you some time and money in other areas in addition to your will. For example, you may also need some help in completing your health care planning, and elder law attorneys are very good at this. For more information on how to find this type of attorney, look at the Web site of the National Academy of Elder Law Attorneys.[4]

ADVANCE CARE PLANNING

"Advance care planning is making decisions about the care you would want to receive if you happen to become unable to speak for yourself."[5] An advance directive is also referred to as a living will, the written document that lays out your wishes with regard to your health care and that designates a spokesperson to relay your wishes to the health care providers who are caring for you.

To understand how we came to endorse and promote advance directives, we need to look at the legal decisions over the last 30 years that in essence "affirmed the right of people to refuse unwanted medical treatment." In other words, these documents are a type of informed consent that recognizes a patient's autonomy in decision making. In 1990, Congress enacted the Patient Self-Determination Act, a law that requires health care institutions that receive Medicare and Medicaid funds to provide patients with information about advance directives. The purpose was to increase awareness and to encourage patients and health care providers to make use of advance directives. A further aim was to avoid the ambiguity regarding decision making, as was evident in the Nancy Cruzan case. Supreme Court Justice Sandra Day O'Connor, speaking about *Cruzan v. Director, Missouri Health Department*, said that "advance directives could dispel such ambiguity."[6] Advance directives include your wishes regarding the kind of treatments you would want to have and the kind of treatments you do not want to receive if you are unable to speak for yourself. The document can be more general or very detailed, as long as it clearly portrays your wishes. The purpose of this document, however, goes beyond just making sure that a person's wishes are known and followed. Properly executed advance directives "reduce the likelihood of conflicts between family members (and close friends) and health care providers and minimize the burden of decision making on family members or close friends."[7] The question of who should be involved in the discussion about health care planning is often raised. This depends of course on the individual, but in general close family members and/or friends, in addition to your primary care physician or other physicians. The point is that you get as much help and support as you want to make these important decisions.

In setting up your advance directive, you will need to answer two important questions. First, who will you designate as your health care proxy? A health care proxy is a person whom you choose to speak on your behalf when you cannot speak for yourself. This can be a family member or a friend. It is very important that your proxy understands that his or her role is to relay *your and only your* decisions. This person may not always agree with your wishes but must be able and willing to act on them, separating his or her own feelings from yours. The person should be someone you know well and trust and can talk to openly, someone who is strong enough to handle any possible conflicts with other family members or with physicians, and who is likely to be there in the future should you fall ill.

The second question is whether you want to receive or decline life-sustaining treatments in case you have a life-limiting illness. If you choose not to have any life-sustaining treatments, you can request what is called a DNR order from your doctor. This stands for "do not resuscitate," and it means that you do not wish to have "a medical procedure which seeks to restore cardiac and/or respiratory function to individuals who have sustained a cardiac and/or respiratory arrest."[8] This set of medical procedures, commonly referred to as cardiopulmonary resuscitation, or CPR for short, is designed to reestablish the circulation of blood flow through the heart and to support the flow of oxygen to the lungs. When trained medical personnel, such as emergency medical technicians or paramedics, are present, oxygen is usually provided via a tube inserted through the mouth into the windpipe, and, depending on the circumstances, chest compressions may be used to help the heart pump blood. In other cases, the heart may need to be shocked with a small amount of electricity to reset its rhythm so that it can beat and pump properly again. If you have ever witnessed such a resuscitation, you may have been shocked at what appears to be a rather "aggressive" treatment. CPR works well if it is started and performed correctly soon after a patient collapses and on proper examination is found to have no pulse and no respirations. Unfortunately, CPR often does not work very well in seriously ill patients and in many older patients who have multiple medical conditions. Although it is sometimes possible to get the heart beating again, the patient may be left with significant brain damage and require the support of a ventilator to breathe. This is, therefore, a very important decision, and you should make sure to ask your doctor about it in some detail.

To make it very clear, a DNR order refers only to the CPR procedures described herein. Having a DNR does *not* mean that you wish to decline other treatments, such as intravenous fluids for hydration, antibiotics, pain medications, or even nutritional support. Unfortunately, there is a common misconception that once a patient has a DNR order, no further aggressive treatments should be undertaken. Nothing could be more wrong.

RESIDENTIAL OPTIONS OR WHERE'S BEST TO LIVE

The American dream has always been having one's own house to enjoy "home sweet home." However, at one point or another, your house may no longer be what you and your spouse or partner really need. When thinking about possible living options, important factors to bear in mind include your safety and whether you can get the help you need. Again, this is not something you need to decide by yourself. Family members and friends can help, and your physician may also have some suggestions. Many different options are available, any one of which may be a good choice depending on your specific circumstances.

Your House

Let's start with your house. If you are living in your own house, but need some help, often depending on your medical condition, you may be able to find and obtain home health care services. Home health care may include some home care services like housecleaning, cooking, and other chores around the house. Typically, however, home health care refers to more medically oriented help in the home, such as nursing care or physical and occupational therapy. Older adults who have recently left the hospital or a short-term rehabilitation facility and who need some continued help with bathing and dressing, as well as those who would benefit from some additional rehabilitation therapy, are ideal candidates for these services.

The cost of home health care services can vary widely in different areas and states. Some such services are paid for privately, but funding is also available through "Medicare, Medicaid, the Older American Act, The Veteran's Administration, and private insurance."[9] Medicare is the largest single payer of home health care services, but strict requirements need to be met. Besides the fact that a patient must be homebound and under the care of a physician, he or she must also meet the need for these services, and the home health agency must be certified by the Medicare program. If you elect to pay privately for home health care services, you will have a large number of private home care agencies from which to choose. However, you need to do your homework carefully and interview several agencies before making a decision to hire one. Your local area agency on aging or department of public health can often provide further help and useful information.

Another option is an adult day program. These programs can be very helpful in providing some well-deserved and needed respite for caregivers, as well as different activities and a change in routine for the patient. Sometimes, it is wise to start looking at other living options, especially if your needs or those of a loved one seem more complex than a home health care agency can meet. This is especially the case if you are having difficulties with weekend and holiday coverage, and you begin to feel like an employment agency yourself.

Even if you do not have any medical problems, your house may simply have grown too big for one or two people and the upkeep and expenses may have become burdensome.

"Villages" or "At home" Organizations

Before you plan on moving out of your house, you may want to consider the possibility of forming a "village" or "at home" organization in your community, which will transform your current community into a virtual retirement community. You can find these "villages" in almost any state—there is even one in Australia! A village is essentially a membership organization created by residents of a community "as an alternative to moving from their houses to retirement or assisted living communities."[10] Usually, any one village has a minimum of 150 members, who pay monthly fees of several hundred dollars. In return, members receive home care services and transportation at a reduced rate, and have preferred contracts with a variety of vendors that provide services like housekeeping, home repair, and yard work. You can also take advantage of a number of social affairs organized by the community. These neighborhood groups are nonprofit organizations, have a board of directors and a business plan, and are involved in fundraising. If you are interested in organizing such a village in your community, you may want to purchase a manual from the Beacon Hill village Web site[10] or attend a national conference on how to go about setting up a village in your community.

Subsidized Senior Housing

State and federal programs are available that pay for housing for older adults with low to moderate incomes. These facilities provide independent living in apartments, while offering some assistance, such as laundry and shopping.[11]

Independent and Assisted Living

Nowadays, the number and types of facilities that offer a variety of residential options continue to grow, giving you lots of options.

In independent living residences, older adults are able to live independently but, at the same time, can take full advantage of various services and amenities, such as housekeeping, restaurant-style meals, and fitness facilities. They can also join in any of the social and cultural or educational activities that are offered. This appeals to many people, offering a quality of life they may not have been able to enjoy at home. Some of these independent residences are connected to and part of larger facilities that also provide assisted living. The assisted-living sections provide older adults with assistance in some activities of daily living like bathing, dressing, doing the laundry, and taking medications properly; they are therefore bridging the "gap between independent living and nursing homes."[12] These assisted-living areas are not meant for people who require a great deal of medical care. Instead, they provide a personalized service plan for each resident, which may include three meals a day (often served in a restaurant-type setting), 24-hour supervision, housekeeping and laundry services, some cultural activities, and some minor medical assistance, such as helping with taking medications properly and on schedule. A resident who requires more help with personal care may be able to transfer into an assisted-living apartment, while a healthy spouse or partner may stay in the independent section and, therefore, remain close by.[13]

Some facilities, in addition to their independent and assisted-living sections, have their own nursing facility. These are commonly referred to as continuing care retirement communities (CCRCs). The advantage of these larger communities is that once residents move into the community, they can remain there even if their health declines and they need more assistance and eventual nursing home placement.

Unfortunately, none of these different living options are inexpensive and with a few exceptions, they need to be paid for privately. It is a good idea to consult with your financial planner and lawyer, especially if you are planning to move into a CCRC.

Board and Care Homes

Other types of assisted-living-like facilities include board and care homes and congregate housing. These two housing options for seniors have been around long before today's assisted-living facilities started appearing on every street corner. And the differences between these various housing options have become less distinct, especially with more and varied services being offered today at assisted-living facilities.[13] So what exactly is board and care? "A board and care home is a housing facility for seniors or individuals with disabilities who want to be in a group living situation" . . . "when 24-hour, nonmedical supervision is needed or desired." These facilities vary from converted single-family homes with up to six residents, to larger apartment buildings with 100 or more residents. The hallmark of board and care facilities is the daily contact with the staff and a communal meal. It is important to note that government funding can sometimes cover the cost of living in these facilities.

Another difference between this type of housing and the newer types of assisted-living facilities is that board and care homes are subject to state licensing laws and are, therefore, held to certain "recognized standards of care." Before you consider moving to a board and care home, it is advisable to carefully inquire about the standards of care and recent monitoring reports.[13]

Congregate Housing

As mentioned before, congregate housing is another type of assisted-living-like facility. "Congregate housing started as a type of subsidized senior housing supported by government programs and by private charities. Nowadays, many forms of senior group living arrangements may be called 'congregate housing.'" Residents in this type of housing may have to share a room and bathroom and the main "services" are the "opportunities for social and recreational activities in a community of seniors," while other types of housing arrangements may also offer communal meals. Similar to other types of assisted-living arrangements, no medical supervision or care is provided in this setting. These facilities are ideal for seniors who do not want to live alone or have the daily chores of housekeeping and meal preparation but still want to live in a senior apartment.[13]

Nursing Homes

When medical care and around-the-clock personal care are needed, nursing homes are often the best choice. Unfortunately, nursing homes have not always had the best reputation, and the reports you can obtain about a facility are not always easy to understand. If a loved one has to go to a nursing home, the best advice is to personally tour the facility ahead of time and ask other family members who have loved ones in the facility about their experience with the care provided by the staff. In most nursing homes, skilled nurses and nursing aides are present at the facility 24 hours a day. In general, doctors, nurse practitioners, or physician assistants visit their patients once a month, unless there is an urgent need to see a patient more often. Some medical care is available, such as administration of intravenous fluids and antibiotics, and wound care. Physical, occupational, and speech therapy are usually also available.

Nursing homes are regularly inspected by a state agency. These inspection reports are public information and must be clearly displayed in the facility for family members and visitors to see. Payment for nursing home care is through private pay, Medicaid, or long-term care insurance. Medicare pays for only the first 100 days in a skilled nursing facility after a patient leaves the hospital. To find nursing homes in your area, see summaries of recent inspection reports, and compare different nursing homes, go to the Medicare Web site.[14,15]

PREPARATION NOW ALLOWS RELAXATION LATER

Don't let these important issues hang over your head. By doing your homework and making sure your personal paperwork is in order, you can relax knowing that your wishes will be carried out in the future. You will also save your family a great deal of worry, heartache, and even legal complications later on. And that's a good formula to allow you to make the most of the senior years of your life, enjoying your family and friends and your time together.

REFERENCES

1. Law Offices of Aaron Larson, "Your Last Will and Testament," ExpertLaw, http://www.expertlaw.com/library/estate_planning/wills.html.
2. MedLawPlus.com, "How to Create a Last Will and Testament: Step-by-Step Instructions with State Links," http://www.medlawplus.com/library/legal/lastwill andtestamentform.htm.
3. Alabama State Bar, "Last Will and Testament," http://www.alabar.org/brochures/ last_will.pdf.
4. National Academy of Elder Law Attorneys, Inc., "About NAELA," http:// www.naela.org/About_WhatIsNaela.aspx?Internal=true.
5. Caring Connections, "Advance Care Planning," http://www.caringinfo.org/Planning Ahead/AdvanceCarePlanning.htm.
6. Marilyn Jane Field and Christine K. Cassel, eds., *Approaching Death: Improving Care at the End of Life* (Washington, DC: National Academies Press, 1997), http://www.nap.edu/openbook.php?record_id=5801&page=R1.
7. Ethics in Medicine, "Advance Care Planning," University of Washington School of Medicine, http://www.depts.washington.edu/bioethx/topics/adcare.html.

8. Department of Bioethics, "Policy on Do Not Resuscitate," Cleveland Clinic, http://www.clevelandclinic.org/bioethics/policies/dnr.html.
9. Eldercare Locator, "Fact Sheets: What Is Home Health Care?" http://www.eldercare.gov/Eldercare.NET/Public/Resources/fact_sheets/home_care.aspx.
10. Beacon Hill Village, "Welcome to Beacon Hill Village . . . Where City Living Just Got Easier," Beacon Hill Village, http://www.beaconhillvillage.org.
11. U.S. Department of Health and Human Services, "Nursing Homes: Alternatives to Nursing Home Care," http://www.medicare.gov/nursing/Alternatives/Other.asp.
12. Assisted INFO, "What Is Assisted Living?" http://www.assistedlivinginfo.com/alserve.html.
13. Helpguide.org, "Assisted Living Facilities for Seniors," http://www.helpguide.org/elder/assisted_living_facilities.htm.
14. U.S. Department of Health and Human Services, "Nursing Homes: Paying for Care," http://www.medicare.gov.
15. National Institute on Aging, "AgePage: Nursing Homes—Making the Right Choice," http://www.nia.nih.gov/HealthInformation/Publications/nursinghomes.htm.

17

Enjoy the Passage of Time

Life really is a journey from birth to old age. Every day, every one of us gets a little bit older, and there is nothing any of us can do to stop or reverse this process. Face lifts, tummy tucks, or liposuction may make you look younger on the surface (or so you think), but they do not change your age. And although modern medicine can do wonderful things, in reality, no medications, no technology, and no doctors can make us younger again. So, at the end of the day, it is up to each of us to make the best of our passage of time. For some, especially those of us who are blessed with good health, the journey may appear easier than it does for others. But don't be fooled into thinking that the grass is always greener on the other side. Regardless of your circumstances (or those of others), much of how successfully you age and enjoy the passage of time is up to you. Although I wouldn't go so far as to call the following three tips the secrets of aging, I urge you to consider and apply them to your life to make the passage of time as pleasant and gratifying as possible.

Commit to Doing the Right Things

First, you need to really want your passage of time to be successful for it to be successful. Nobody ever said that getting older was going to be easy. To the contrary, it takes hard work, perseverance, and a lot of self-discipline, including eating right (see Chapter 5), exercising regularly (see Chapter 6), paying careful attention to your health (see Chapter 8), and maintaining good relationships (see Chapter 15).

Accept Some Limitations

Second, you have to accept some of the limitations that often come along with age. Your body may have picked up a few "dents and scratches" along

Although not strictly a patient of mine, I recently met again a previous neighbor and I was amazed at how well he looked. When I had last seen Jim, he was overweight and convinced that mowing his lawn was the only exercise he needed at his age. Jim told me that his older brother had passed away from a heart attack two years earlier, and he realized that he would likely suffer the same fate if he did not change his lifestyle. He joined a gym, changed his diet, and lost 30 pounds. He even took up running and is thinking about running in the Boston marathon!

the way, and you need to learn how to deal with them. Becoming frustrated and angry—or worse, depressed—does not help you or anyone else. There is no question that serious medical conditions, like a stroke, heart attack, and especially a diagnosis of cancer, are very difficult and challenging, even for the strongest among us. But even despite a healthy lifestyle, any of these things *can* happen, and help and guidance is available. You do not have to do it alone, nor should you try.

Bear in mind that accepting one's limitations does not mean giving up and letting fate take over. It means adapting and compensating for any limitations that result from your medical condition(s) so that you can continue to enjoy your life and as many activities as possible.

After a massive stroke, one of my older patients was left with some severe disabilities. He came to my office and told me that no way in hell was this stroke going to keep him from his favorite pastime of going to the casinos. He was determined to walk upright again into the casino for a good game of blackjack. And he eventually did. He walked into the casino on his own power—not very fast, but by himself with just a cane. Incidentally, he did lose quite a bit of money gambling that day, but he told me "that's the price I had to pay."

Another patient of mine had crippling rheumatoid arthritis, forcing her to become increasingly dependent on multiple caregivers to remain living in her own house. She made it her mission in life to arrange for a patchwork of caregivers, because she wanted to be able to sit on her porch and enjoy the beautiful sunset every evening. She told me watching the sunset gave her the strength to face another tomorrow.

Yet another example was an older couple who did not want to move into their child's house. Independence was their goal, and they worked hard at preserving it. Ultimately, they decided to move to a senior housing apartment and, although this was not the same as being in their own house, it allowed them to retain the independence they cherished.

A common theme among all these individuals is that they wanted to be in control of their lives. By accepting reality, making changes in their lifestyle, and working around their particular obstacles, they all were successful in their own pursuit of happiness.

LIVE FOR TODAY

Last, but not least, focus on living life now! Be part of today, "living in the current time." It's fun to occasionally reminisce with old friends, but it's not healthy to live in the past or to keep looking back at what supposedly were the "good old days." Stop thinking or saying, "when I was younger, we did not do this" or "we never had that." Open your mind and heart to new ideas and ways of doing things. Know something about the music your grandchildren listen to, read or be aware of new books, learn how to surf the Web, and keep on top of current events. This does not mean that you need to like the music, read all those books, or embrace the latest technological gadgets. However, you might well be surprised to find that you actually like some more modern music or enjoy using e-mail to stay in touch with your family and friends.

Speaking about the past, it is also important to let go of old resentments. If you need to, make up with family members and former friends. Think carefully about holding a grudge against anyone. It serves no purpose, does nothing for your health, and will not make you happier.

Keep the past for all the good memories, forget the bad ones, and use those wonderful memories to help you get through tough times.

A dear patient of mine who started suffering from insomnia after her husband passed away once told me that she finally found a cure to her difficulties falling asleep. She started thinking about what she liked most when she and her husband were still living in New York City. Her favorite pastime was to go to the museum of fine arts. Now when she lies awake at night, she tries to remember all the details of what she had to do to get from her uptown apartment to the museum, such as which subway station she had to use, what train she needed to take, and where she got off. She imagines taking the long escalator down to the subway station, waiting patiently for the train to come, always trying to board the first car, counting the stations until she reached her destination, and finally walking to the museum. She proudly told me that she has never reached the museum in her thoughts because she always falls asleep somewhere on the subway.

The Very Last Word

So, yes, aging brings many changes—physical changes, changing roles and relationships, possibly a changed living situation, and many more. Many of these changes can be challenging and may elicit strong emotions. Some of these changes will be easier to adapt to than others, but I think it's fair to say that they will have an effect on your mental well-being. However, if you can approach the changes of aging with a positive attitude by understanding, accepting, and making peace with the process, I guarantee that people will notice and respond. You will be happier and more satisfied with yourself— and with others, too. Undoubtedly, your days will be much more contented and fulfilling. Enjoy the passage of time!

Appendix: A Dozen Useful Web sites

I thought it would be helpful to share with you some of the Web sites I use in my daily practice and when I wrote this book. An overwhelming number of Web sites are available on health and aging, even without the slew of anti-aging sites. However, I find that I always go back to these 12 Web sites because of the high quality of the information provided. Good luck, good health, and happy browsing!

1. **www.aarp.org**
   The American Association of Retired People is a well-known and respected organization with a helpful Web site that provides information on a variety of topics, including numerous health issues. Just click on the health tab for further information.
2. **www.alz.org**
   The Alzheimer's Association is a national organization whose mission is to "help fight Alzheimer's disease through vital research and essential support programs and services." The Web site is very easy to navigate and provides excellent information on Alzheimer's disease under the Alzheimer's disease tab. If you are interested in other dementias, use the "Related Dementias" field under the Alzheimer's disease tab. Caregivers can find helpful information by clicking on the "Living with Alzheimer's" tab.
3. **www.cdc.gov**
   The official Web site of the Centers for Disease Control and Prevention is a useful place to start a search on topics on aging. Just enter the word *aging* in the search field, and be prepared to spend hours reading the vast amount of information on a variety of aspects of aging.
4. **www.caregiver.gov**
   This Web site of the Family Caregiver Alliance provides comprehensive information for caregivers on a local, regional, and state level. It is referred to as a "one-stop shopping center for caregivers." The Web site also offers some information fact sheets in both Spanish and Chinese. With the "Family Care Navigator," it provides caregivers a state-by-state list of resources.
5. **www.eldercare.gov**
   This useful Web site of the Department of Health and Human Services will bring all the information about elder care services in your geographical area to your "doorstep."

Just enter your city, zip code, or county, and you will find information about the available services for yourself or a loved one in or around your hometown.

6. **www.healthinaging.org**

   This is the Web site for the Foundation of Health in Aging, a nonprofit organization founded by the American Geriatrics Society (AGS) in 1999. Its goal is to link elder research and the public with the practice of geriatrics that is the clinical care of older adults. Under the tab "Aging in the Know," you will find up-to-date information about aging for consumers. Family caregivers will find useful information when clicking on the "Eldercare at Home" tab, and the tab "Health in Aging Stories" provides for enjoyable and inspiring reading.

7. **www.icarevillage.com**

   This relatively new Web site on "everything eldercare" offers a novel and easy way to navigate through a vast array of information. Clicking on the different tabs will provide good and helpful information, ranging from specific disease descriptions to caregiver, legal, and financial advice. The "Ask the Experts" tab will allow you to watch videos and encourage you to ask questions. If you choose to become a gold member, you can also schedule a virtual meeting with different experts for a predetermined hourly rate.

8. **www.mayoclinic.com**

   I have used this very helpful Web site extensively myself. I regularly print the Mayo Clinic's handouts on certain disease states for my patients and/or their caregivers. Under the heading of "Diseases and Conditions," you can search for information on a disease by clicking on its first letter. The disease descriptions are precise, up to date, and written in easy-to-understand language.

9. **www.nccam.nih.gov**

   If you are interested in complementary or integrative medicine, please look at this Web site of the National Center for Complementary and Alternative Medicine (NCCAM). The best way to start browsing this information-packed site is to click on the "A–Z Index of Health Topics" tab. You can spend hours on this Web site. The information on herbal and other complementary medicinal approaches is scientific and honest.

10. **www.nia.nih.gov**

    This is the Web site of the U.S. National Institutes of Health, featuring the National Institute on Aging. I find the tabs "Alzheimer's Disease Information" and "NIHSeniorHealth.gov" the most useful. You will find them under the heading Health Information. When you click on NIHSeniorHealth.gov, you will find health topics either listed by first letter or by general categories. The healthy aging section is particularly useful.

11. **www.cms.gov**

    This Web site of the Centers for Medicare & Medicaid services is very useful but equally overwhelming and typical of government bureaucracy. You need to know where to find the information, or you may spend a long time looking for it. The information on screening for different disease states is quite helpful, and it is available on the home page under the heading of "Prevention."

12. **www.drugs.com**

    Anything you ever wanted to know about medications is readily available on this Web site. The "Pill Identifier" tab is extremely useful when neither you nor your physician knows what pill is in the box! Other useful tabs are those labeled "Side Effects" and "Natural Products." The "International" tab helps identify those mysterious medications prescribed outside the United States.

INDEX

Page numbers in italics refer to tables.

About the Author

JUERGEN BLUDAU, MD, was born in Germany and educated in England. He received his medical degree from the Royal College of Surgeons in Ireland and completed his postgraduate studies in the United States. He is a board-certified, Harvard fellowship—trained geriatrician and is currently the acting clinical chief and director of clinical geriatric services at Brigham and Women's Hospital, Division of Aging. Dr. Bludau is an instructor in medicine at Harvard Medical School, a clinical assistant professor of medicine at Nova Southeastern University, and a member of the scientific advisory board of the Gerontological Economic Research Organization in Kreuzlingen, Switzerland. Dr. Bludau regularly speaks at local, national, and international conferences. His interests are the primary care of dementia patients, the development of improved out- and inpatient geriatric services, and the geriatric education of nurses. To that end, he has developed a curriculum for practicing nurses and has given several courses at Beijing Hospital No. 1 and Fudan University School of Nursing in Shanghai. Dr. Bludau resides in the Boston area with his wife and their three children.